Rambling Along
the Royal Canal

About the Author

On retiring from his position as telecommunications technologist in ESB, Tom Dredge immersed himself in his passions of hill-walking and writing. A member of Bealtaine Poets, Boyne Writers and Leixlip Writers, his poetry has appeared in numerous poetry magazines. He was accepted into the National Mentoring Programme, funded by Kildare Arts Service in collaboration with the Irish Writers Centre and the Arts Council, which led to the completion of *Rambling Along the Royal Canal*.

Rambling Along the Royal Canal

A Journey into the Heart of Ireland

Tom Dredge

The Liffey Press

Published by
The Liffey Press
'Clareville', 307 Clontarf Road
Dublin D03 PO46, Ireland
www.theliffeypress.com

© 2025 Tom Dredge

A catalogue record of this book is
available from the British Library.

ISBN 978-1-0686645-5-7

All rights reserved. No part of this publication may be reproduced or transmitted in any form or by any means, including photocopying and recording, without written permission of the publisher. Such written permission must also be obtained before any part of this publication is stored in a retrieval system of any nature. Requests for permission should be directed to The Liffey Press, 'Clareville', 307 Clontarf Road, Dublin D03 PO46 Ireland.

Printed in Northern Ireland by W&G Baird

Contents

Map of the Royal Canal — vii

Route Maps — viii

Acknowledgements — x

Introduction — 1

1 **Dublin Docklands to Drumcondra** — 3
   Balladeers, Drovers, Playwrights and Lockkeepers

2 **Drumcondra to Broadstone** — 18
   Street Soccer, Mountjoy, City Basin and Broadstone

3 **Broadstone to Glasnevin Cemetery** — 28
   Poets, Broadcasters, Pacifists and Liberators

4 **Glasnevin Cemetery to Broombridge** — 34
   Hedgerows, Trains, Equations and a Hanging Judge

5 **Broombridge to Blanchardstown** — 43
   Parks, Mansions, Astronomy and Barges

6 **Blanchardstown to Confey** — 56
   Gunpowder, Tragedy, Castles and a Priory

7 **Confey to Leixlip** — 72
   An Aqueduct, a Spa, a Brewery and a Writer

8 **Leixlip to Maynooth** — 81
   Spooks, Follies, Dukes and Seminarians

9 **Maynooth to Kilcock** — 100
   Water Polo, Markets, Accordions and Missionaries

10	**Kilcock to Enfield**	110
	Sustainability, Reeds, Buzzards and Conversations	
11	**Enfield to Hill of Down**	123
	Bealtaine, Ribbonism, Herons and a Missing Hill	
12	**Hill of Down to Killucan**	137
	Eskers, Old Inns, Deep Space and Camillians	
13	**Killucan to Mullingar**	151
	The Summit, Squirrels, Pipers and Lilliputians	
14	**Mullingar to Coolnahay**	174
	Studs, Genealogy, Local Lore and a Tea House	
15	**Coolnahay to Ballynacargy**	186
	The Descent, Barrows, Garrisons and a Raffle	
16	**Ballynacargy to Abbeyshrule**	199
	Secretive Mammals, Planes, Bog Oak and a High Cross	
17	**Abbeyshrule to Ballymahon**	218
	The Inny, Evictions, Bianconi and a Pleasure Park	
18	**Ballymahon to Mosstown**	228
	Authors, a Medic, an Ancient Trackway and a Notorious Banker	
19	**Mosstown to Killashee**	248
	Swimmers, the National Famine Way, Dams and Merchants	
20	**Killashee to Cloondara**	261
	Raised Bogs, the Táin, a Glorious Harbour and the Shannon	
21	**Cloondara to Longford Town**	278
	Butterflies, a Buried Harbour, a Cathedral and a Workhouse	

Bibliography   299

Index   302

Maps

Map of the Royal Canal (source: Waterways Ireland)

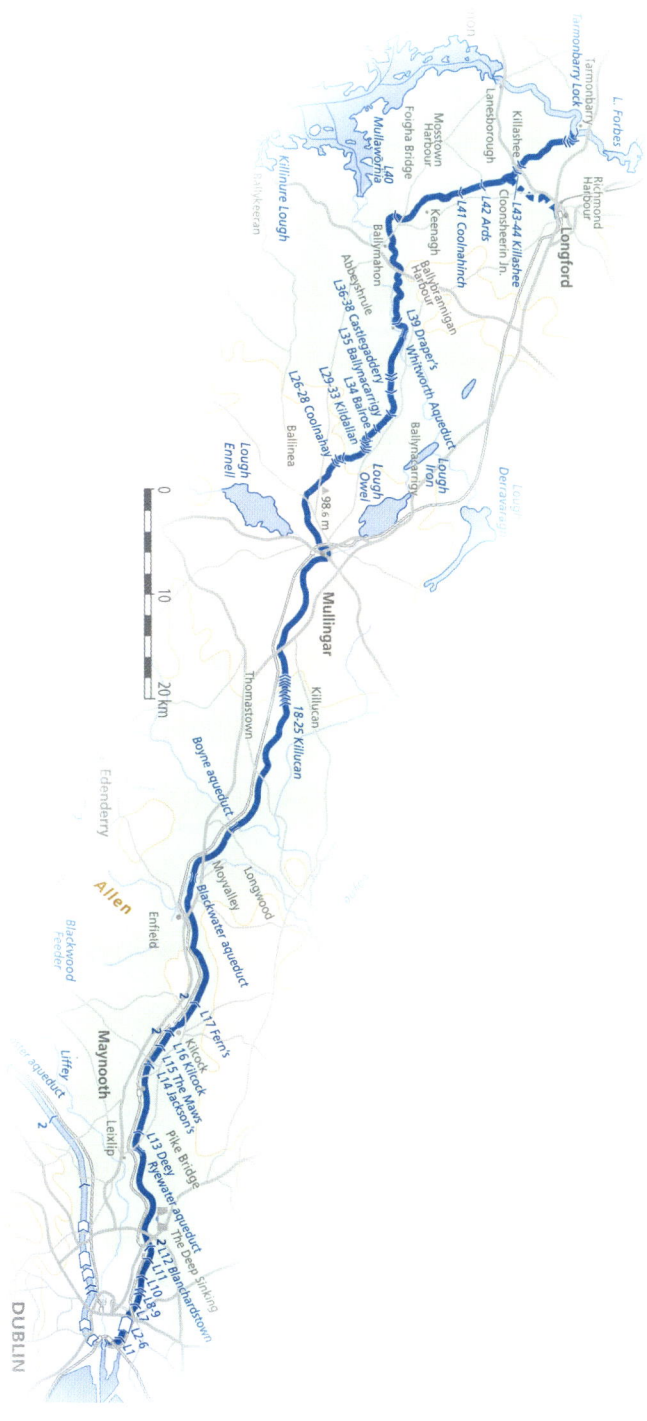

Rambling Along the Royal Canal

Map 1: Spencer Dock to Leixlip – 20.70 km (chapters 1-7)

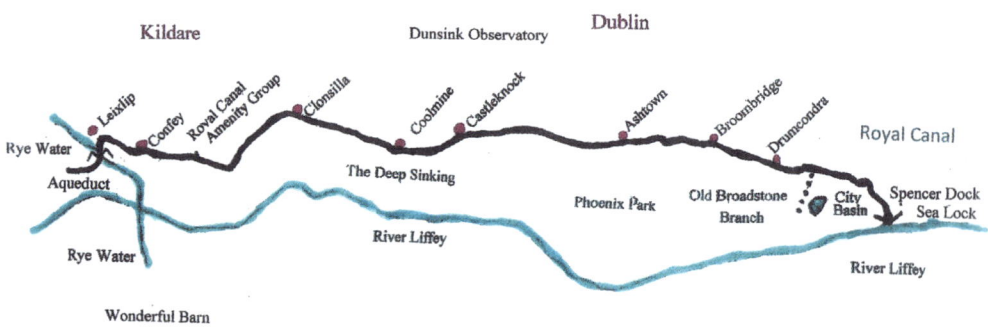

Map 2: Leixlip to Moyvalley – 30.70 km (chapters 8-11)

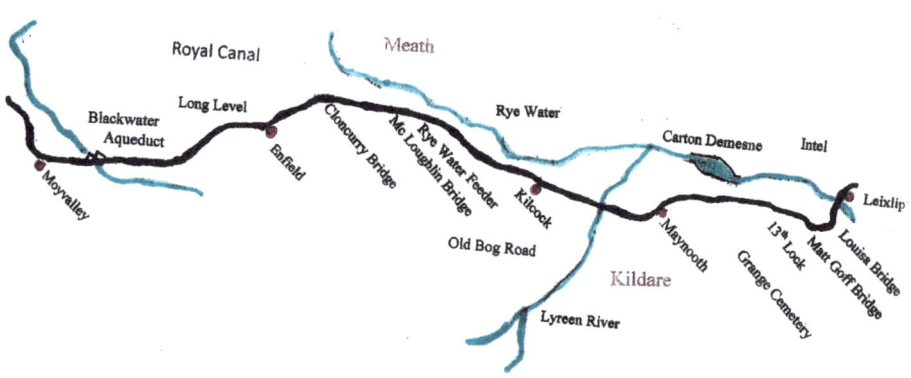

Map 3: Moyvalley to Baltrasna – 29.05 km (chapters 12-13)

Route Maps

Map 4: Baltrasna to Abbeyshrule – 32.35 km (chapters 14-16)

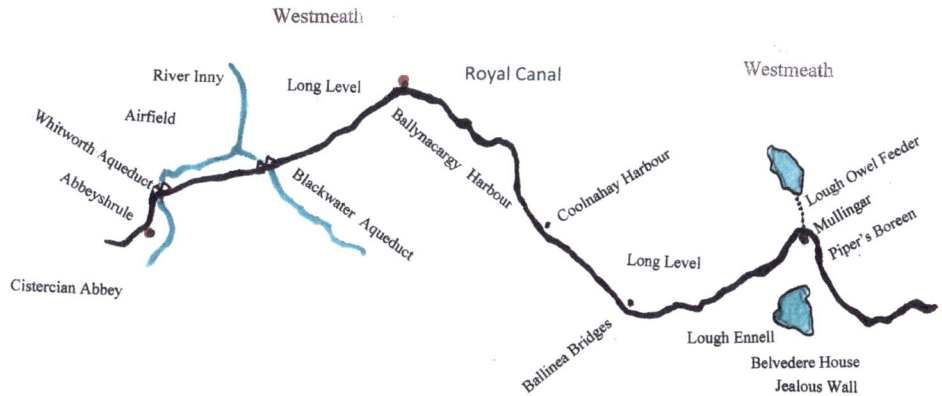

Map 5: Abbeyshrule to Cloondara – 32.80 km (chapters 17-21)
Longford Branch – 8.5 km

Acknowledgements

Many individuals and organizations helped me along the way to publication.

My acceptance into the National Mentoring Programme, funded by Kildare Arts Service in collaboration with the Irish Writers Centre and the Arts Council, offered me the opportunity to work under the guidance of Alannah Hopkin. Alannah proved to be an exceptional mentor, greatly improving my editing skills, and offering endless advice and tireless encouragement. For her dedication to my work I am truly grateful.

Thanks to David Givens of The Liffey Press for having faith in my book. David used his skills, knowledge and expertise as a publisher, blending text and photographs to compile a beautiful finished piece of work. It has been a pleasure working with him.

Thanks to Éanna Ní Lamhna for generously agreeing to launch my book. Éanna's dedication to the world of nature, biodiversity and care for our planet has been an inspiration to me as I investigated the flora and fauna along the banks of the canal.

I extend a big thanks to my wife, Helen, who has been my tireless editor, map maker and motivator, from the beginning to the end of this project. Thanks also to both my sons, Raymond and Stephen, for the endless support they offered me, reading, editing and making invaluable suggestions regarding the project.

Thanks to Carmel McLoughlin and Breda Fay for supplying me with invaluable references in the form of books and pamphlets. Thanks

Acknowledgements

to Louise Dredge for her advice and guidance. I give a special thanks to Jenny Wren for navigating us in her barge along the canal, while enthusiastically sharing her many wonderful stories and canal lore.

I am most grateful to Fingal County Council Arts Office for supplying me with sponsorship for my book. I also extend my thanks to the Inland Waterways Association of Ireland (IWAI), the Royal Canal Amenity Group and Waterways Ireland who have helped by supporting and promoting my book.

A special thank you to the Bealtaine Poets for their constant encouragement, to the Boyne Writers Group for their excellent critiquing and to the Leixlip Writers Group in whose anthology an extract from the book appeared.

Royal Canal in Dublin

Introduction

Water enthrals me. It always has. Whether it be the lashing of wild waves over a pier wall, the soft lapping of lake water on a shore, or the rush of canal water from the high level above, down into the chamber beneath, I am hooked by the sights and sounds of this liquid entity.

As a teenager, I lived a stone's throw from the Grand Canal, along whose banks I loved to walk. Sometimes I would try to net pinkeens, my efforts frequently thwarted by the laws of refraction. Occasionally I would witness a couple of brave lads jumping into the lock chamber, having a swim and climbing up the breast gate to regain a foot on terra firma. This was out of the question for me as I had yet to master the art of swimming.

In later years, as a married man, I settled close to the banks of the Royal Canal. Its towpaths became my favourite choice for an enjoyable walk. When work took me to the midland counties of Ireland, I began to discover other sections of this marvellous waterway.

Then, in 2015, I finally realised my dream, walking its full length from the River Liffey to the River Shannon, over ten non-consecutive days. My journey covered spring and summer allowing me to see the changes that took place along the waterway during those two seasons.

I enjoyed losing myself in the beauty of the flora and fauna along its banks, and a keen interest in art, literature and music meant looking for connections to those disciplines. My curiosity was further aroused by historical, cultural and engineering links along the canal.

I became more passionate about the walk with every day, speaking to different people along the route and discovering just how diverse this wildlife habitat is. It takes you through city, suburb, town and village on tarmac, gravel, stone, grass and mud. I felt a need to encounter this biosphere up close and to let the aura surrounding each day flow onto my page as I experienced it, leaving research and detail till later.

Much has changed of course since 2015. Even back then the first signs of the Royal Canal Greenway were starting to appear in County Westmeath. Now that this greenway is close to completion, the towpaths have become accessible to young and old with its safe, level tarmac paths. Still, I count myself lucky to have experienced it in all its fully fledged greenery, before the transformation of its grassy banks.

Entrance to Spencer Dock amd lifting bridges

1.

Dublin Docklands to Drumcondra

Balladeers, Drovers, Playwrights and Lockkeepers

The Royal Canal Company was formed in 1789 by a group of businessmen and politicians with the aim of providing passage for goods and passengers between Dublin and the River Shannon.

During the early part of the eighteenth century, commercial goods were transported either on winding roads or along meandering rivers. However, there was an urgent need for a direct route that would connect Dublin to the River Shannon for the transportation of a variety of goods in either direction. The concept of achieving this by connecting various rivers proved impractical as some rivers were unsuitable for navigation. In the latter part of the eighteenth century, the solution to this problem was the construction of the Grand Canal, followed ten years later by the Royal Canal.

The main harbour for the new Royal Canal waterway was at Broadstone in the heart of Dublin, remaining so for a number of decades. In 1845, after the Midland Great Western Railway Company acquired the Royal Canal, goods continued to be carried by canal for some further decades, albeit at a slowly dwindling rate. In 1873, when Spencer Dock was completed and opened by the railway company, it incorporated a sea lock allowing small vessels access to the railway and canal from the River Liffey. Spencer Dock then became the main point from where barges began their long journeys inland, along the canal towards the River Shannon. Commercial traffic continued to use the canal's Broadstone section until 1879, after which the harbour was filled in.

The popular means of transporting people during the eighteenth century had been by horse-drawn coaches and cars. However, this all changed with the construction of canals in Ireland, which offered passengers cheaper fares, a more reliable service and a comfortable mode of transport. The passengers could enjoy the scenery at their ease and could also dine on board. Some coaches, such as Bianconi coaches, began to operate as feeders to and from various locations along the canal route, so that passengers could be transported from the canal to their chosen destination.

So today, late in the month of February, I begin my long trek. As I board with growing excitement the train from my home in Leixlip to Dublin, I imagine the enthusiasm that would have filled the hearts of those Antarctic explorers, Shackleton and Crean, as they began their adventure. My journey, though less formidable, has been eagerly awaited as I set out to walk the 146 kilometres of the Royal Canal taking me from the River Liffey to the River Shannon.

Spencer Dock sea lock

I arrive at Dublin's Docklands, where the Royal Canal meets the River Liffey, and where cargo from endless boats was loaded for dispersion across the country. A variety of goods were transported including, porter, coal, turf, manure and building materials. I can almost hear the shouts of stevedores and the roll of wooden casks of porter over cobbles, visualising dockers toiling at this strenuous work. Time brought progress in the mass transportation of liquids, eliminating the need for casks to the point where Guinness was largely transported in tankers, resulting in a drastic loss of jobs for dockers.

Standing at Spencer Dock, I imagine sitting on the bow of a narrowboat as the bridge lifts up, the sea lock opens and the boat enters the canal waterway from the Liffey. However, my journey is of a different kind. I am thrilled to be taking my first steps along the canal towpath, by the side of the glass cylindrical structure of the Convention Centre.

I walk out onto a pedestrian bridge spanning the canal, close to the sea lock. From here I can see Spencer Dock Bridge to the north, which carries road and pedestrian traffic, as well as the LUAS, over the waterway. Built in 2009, it has resulted in Upper and Lower Mayor Street being reunited for the first time since the 1790s, when construction of the canal bisected it.

Sheriff Street Drawbridge and Luke Kelly statue viewed from Canal Walk

This 40-metre concrete span, designed by Amanda Levete Architects, curves and widens, reflecting a manta ray's pectoral fins in motion, as envisaged in its original design.

Strangely enough, viewed from the bridge by the sea lock, it appears to rise from its central base and spread out like the giant tail of a diving humpback whale. Walking on a smooth tarmac towpath I am soon passing beneath it.

As I approach the Sheriff Street Drawbridge, I am struck by this imposing piece of legacy engineering, which although in need of maintenance, is a compelling construction. The mechanics of this structure rise high above the road, resembling a dinosaur frozen in time, ready to shake the very foundations of Sheriff Street.

This drawbridge crosses Spencer Dock and is currently inoperable, and along with an 110kv electric cable, obstructs navigation at this point. However, by careful management of the water level, it is possible for boats to achieve a passage.

After just 300 metres my towpath trail has come to a stop at the base of a stairwell, leading me up to Sheriff Street Upper. Just across the road is a commuter train stop, Iarnród Éireann's Docklands Station, serving Maynooth/Longford.

There are two commemorative stone plaques on either side of the road with the inscription *Midland Great Western Railway of Ireland* circling the date '1845'. This is the year that company purchased the Royal Canal, with the intention of laying its tracks along the waterway's bed, a plan which, thankfully, never came to fruition. It was also coincidentally, the year the Great Famine began. The tonnage of goods carried on the canal rose to its highest level ever of 112,181 tons in 1847.

Both plaques are divided into four sections containing elaborate emblems, one bearing the inscription *Spencer Dock 15th April 1873*.

Standing on Sheriff Street Bridge I see that both the canal and railway slowly begin a more westerly course after it. They will pass by Croke Park which looms on the horizon. Unfortunately, I am unable to continue as I am confronted with a wasteland of overgrown lank

New cycle and walkway up to Newcomen Bridge

and scrawny late winter grasses, a few struggling deciduous trees, and some scattered semi-foliated bushes. Buddleia raises its head above the railing and its long conical spikes are a withered brown. I must now temporarily divert back onto the concrete thoroughfares of the north inner city.

Since 2020 a new route has been opened through this railway land, from Guild Street along the banks of the canal. Much of the wasteland has now been converted into a beautiful linear park, which eventually rises up onto a sweeping new cycle/pedestrian bridge crossing the railway line, bringing you alongside Newcomen Bridge. This route is a wonderful amenity, used by local people, workers, students and those just out for a leisurely stroll or cycle.

My diversion takes me by the church of Saint Laurence O'Toole, standing at the corner of Sheriff Street Lower and Seville Place. Completed in 1858, it is an impressive example of the Gothic Revival in architecture. Its high spire is a well-known local feature, and was said to be the last landmark visible to emigrants departing from the North Wall, during the nineteenth and twentieth centuries.

Saint Laurence O'Toole was born in 1128, at Castledermot, County Kildare. He was Archbishop of Dublin during the Norman invasion

Photo in Saint Laurence O'Toole Church of cattle drovers

and took part in negotiations with the English. He died in 1180 and is buried at Eu in Normandy, France. After he was canonised in 1225, a small bone from his hand was brought from Eu and placed in a shrine in this Dublin church.

I enter the church and locate this inconspicuous, golden shrine, in which the finger bone is illuminated. There is a statue of the saint beside it. Coloured light from the stained glass windows floods the church interior. In the porch, I notice some photographs, images of former times, depicting customs almost forgotten, such as a Corpus Christi procession. Others portray activities that occurred in this area in the past, such as cattle drovers driving their herd to the docks for export.

This is of particular interest to me as my grandfather, who lived in Cabra, was a drover. I remember stories of my grandmother bringing down sandwiches and tea in a milk bottle to him at the cattle market at Hanlon's Corner. I was always fascinated by the practice of driving herds of cattle through the streets of Dublin, back then in the 1950s. At that time this market had been the busiest of its kind in Europe. Prices set at the cattle market in Dublin would affect prices at fairs and markets throughout the country. It closed in the 1970s and social housing was built on the site. The area had acquired the name Cowtown and some of the street names reflect this such as Red Cow Lane and Oxmantown Road.

Another photo is of Luke Kelly, who was born in Sheriff Street in 1940. He is accompanied by Ronnie Drew and a young woman, as they stand on a ship waving.

In 1958 Luke moved to England. He acquired a banjo and played at folk clubs. His love of music was fuelled by the folk revival and in particular by Ewan MacColl. He was also influenced by US songwriters like Pete Seeger and Woody Guthrie.

Later, back in Dublin, he joined Ronnie Drew's Ballad Group. When a new name was sought for the group this avid reader suggested The Dubliners, having read James Joyce's short story collection.

Luke chose carefully the songs he sang, such as *The Auld Triangle* and *Dirty Old Town*. He had a talent for interpreting songs like no one else. He delivered each with clear diction and unrivalled passion, creating a work of art suspended in space for the duration of the recording. Many people, local, nationwide and worldwide, felt the loss when he died of a brain tumour in 1984 at the age of forty-three. In 2019, on the 35th anniversary of his death, two sculptures of Luke were unveiled on either side of the Liffey.

Looking up the street from the porch of the church, in this mainly working class area, a litany of talented people from Sheriff Street, the North Wall and the general area around the docks floods my mind.

Barry Keoghan, a young man who was born in this area in 1992, saw an ad in the window of a shop on Sheriff Street, answered it, and in 2011 ended up with a part in Mark O'Connor's film *Between the Canals*. In 2013 he landed a part in *Love/Hate*. After his success in that TV series, he found himself working with some of the biggest names in Hollywood, such as Angelina Jolie in *Eternals* in 2021. In 2022 he won a BAFTA Award for Best Actor in a Supporting Role for his part in Martin McDonagh's, *The Banshees of Inisherin*. In 2023 he took the lead role in Emerald Fennell's box office success, *Saltburn*.

Leaving St. Laurence's church, I turn onto Seville Place. I notice a stone plaque on the wall of a school to my left, which reads as follows:

> TO THE MEMORY OF
> FRANK CAHILL
> PUPIL AND BELOVED TEACHER
> IN THESE SCHOOLS FOR FIFTY YEARS
> DIED 19th OCT. 1957
>
> ERECTED BY
> HIS GRATEFUL PUPILS AND FRIENDS

What a lovely tribute to a local man! Frank was a friend of the playwright Seán O'Casey. According to the actor, critic and theatre director Gabriel Fallon, Frank was with Seán one night on their way home from the Abbey Theatre when they stopped before parting at the Five Lamps, at the end of Seville Place. The two men were discussing the play they had just watched and neither had enjoyed it. Frank then said:

'You know Seán, you could write a better play than the one we saw tonight!'

Seán pondered the idea for a moment and replied, 'D'ye know Frank, I believe I could.'

Thanks to Frank for setting Seán on the road to the Abbey.

Strolling further along the street, I arrive at number 44, a worn, redbrick end house on Marion Terrace, Seville Place. This is where Jim and Peter Sheridan grew up. In the early 1970s they took over the Projects Arts Centre in Dublin and turned it into the focal point of alternative theatre in Ireland.

In 1989, Jim's first step into film directing came with *My Left Foot* starring Daniel Day-Lewis, who won an Oscar for his portrayal of Christy Brown, the novelist and poet who suffered from cerebral palsy. Jim has earned worldwide renown through his writing, producing and directing of high quality films, including: *The Field* (1990), *In the Name of the Father* (1993) and *In America* (2002). In 2015 he was the recipient of a Lifetime Achievement Award at the Irish Film and Television Awards.

Peter Sheridan is famous in his own right for his plays and memoirs. His stage work includes *No Entry*, *Diary of a Hunger Strike* and *Liberty Suite*. I have recently read his memoir, *Break a Leg*, a fascinating look at his involvement in theatre. It reads like a novel filled with life, sadness, joy, humour, self-recrimination and above all his love of the theatre and writing. In 2014 Peter had the honour of being writer in residence at Farmleigh House.

Further along Seville Place a railway wall rises above me, incorporating an old arch which is the entrance to the Dublin Dockland Boxing Club. Another arch displays two crests and the name C.L.G. Naomh Seosamh / Buachaillí Uí Chonaill, the local GAA Club. It is a hopeful sign in the inner city to see two clubs in close proximity providing much needed amenities for local young people.

In fact, boxer Kellie Harrington grew up on nearby Portland Row. Winning gold in the Lightweight division in the Tokyo Olympics 2020, held in 2021 as a result of Covid 19, crowned her career. Along with Emmet Brennan, another Olympian from the area, she was driven through their old neighbourhood on an open-top bus as locals ran after it, chanting with joy. She put the proud community of Portland Row on the national and international maps. Kellie was awarded Honorary Freedom of Dublin City in June 2022. It was a pleasure to see her as Grand Marshall of the St Patrick's Day Parade. She also features on one of *An Post* stamp collections celebrating Irish sports women.

At the end of Seville Place, I turn onto the traffic-busy North Strand Road. A stone monument here commemorates those who lost their lives during the Second World War, when German bombs were dropped on the North Strand in May 1941, despite the fact that Ireland was neutral at the time. It resulted in the loss of over forty lives, the infliction of many injuries and the destruction of hundreds of homes.

I have a childhood memory of my parents speaking to me and my siblings of the great tragedy. They told us about the shortage of food

Towpath arches with safety barriers, Newcomen Bridge

supplies and coal, an inconvenience of minor importance after the bombs fell. A special mention was given to the unpalatable shell cocoa, which they had to drink in place of tea.

Arriving at Newcomen Bridge and the 1st Lock, I re-join the towpath and continue my journey by the Royal Canal. The bridge is named after Sir William Gleadowe Newcomen, a canal company director. Many of the earlier bridges, dating back to the canal's construction, were named after the company's directors or shareholders, thus immortalizing their names in stone. These splendid works were made from natural stone which was quarried, and then cut to the required size with hammer and chisel. Each piece is unique giving each bridge a distinctive look. The majority are built from cut limestone, but a small few, such as Newcomen Bridge and Clarke Bridge, are constructed from cut granite.

The fact that these bridges are still in use today is testament to the quality of the stone used and to the skill of the workers. However, Newcomen Bridge collapsed during construction and had to be rebuilt. Unfortunately, two workers lost their lives in that tragedy.

Newcomen Bridge carries the North Strand Road over the canal and in recent years a steel pedestrian bridge has been installed parallel to it. An unusual feature of this structure is that it is only one of two which have a separate arch for the towpath. However, as it opens out onto an operational railway, access to the arch is restricted for safety reasons.

Before moving on, I look back toward the section of railway land closed to the public which I have just circumvented. Just 100 metres off is a railway lifting bridge that carries a single track loop line at low level across the canal. It marks the end of Spencer Dock. Apparently it was named Effin Bridge by the numerous boat people who cursed it whenever they missed its scheduled lifting time. It is clogged with an unbelievable assortment of rubbish, from plastic bottles to car wheels, tin cans and lengths of wood.

In Dick Warner's superb TV series *Waterways: The Royal Canal*, in which he takes the 70 foot barge *Rambler* along the Royal, he tells us that it took the crew half a day to travel the one kilometre from the sea lock to Newcomen Bridge. Insufficient depth of water, along with the enormous amount of debris present at this lifting bridge, contributed to the delay.

Re-joining the towpath, I pass by the 1st Lock. The old, white-washed lockkeeper's cottage is on the opposite bank, the first of many I shall encounter along the canal. The windows are boarded up and the side wall plastered with graffiti, but the structure looks solid, with the slated roof intact. Some of the original lockhouses have either fallen to ruin or have been completely demolished. However, there are still enough to remind us what they looked like, and also the essential work of their inhabitants in ensuring the passage of barges along the canal.

A two-roomed lockhouse came with the job, providing a home for the lockkeeper and his family. A lockkeeper was on duty twenty-four hours each day, seven days a week. He had to tend to boats day and night, regulate the flow of water and check the towpath banks regularly for a distance of perhaps three miles either side of the lock. This meant that he could not always be present when a boat arrived. In such a case, it frequently fell to his wife to operate the sluices and swing the lock gates.

Lockkeepers today have a different role than that of their counterparts in former times. Boating now takes place mainly during daylight hours because the canal is now used for pleasure rather than trade. The lockkeepers work eight to ten hours a day, seven days a week from March to September. From October until February they work 10 hours a week, at their own discretion.

As I walk along the tarmac towpath it feels like stepping onto a red carpet that will take me all the way to the Shannon. I pass two swans lost in a glide of serenity on the calm water. Up ahead is the beautifully preserved cut stone granite of Clarke Bridge, at the junction of Summerhill Parade and Ballybough Road. It is named after Edward Clarke, another canal director.

Croke Park from canal bank

Walking under its splendid arch, I am faced with the towering edifice that is Croke Park, the 80,000 plus capacity GAA stadium, and headquarters to the Gaelic Athletic Association. This stadium is hallowed ground to all those county teams who train hard so that they might get a chance to compete here in the later stages of the league or championship. It is named after Archbishop Thomas Croke and stands on the far bank, butting right up to the canal.

The wind is channelled along this section as if propelled by a large fan and I have to hold on tightly to my cap. I pass under a number of footbridges allowing access to the grounds.

Besides GAA hurling and football matches, the stadium has been used for other sporting events. Muhammad Ali defeated Al 'Blue' Lewis here in July 1972. He was to return, almost 30 years later, with the athletes of the US Special Olympics team to a rapturous welcome.

Big names from the world of music have also played here including U2, Tina Turner, Robbie Williams, The Police, Garth Brooks and Neil Diamond.

In the past, 'foreign' games were forbidden in the GAA grounds by Rule 42. When Lansdowne Road, the home of Irish rugby and soccer, was being redeveloped into the Aviva Stadium from 2007-2010, a historic change to this rule took place. It paved the way for non-GAA games to be played in the sacrosanct grounds. The second rugby match to take place here was Ireland versus England. It was surrounded by controversy, since it involved playing *God Save the Queen* in a venue where British soldiers had killed fourteen spectators on Bloody Sunday, 1920. But time had moved on and both anthems were greeted with respect. Ireland had much to celebrate, when it was all over, having beaten the English 43-13.

Looking ahead from Clonliffe Bridge, I notice that the concrete towpath is blocked by a metal rail barrier so another detour is required, forcing me to walk down Russell Street.

Brendan Behan was born in No. 14, in one of the tenements that lined these streets in former times, replaced now by two-storey, red-brick, terraced houses with small, neatly-kept gardens.

Looking back from Clonliffe Bridge

The Behans surely encapsulated the social and political history of their time: socialism, workers' rights, republicanism and the Irish language to name a few. Brendan's mother, Kathleen Behan, came from a republican background. Her brother, the poet Peadar Kearney, wrote 'A Soldier's Song', which became our National Anthem. She had two sons, Rory and Sean, with her first husband Jack Furlong, who died from the great influenza epidemic in 1918.

In 1922, at the beginning of the Civil War, Kathleen met Stephen Behan. He was arrested by the Free State and spent two years in Kilmainham Gaol, during which time Brendan was born in 1923. Kathleen reared her family in a tenement owned by Stephen's mother in Russell Street. The other children born to Kathleen and Stephen were Seamus, Dominic, Brian, Carmel and also Fintan who died young.

Kathleen was always singing and in 1981 she released her first long-playing record, *When All the World Was Young*. Her love of music was certainly passed on to her children and to Dominic in particular. Besides being involved in fighting for workers' rights and becoming prominent in the Dublin Unemployed Movement, Dominic was also a playwright, novelist and broadcaster, and is regarded as one of the most influential Irish songwriters of the twentieth century, having written such well-known songs as 'Liverpool Lou', 'McAlpine's Fusiliers' and 'The Patriot Game'.

Kathleen gives a vivid description in her autobiography, *Mother of all the Behans,* of how these tenement dwellers, or 'The Rustlers' as they were known, overcame poverty through their great community spirit and camaraderie.

As I walk down Russell Street I envisage gangs of children, of all ages, playing together on these streets. I can almost hear the rhymes being sung by girls while skipping. I can see ropes tied to lamp-posts being used as swings, and boys playing with sticks and hoops or self-made footballs.

Brendan's membership of the IRA landed him first in a borstal in England and later in prison in Ireland. However, he used his time of incarceration to develop a keen love of literature and to become a fluent Irish speaker. He went on to write some classics of twentieth century literature, including his plays *The Quare Fellow* and *An Giall*, which he translated to English as *The Hostage*.

Brendan's autobiographical novel *The Borstal Boy* was an immediate best seller. There is a wonderful passage at the end describing Brendan on deck as the boat sails into Dun Laoghaire, after his expulsion from Britain. In it he picks out all the landmarks around Dublin Bay including the mountain peaks, the church spires (Saint Laurence O'Toole's being one of them), and also the Poolbeg Chimneys.

View of 2nd Lock at Binn's Bridge on South Side of Bridge

Brendan died in 1964 at the young age of forty-one. But what a legacy he left behind!

At the end of Russell Street I turn onto the North Circular Road and continue as far as Dorset Street. I can now rejoin the canal towpath at Binns Bridge. When I reach it, I discover a man fishing on the narrow bank of green between the canal and the railway line, totally absorbed in his pastime. I pause for a short while on the bridge, reflecting happily on today's walk.

As I travel home by train, I recall the many engrossing people and places that I discovered. From the quays I have encountered unexpected diversions which, surprisingly, have led me into unfamiliar parts of the north city, where every street seems to have its own unique story to tell.

2.

Drumcondra to Broadstone

Street Soccer, Mountjoy Prison, City Basin and Broadstone

Three days later, on the second day of my canal walk, I get into full throttle and expect to cover the 16.5 kilometres from Binns Bridge, Drumcondra, to Cope Bridge, Leixlip. On this overcast day, I take the train from Leixlip to Drumcondra station and walk to the canal.

Standing on Binns Bridge, I get to thinking about some well-known personalities that came from around here. The football pundit, Eamon Dunphy, always an advocate of children playing street football, came from this locality. I can imagine him, back in the days when traffic was very light, kicking ball with his mates up some side street near here, four coats laid out to form two goalposts.

Eamon also became involved in the famous seven-a-side tournaments played on tarmac in the Gloucester Diamond, a short walk from here. Thousands gathered around the pitch, while others watched from the tenement windows and roofs. Young lads honed many useful skills from playing in such tight spaces.

In 1978, Eamon ended his career in professional football to concentrate on a career in journalism and writing. In the 1980s he appeared regularly on Irish television as a football analyst.

The fine, cut limestone structure of Binns Bridge is named after John Binns, one of the founders of the Royal Canal Company. He had previously been a director of the Grand Canal Company and has the distinction of lending his name to a bridge on both canals. The 2nd Lock, the deepest on the Royal Canal, is also located here. It is unusual in that its lower chamber has been constructed under the bridge, with the Drumcondra Road traffic passing over it. The 2nd Lock is the first of a succession of double-chambered locks through which the canal rises steeply out of the city. Double-chambered locks are used when the canal must make a change in level greater than could be achieved by a single chamber. The lockkeeper's cottage was located on the opposite bank close to the bridge.

Leonardo da Vinci invented the mitre lock gates in 1497, which are still in use today. The gates at the canal high level are called breast gates and those at the lower level tail gates. The lock chamber, which is in between the two sets of gates, is filled or emptied as required by raising or lowering the sluices within those gates. The gates are opened and closed manually by pushing on the balance beam of the gate. When closing the gates it is important that the mitred edges meet cleanly.

Pigeons dominate the canal bank here, while mallards rule the water. A lone swan preens itself on the bank, the webbed feet looking unnaturally large out of water. A solitary heron appears less shy than his country cousins, yet still moves from bank to wall avoiding close contact with me.

A wonderful John Coll sculpture on the bank depicts Brendan Behan sitting relaxed on a bench, observing a pigeon perched on the other end.

Sculpture of Brendan Behan at Binns Bridge

The nonchalant pose perfectly reflects the man. Four intertwined triangles form part of the upright back section of the bench, which displays quotations from the playwright and poet, including the poignant poem 'Loneliness', or 'Uaigneas' as it was called in the original Irish.

I smile as I recall how passing this sculpture one day, I noticed that Brendan had acquired a pair of sunglasses, a nice expression of Dublin wit. I sit down beside him for a short interval, hoping to soak up just a fraction of his genius.

I commence today's journey along the towpath, passing by the occasional native tree. As I look across the rail line to the far side of the Whitworth Road, I see terraces of elegant red-bricked houses, some with bay windows. Old-style lamp posts along the canal banks help add to the historical character of this area.

As I pass the double-chambered 3rd Lock, I notice a long jetty on the far bank which is slightly staggered to accommodate a beautiful oak tree growing there. It marks the end of some domestic housing, as the high walls at the back of Mountjoy Prison rise imposingly in their place.

3rd Lock looking west

This was Brendan Behan's home from 1942-1946. Opened in 1850, it is commonly referred to as The Joy, and was named after Luke Gardiner, Lord Mountjoy, who was responsible for building Mountjoy Square, Gardiner Street and Blessington Street.

The words and tune of 'The Old Triangle', from Brendan's play *The Quare Fellow*, resound poignantly in my head, as visions of mice scurrying around his prison cell rise before me. That old metal triangle still hangs in The Joy, though it is no longer used to waken prisoners in the morning. The jingle jangle is gone. I wonder what has replaced it?

Drumcondra to Broadstone

The wall of Mountjoy Prison continues along the far bank past the doubled-chambered 4th Lock. It then runs behind the Dakota Court apartments, just before Cross Guns Business Park.

These apartments are built on much of the original junction between the Broadstone Line and the branch heading towards Spencer Dock. Broadstone Harbour was infilled back in 1879, whereas the rest of this channel between Broadstone and the 5th Lock did not meet the same fate until 1927. In the 1930s the area was converted into a very beautiful linear park, much frequented by the public.

Making a small detour I walk towards the site of the former Broadstone Harbour, the original canal terminus. This harbour was constructed close to the city markets, a major trading area of the city, and close to many institutions including the Richmond Penitentiary, the Richmond Lunatic Asylum, the North Dublin Union Workhouse, the Female Penitentiary, the Linen Hall and the Queen's Inns.

I traverse Cross Guns Bridge at Phibsborough and follow the sweeping wall of Mountjoy Prison which becomes the eastern boundary of the linear park.

The back of Mountjoy Prison viewed from the canal

Cross Guns Bridge

Strolling along, I arrive at a very impressive red brick building, over which is etched, PUBLIC LIBRARY and ERECTED 1934, just seven years after this section of the canal was infilled.

Entering the grounds of the library from Blaquiere Bridge, I examine a sculpture which represents the flow of water, set at the edge of a miniature, man-made pond, with an olive tree in the background. Stepping stones, some with inscriptions, run in a semicircle about it. As I read them, I realize this is the first sentence from James Joyce's novel, *Finnegan's Wake*.

> *riverrun, past Eve and Adam's, from swerve of shore to bend of bay, brings us by a commodious vicus of recirculation back to Howth Castle and Environs*

Returning to Blaquiere Bridge, under which the canal once flowed, I cross the North Circular Road. A sign here indicates Inns Quay Ward, and at the far end Arran Quay Ward, the bridge marking the boundary between these two electoral divisions.

Behind the railing of the bridge is a monument depicting a soldier on one knee holding a rifle. An inscription in Irish is in remembrance of members of C company who fought for the freedom of Ireland.

Descending a series of steps from the bridge, I return to the linear park, a peaceful tree-lined enclave surrounded by the bustle of the city streets nearby. A stone wall to my left now becomes its boundary.

I soon arrive at a mysterious, black metal door. On entering, a host of pigeons come swirling down in a flutter and land on the railing in front of me. The long curve of a human arm spreads a semicircle of temptation and the avian flock zone in on the coveted bread. On the water below, tufted ducks wait for the crumbs to fall from above, a change from the marine invertebrates and aquatic plants that they normally dive for. Two swans spread their wings and fill the air with their swooshing sound, as they fly to the far end of this artificial lake.

Linear Park looking towards Blaquiere Bridge

The Old City Basin was originally called the Royal George Reservoir, marking the Golden Jubilee of King George III. It covers an area of approximately 1.75 acres, and the soil excavated from it was used to build up the harbour at Broadstone. On completion in 1809, it was filled with water from the Royal Canal to feed the expanding north side of Dublin, which it served for nearly sixty years. Over time, there were many complaints regarding the quality of the water. The primitive filter system of a wire mesh with a gravel bank across its centre stood little chance of achieving its purpose, with locals washing clothes in the canal, dogs paddling in it, and cattle boats pumping their bilge into it. In 1868 the new Vartry Water Works was built, from which the city then got its water supply, and so the basin became more or less redundant.

A high stone wall encloses this hidden park. The Old City Basin is made up mostly of water, which is now fed from the mains water supply. An artificial island, densely planted with trees and shrubs, has been created in its centre, a haven for the feathered residents. I stroll along the pathway by the protective rail that surrounds the water.

Plaque to commemorate the opening of the City Basin Park

Young mothers push their small children in buggies and two young men sit chatting on a wrought iron bench. Under a tree by the water's edge, a fairy garden is dotted with toadstools and fairy charms, a tiny wonderland for city children visiting this wildlife gem.

An information sign here explains 'food chains' and the 'food web' within the basin and the network of inter-relationships between animals and plants. A sign urges people not to feed bread to ducks and swans, as it is neither good for the birds or the water. It suggests alternatives such as lettuce, celery, bird seed or mealworms.

I pass the stone control building for this reservoir where the water supply enters. Beyond it is a Tudor Revival style gate lodge with the inscription, The Lodge 1811, on the apex, built as a residence for the basin keeper.

The impressive bronze works of local sculptor Austin McQuinn, called *Natural Histories*, are mounted within niches along the park's north wall.

Old Basin Keeper's Lodge

Lovely stonework and benches in City Basin Park

Further on, a plaque bears a poem, called 'The Basin in Blessington Street', by Noel Manly. He talks of this 'quiet oasis, far from the blare of the city strife', which sums up my thoughts precisely.

Reluctantly exiting the Basin's retreat, I continue along the grassy park past two newly refurbished houses, which at one time made up the Royal Canal ticket office. Beside them, backing onto student accommodation, is the Broadstone Community Garden, full of thriving vegetables and flowers, grown and cared for by the local people.

I arrive at a circular area high above the surrounding streets and I am now looking down on Broadstone and Constitution Hill. To my left is the impressive King's Inns building, designed by James Gandon in 1785, with its large grounds. To my right is the old Broadstone Railway Station.

Constitution Hill was substantially lower than the level of the canal, so Foster Aqueduct, named in honour of John Foster, the last speaker of the Irish House of Commons, was built to allow the canal to cross over it. Once this was complete, a large harbour was dug to serve as a terminus. The aqueduct was a fine example of early nineteenth century engineering. Its main arch had a span of 30 feet, with two smaller arches for pedestrians. A breach in this structure would have caused devastating flooding in Dublin, but it was well up to its job. In 1951, it was demolished to facilitate the widening of Phibsborough Road.

There was a Royal Canal Hotel at Broadstone and another at Moyvalley, where passengers could enjoy hospitality before boarding the passage boats. Two boats departed from Dublin each day, one early in the morning and the other at 1:00 pm, which stopped overnight at Moyvalley before continuing to Mullingar, with similar arrangements for the return journey.

Broadstone Harbour was a busy place in the early 1800s. Boats arrived daily from the midlands, delivering cargoes of cattle and pigs, as well as turf and agricultural produce. On the return journey, the same boats would be laden with such items as coal, casks of porter and tea.

A painting titled 'Broadstone Harbour in 1818' by Samuel Brocas, illustrated in Ruth Delany and Ian Bath's *Ireland's Royal Canal, 1789-2009*, depicts a wide basin of water against a backdrop of city dwellings, including the Four Courts, with the Dublin Mountains in the distance. The barges carrying cargoes of turf are docked in the harbour and on the banks are stacked large heaps of turf and building materials. The area is a hive of activity, with men dragging boats to the bank, local people carrying away baskets of produce and horse-drawn carts being loaded. Amidst all this activity, two members of the local gentry in very fine attire, a lady in an elegant gown and a gentleman in top hat and tails, stroll along the banks of the harbour.

I have made some amazing discoveries by taking this detour along the old Broadstone branch of the canal. It was a journey back in time to a very different Dublin. It showed me how Dublin has changed to accommodate the city dwellers of today, while managing to retain the Old City Basin in all its former glory.

3.

Broadstone to Glasnevin

Poets, Broadcasters, Pacifists and Liberators

Leaving the site of the former Broadstone Harbour, I re-join the canal by walking up Constitution Hill, along the Phibsborough Road, and eventually arriving back at Cross Guns Bridge. Back on the towpath, I stroll by the waterway with my sights on Glasnevin.

The official name for Cross Guns Bridge is Westmoreland Bridge, because in November 1790, John Fane, Earl of Westmoreland, laid the first stone of the double-chambered lock at this location. Listed as the 1st Lock when Broadstone Harbour was the terminus, it was renamed the 5th Lock when Spencer Dock became the new destination.

The original bridge was apparently removed. The current one was rebuilt circa 1864. Unusually, the safety barrier is constructed of cast iron, with elaborate curved lines, and is finished with a pale-green paint. It has a different decorative charm to the cut stone. The name Cross Guns refers to an inn which was situated north of here at Hart's Corner.

While taking some photographs from the lock, I strike up a conversation with a man who is standing on the bank feeding the ducks.

'It's lovely around here,' I say.

'Ah, sure it's amazing. Where are you from yourself?'

'Further up the canal, at Leixlip.'

'We're blessed, so we are, to have the canal on our doorstep.'

Then he went on to relate some antisocial behaviour. 'Ye get some lads dealin' drugs just up the way there.'

'Yeah! That's a pity. There's so much of it going on about the city.'

He pointed out a stone wall along the far bank, which had been graffitied. A mesh wire fence had been erected on it, topped off with barbed wire to keep out trespassers.

'Some new age travellers moved in there a while ago, into that old building with the galvanised roof. They've basically created a ladder for themselves by removing some stones from this side of the wall for a foothold and cut a hole through the mesh wire for access.'

Looking towards the 6th Lock

Changing the subject he then asks, 'Are you out for a walk?'

'Yeah, I'm walking the canal today from Binns Bridge to Cope Bridge in Leixlip.'

'Go on with you then and get your walk in,' he says jovially. 'You've a long way to go.'

Immediately after the 5th Lock, I discover that the canal expands to form a harbour. On the far bank stands an old, grey stone building, formerly Mallet's Mill Iron Works, the site being leased by Robert and John Mallet in 1822. The Royal Canal Company referred to all industrial buildings as mills. It is good to see that the building has been preserved, having been converted into apartments.

John Mallet's son, Robert, who designed the floors of the Scherzer Bridges at George's Dock and Spencer Dock, was an early pioneer of seismology, the study of energy released by volcanoes. Today, he is considered the father of seismology and is credited with coining the term.

I am soon approaching the double-chambered 6th Lock. Some houses line the far bank, as the waterway narrows to its normal width again.

The village of Glasnevin is to the north and is steeped in history. Its Irish name is Glas Naíon, meaning 'stream of the child'. It is believed

Double-chambered 6th Lock

this stream ran through a monastic settlement here. It was by the banks of the Tolka River in Glasnevin that St. Mobhi founded a monastery and monastic school in the sixth century. A local church and road are named after him. Among his pupils were St. Canice of Finglas, St. Colmcille of Iona, and St. Comgall of Bangor. On his death, his girdle was brought to Colmcille who said: 'Good was the man who had this girdle, for it was never opened for gluttony, nor closed on falsehood.'

In the eighteenth century, the poet Thomas Tickell owned land around Glasnevin. He built a big house here in 1740 on a hill rising high above the Tolka valley. The house and lands were acquired by the Royal Dublin Society in the 1790s, with the aim of establishing Ireland's first botanic gardens, which still thrive to this day.

One of the most deeply engrained memories from my childhood is the fire and spirit in the voice of the Glasnevin-born Michael O'Hehir filling our living room with the progress of a GAA match or a horse race. In the days before television, a large portion of the country would gather around their radios, listening to his running commentaries. When Ireland's first national television station, Telefís Éireann, was founded in 1961, Michael was appointed head of sports programmes.

In November 1963, O'Hehir was on a trip to New York which coincided with the assassination of President John F. Kennedy. The responsibility to report on the funeral fell to O'Hehir and his coverage on Telefís Éireann won him praise, both in Ireland and the U.S. He died in 1996.

Close to the 6th Lock, on the north path, there is a galvanised steel, palisade fence which marks the boundary of Glasnevin Cemetery, also known as Prospect Cemetery. It is the final resting place of many famous Irish people. Its plots are burning with the bones of revolutionaries, peaceful or militant, spurred on or tempered by the pens of authors and religious figures.

Prior to its opening, Irish Catholics had no cemetery of their own because the Penal Laws had curtailed the performance of Catholic services. Daniel O'Connell (1775-1847), known as 'The Liberator', prepared a legal case to challenge this situation. He then pushed for a cemetery where both Catholics and Protestants could be buried, which eventually led to the opening of Prospect Cemetery, the first burial taking place there in 1832.

Daniel favoured reform by non-violent methods. He was a skilful lawyer and a charismatic orator. He campaigned for Catholic Emancipation, which he secured in 1829, giving Catholics the right to sit in the Westminster Parliament, denied for over 100 years.

In 1847, while on a pilgrimage to Italy at age seventy-one, he died in Genoa. According to his dying wish, his heart was buried in Rome and the remainder of his body was interred in Glasnevin Cemetery. It lies in an oak coffin beneath a large altar stone of black Kilkenny marble.

O'Connell Tower in Glasnevin Cemetery

O'Connell Tower

The round tower above the crypt, called the O'Connell Tower, is a distinctive landmark on Glasnevin's skyline, clearly visible from the canal bank, standing at 51 metres tall.

Another major political figure, Charles Stuart Parnell, rests here in Glasnevin. During the latter part of the nineteenth century he worked to achieve Home Rule, as well as the rights of tenants to their land. Despite his affair with a married woman, Kitty O'Shea, and the failure of his Home Rule Bill, his funeral when he died in 1891 at the age of forty-four was the largest ever seen at Glasnevin. Mourners took sprigs of ivy from the cemetery walls to wear in their buttonholes, giving rise to the denoting of Parnell's Remembrance Day as 'Ivy Day'.

One of the most courageous, though less well-known, of our revolutionaries interred here is Anne Devlin. When Robert Emmet's party began to draw up plans and preparations for the rebellion of 1803, Anne Devlin was taken on, ostensibly as a housekeeper. In fact she facilitated communications between the leaders of the planned insurrection, constantly putting herself in danger.

The rebellion failed, however, and Anne Devlin was imprisoned. Despite being constantly interrogated, insulted and tortured, she refused to inform on Emmet and his followers. She was released three years later, penniless and in poor health.

Sir Roger Casement, who was born in Dublin in 1864, also rests here. While working for the British Consulate in remote regions of the Upper Congo, and later in a remote tributary of the Amazon, he observed colonialism in its most brutal and degrading form, which he presented in his reports, earning him a knighthood. In 1913 he retired from the Foreign Office and began to play a significant role in

Irish affairs. He was the principal organiser of the Howth gun-running in 1914. Some of these weapons were used in the Easter Rising.

On Good Friday 1916, after landing at Banna Strand with a German arms ship and submarine, Casement was arrested, tried for treason and hanged. He was buried in quicklime in the cemetery at Pentonville Prison, London. In 1965, his body was exhumed and repatriated to Ireland, and half a million people filed past his coffin in Arbour Hill, before being taken to his final resting place in Glasnevin Cemetery.

Resting among all those involved in Ireland's search for freedom is one of my favourite poets, the English Jesuit, Gerard Manly Hopkins. The themes of his poems mainly concern the natural world and religion. He began eventually to experiment with unusual metres and rhythms and in particular, sprung rhythm. This influenced the rise of free verse in the early twentieth century. His fascinating use of imagery marks him as a poet with a great vision, whose poetry outshone the mostly traditional poetry of his age.

His well-known poem 'Spring' was part of the second level English curriculum for many years.

> *Nothing is so beautiful as Spring –*
> *When weeds, in wheels, shoot long and lovely and lush;*
> *Thrush's eggs look little low heavens, and thrush*
> *Through the echoing timber does so rinse and wring*
> *The ear, it strikes like lightnings to hear him sing ...*

In 1884, Hopkins was appointed professor of Greek literature at University College Dublin. He died of typhoid fever in 1889 and was buried in Glasnevin Cemetery.

It is now time to leave the 6th Lock and this notable cemetery behind and continue on my journey.

4.

Glasnevin to Broombridge

Hedgerows, Trains, Equations and a Hanging Judge

With the end of February approaching, even within this urban setting, I can sense spring awakening in the hedgerow. The Irish native hedgerow is made up mostly of hawthorn, blackthorn, bramble, holly, crab apple, hazel and birch. This mix is important for wildlife diversity, supporting species such as badgers, owls, stoats, hedgehogs, as well as a variety of plants, birds and insects. Hedgerows provide food and shelter for pollinators and can help to alleviate flooding. Here on the north bank, along the boundary fence of Glasnevin Cemetery, is a magnificent tangle of shrubs and trees, creating a perfect native hedgerow.

The blackthorn is just starting to bloom and will soon be covered with starry white flowers, before any leaves appear, as they brave the last of the chilly weather. In Seamus Heaney's translation of the anonymous Irish poem, 'Sweeney Praises the Trees', he refers to the blackthorn as a 'jaggy creel'. The deep-blue fruit of the blackthorn are called sloes. Extreme care is required picking them from the jaggy creel because its thorns, which carry a toxin, can inflict a nasty wound.

The leafy hawthorn waits until May or June to display its blossom, hence its alternative name, the Maybush. The small, shiny, bright-red berries of the hawthorn are called haws.

Brambles, which produce blackberries, are also in abundance along much of the canal route. When autumn comes, foragers will set forth with bowls or bags, collecting sloes, haws and blackberries, from which delicious jams and jellies can be made.

Beyond the 6th Lock, the cemetery's boundary fence is moving slowly away from me, as Phibsborough merges into Cabra. Soon after I pass a row of red brick artisan cottages, some of which have been refurbished and extended, with gardens that can be accessed from the towpath. These are the Coke Oven cottages built in the mid-nineteenth century and one of them housed the Station Master for the Midland Great Western Railway. Over the next kilometre I will learn that this area has always been, and still is, an important railway hub.

The train line below passes under the canal aqueduct here, diverting from Heuston Station into the Phoenix Park Tunnel and on to Connolly Station. This tunnel is 692 metres in length and was opened in 1877. Passenger trains ceased using it on a regular basis around the year 2000. In 2016, the tunnel reopened to commuter trains, facilitating passengers from Kildare and surrounding areas to travel on to Connolly Station and the city centre.

A pair of young swans has drifted close to the bank. Their juvenile feathers are still in the process of turning fully white and their beaks have still yet to gain that magnificent distinctive patch of yellow.

Two young swans

I come across two lads fishing, who have just been rewarded with a fine specimen of pike. It is approximately two feet long and must weigh about five pounds. They agree to pose for a photo. The lad who caught the fish takes its dark speckled back in his hands and holds it proudly, with its white belly facing me, while I focus and snap. I congratulate him and recommence my walk.

On my approach to the 7th Lock, a sign behind a wire mesh fence on Irish Rail land announces, Cabra for Youth, Community Garden-Helping Young People to Grow. It is in its early stages, with the construction of some raised beds in progress. I wish the garden and the youth all the growth they deserve with this inspiring project.

Fine specimen of pike

Ahead of me, I notice two figures standing by a barrier across the towpath. As I get closer, one is taking a gulp from a bottle of vodka and the second guy has his own bottle balancing on the barrier's crossbeam.

'Howeya,' the gulper says to me. His tone is friendly and light-hearted.

'Ah, sure not a bother. How's yourself?'

He nods, indicating he's fine and mumbles something I don't quite catch and so I move safely on.

I enter a short underpass beneath the bridge that carries the Dublin-Sligo line over the canal, which runs on the south side of the waterway, all the way to the Ballinea Bridges west of Mullingar. Emerging at the far side I am confronted by the site of the former Liffey Junction Railway Station and the 7th Lock. A short railway branch that ran from the Liffey at North Wall joined the old Broadstone-Mullingar line at this former hub. This station closed to passengers in 1926.

All that is left of Liffey Junction Station is the remains of an old water tower, and a sluice that provided water to the railway, remnants of our extensive railway heritage. In the past, a regular supply of water was required for steam engines, and with the canal close by, there was no shortage of this commodity.

South of here lies the suburb of Cabra, known as Cabragh until the early twentieth century. Up until the 1930s, it marked the northwestern boundary of Dublin City. The area to the west consisted mostly of fields, used for market gardening and as pastures for the grazing cattle that were destined for the cattle market on Hanlon's Corner.

In 1938 Dublin Corporation announced a new housing development to be called Cabra West, one of the most ambitious housing projects in Europe at that time. This was in response to the dreadful overcrowding and poor living conditions in the tenements of Dublin. Building began in the early 1940s and by 1946 2,249 houses had been built, despite a shortage of building materials during the Emergency years. When German bombs fell on the North Strand in 1941, work intensified on the Cabra West project, providing much needed homes for those unfortunate families left homeless after the bombing.

Cabra residents have many celebrities to be proud of, such as Dickie Rock, who was born in 1946. He fronted the Miami Showband, storming the Irish stages and charts in the 1960s with his own form of Beatlemania. I still remember listening to his hits on our radio, as presenters played such songs as 'From the Candy Store on the Corner' and 'Georgie Porgie'. In 1966 he represented Ireland in the Eurovision Song Contest, with the song 'Come Back to Stay', finishing in fourth place. Dickie embarked on a solo career in 1972.

Tragedy struck in 1975 as three members of the Miami Showband were murdered in a UVF bomb attack, when the band were returning from a gig in Banbridge, County Down.

Dickie continued to tour around the Irish music circuit until he took to the stage for his last gig at the Red Cow Inn on 28 December 2019 at the age of eighty-two.

7th Lock Liffey Junction

Cabra has also been blessed with some great writers, including the award winning journalist Gene Kerrigan. For over three decades he has been a highly influential voice in Ireland, standing up for workers and highlighting injustice in his current affairs column in *The Sunday Independent*.

Kerrigan has also earned renown as an author. In his book *Another Country: Growing Up in '50s Ireland*, he recounts growing up in Cabra, weaving family and street life with the society and politics of the day. He also examines the impact of major figures on Irish society, such as de Valera, Michael O'Hehir and Hector Grey.

A direct antithesis of Gene Kerrigan is the historical figure John Toler, otherwise known as the First Earl of Norbury, whose country residence, Cabragh House, was located here in Cabra. It was demolished in the 1930s to make way for local authority housing.

Toler became known as The Hanging Judge. Allegedly, he thought nothing of cracking jokes while passing the death sentence. He was infamous for his corruption and incompetence. He prosecuted many leading figures within the United Irishmen, including Robert Emmet in 1803. According to most accounts, he constantly harangued and abused Emmet during his famous Speech from the Dock, before sentencing him to hanging. Whatever the truth, we know that Abraham Lincoln knew Emmet's speech off by heart, and it is thought likely that it influenced his Gettysburg Address.

In 1827, Toler was finally discharged at the age of seventy-five, due to his absent-mindedness and his habit of falling asleep during trials. He died ten years later. The ropes for lowering his coffin were too short and a witty lad among the mourners shouted: 'Give him rope galore boys, he was never sparing of it to others.'

As I leave the 7th Lock, the factories of Dublin Industrial Estate come right up to a fence and within minutes I arrive at Broombridge train station and depot, an historic station that has been modernised, accommodating staff facilities and offices. The LUAS terminates here, with connections serving stations into Dublin, and as far south as Sandyford. It also acts as a hub for local buses, linking rail and road infrastructure.

I follow the towpath under the beautiful, old cut stone bridge. It was originally named Broome Bridge, after William Broome, another canal director. It was renamed Hamilton Bridge in 1958, after Sir William Rowan Hamilton, the Dublin-born physicist, mathematician and astronomer from Dominic Street. The transport depot is named Broombridge-Hamilton.

Hamilton, born in 1805, was considered a child prodigy. From an early age he had an astounding aptitude for learning and speaking languages. By thirteen, he had mastered Hebrew and some of the modern European languages.

Approaching Hamilton Bridge

Plaque on Hamilton Bridge

Hamilton developed an interest in mathematics and physics, entering Trinity College Dublin in 1823 at the age of eighteen. Four years later, while still an undergraduate, he was appointed Professor of Astronomy at the college, and in 1827 Royal Astronomer of Ireland. One of the perks of this position was being provided with a fine house beside Dunsink Observatory in Castleknock.

In 1843, while walking from Dunsink with his wife Helen along the Royal Canal, he had a sudden flash of genius and carved his formula for quaternion algebra $i^2 = j^2 = k^2 = ijk = -1$ into the stone of Broome Bridge. Quaternion multiplication is used today in computer gaming and space travel. However, it is generally regarded that his greatest contribution to science is his reformulation of Newtonian mechanics, which is now called Hamiltonian mechanics, used in such areas as the study of electro-magnetism and developments in quantum mechanics. He died in 1865.

A plaque celebrating Sir William's famous equation has been erected on Hamilton Bridge. I examine the grey stone of the bridge for signs of the original carved formula, but to no avail. The plaque will have to satisfy me, along with a recently added portrait of this genius.

Glasnevin to Broombridge

When I look north from here, I can see the vast suburb of Finglas, with a population of over 30,000. Its Irish name, Fionnghlas, means 'white or clear stream'. This little stream is called the Finglas River and it flows into the Tolka. According to tradition, in AD 560 a Christian monastery was founded here by St. Canice. His name is honoured still in many local places such as St. Canice's Church and St. Canice's Primary School. Though it was originally a country village outside Dublin, Finglas became a suburb of the city in the 1950s, when a wave of new housing estates sprung up all around it. Many of these estates were built to house families displaced from the inner city, as a consequence of urban development there. However, with a complex of shops and businesses close to the church and schools, it still manages to retain that village atmosphere.

An interesting article in the *North County Leader* newspaper reports on a local language called 'Fingallian' which is derived from Middle English. It was spoken in the seventeenth century alongside Irish and English. Surviving as an isolated language in North County Dublin until the mid-nineteenth century, it eventually succumbed to English.

Standing on the canal bank, I look across at the houses spreading as far as the horizon. These sprawling working class suburbs would seem to have been a hot bed of encouragement and creativity. It is generally known that the musical roots of U2 and Aslan were nurtured there.

An interesting contrast to such musicians is the Finglas man, Séamus Ennis, who followed a different musical tradition. He is widely regarded as one of the greatest uilleann pipers of all time. He was partly responsible for the revival of the instrument in the twentieth century. I was enthralled too by his singing voice and his rendition of traditional songs. Séamus was also an Irish music collector and his work with the Irish Folklore Commission resulted in the preservation of almost 2,000 Irish songs and dance-tunes. Seamus died in 1982 at the age of sixty-three, spending the final years of his life living in Naul at the northern edge of Finglas. The Seamus Ennis Arts Centre, which hosts many events, is located there.

In 1959, the author and publisher Dermot Bolger was born in Finglas. When he was just eighteen, he established the innovative Raven Arts Press which published debut novels, poetry collections, memoir and English language translations from the Irish. Many of these writers are now well known, such as, Colm Toibín, Sebastian Barry, Paul Durcan and Nuala Ní Dhomhnaill. The aim of the press was best expressed by the man himself:

> *The press never possessed a single unifying intellectual agenda, but was a loose movement for change, its course being dictated by the writers who got involved and who brought others in. It was never run as a business, but it was a huge amount of fun with serious intent, a passion and a pleasure, an adventure undertaken with a genuine love of literature and at times a genuine sense of mischief.*

The Raven Arts Press was eventually closed by Dermot in 1992, allowing him to concentrate more on his own writing.

His novels, plays and poems examine many aspects of Irish life, such as the property boom, football, drink, drugs and political corruption, giving a voice to working class people. This is very evident in his poem, 'Jesus of Clondalkin'.

> *Passing half built apartment blocks investors own,*
> *Passing burnt-out cars, glass shards, twisted chrome,*
> *..*
> *Maybe we are so adrift in our own cares that we fail*
> *To see whip marks, collapsed veins, his crown of thorns.*

With Dermot's words resonating in my head, and thinking of all the creativity nurtured in these working class areas of west Dublin, I leave Hamilton Bridge, heading west once again, open to new discoveries along the way.

5.

BROOMBRIDGE TO BLANCHARDSTOWN

Parks, Mansions, Astronomy and Barges

Beyond Hamilton Bridge, my head begins to grapple with that great man's formula and to contemplate the genius behind it. However, I am quickly brought back down to earth as I pass a cluster of small industrial estates, bordered to the north by Ballyboggan Road and the Tolka River. The factory buildings have a dated look, built of corrugated iron, now rusted, with most windows boarded up. They are behind a metal palisade fence, topped with a predominance of spikes, and abundance of concertina razor wire coils. Part of the fence is covered with a drab display of graffiti, another strand to its ominous appearance.

Further along the fence, a burnt out motorbike is half buried in the bramble. However, in contrast, two preening swans filling the bank with life, oblivious to the destruction close by, are a picture of purity that lifts my spirit.

A new bridge of precast concrete slabs and green metal looms before me to the west. A little beyond it lies the old, preserved stone structure. Its function had been to carry the Rathoath Road over the railway and canal. The level crossing on the adjacent rail line had been one of the busiest in the country, causing delays for traffic, train commuters, and pedestrians alike. It has now been removed, with all vehicles freely traversing across the modern, green arched bridge. The old bridge is now closed on the south side creating a cul-de-sac.

As I approach I can hear whistling. I turn onto the bridge to discover that the whistler is a man in his fifties, wearing an An Post jacket.

'A lovely day,' he says, facing me with a warm glow in his cheeks and eyes.

'It certainly is,' I reply. 'Tell me, how's the new arrangement working out?'

'Well,' he says, 'it appears to benefit everyone. It was feared that it might affect business in Campbell's Garage, situated on the Finglas side of the old road and which had been effectively bypassed by the arrangement. However, as it turned out, most of their customers were local people who remained loyal to them, continuing to fill up their tanks there.'

'Well that certainly says a lot about the people around here,' I say, as I bid him goodbye to continue my journey.

The 8th Lock is just after Reilly's Bridge. Sadly, the former lock-keeper's cottage lies in ruin just off the far towpath.

New Bridge from Reilly Bridge

The newly developed residential area of Rathborne Village, together with Pelletstown, is just off the canal bank and stretches northeast to the River Tolka. As part of this development, the towpath has been resurfaced, public lighting has been installed and an arena-like stepped area leads down to the waterway.

As in the 1940s when Cabra West was built in response to a shortage of housing, this area was planned to alleviate the crisis facing Dublin in recent years. It is being developed as a small village-style community, with local access to shops, bars, restaurants and other services. A vital addition to the neighbourhood since 2021 is Pelletstown Train Station. It connects Pelletstown to Ashtown so that both communities can now access the city or Maynooth.

Having passed the 9th Lock, I arrive at a Waterways Ireland sign announcing my approach to Ashtown. On the far side of the canal are the St. Oliver Plunkett GAA Clubhouse and Sports Grounds, home to the famous Brogan brothers. Their father, Bernard Brogan Sr., won three all Ireland medals. Alan has matched his Da's achievement with his three medals, while Bernard Jr. has surpassed them both by winning seven.

Statue of man operating lock gate

Just before Longford Bridge, there is an attractive stone harbour with some mooring points. On the bank above it there is an aptly placed, life-size, cast-iron statue of a toiling lockkeeper, pushing open a lock gate.

The name Longford Bridge is on a plaque below the capstone, honouring Lord Longford, another canal company director. It carries one-way traffic over the waterway and marks the Dublin-Fingal boundary. With the population explosion in this area, one would wonder how long the out-dated level crossing on the road will suffice, before a new purpose-built bridge becomes a necessity.

Beyond the bridge, the towpath has switched to the south bank and I encounter the double-chambered 10th Lock. The former lockkeeper's cottage, painted a deep cream, with curtains on the windows, is located to the side of the towpath. As final proof that it is occupied, I have just seen a man entering the front door.

Approaching Longford Bridge and the 10th Lock

Ashtown Mill is just beyond the bridge and is set back from the waterway. In the past it used water from the canal as an energy source, and some parts of the mill-race are still visible from the towpath. The water was returned to the canal through a small arch on the city side of Longford Bridge. In 1837 it was a linseed oil mill, but over the years was used for many other purposes, including a candle factory and a polish factory. It has been lying idle for some time now. However, as it is a listed building let us hope that it can be saved and put to good use again.

Ashtown Stables, located beside the mill, offer trekking in the vast Phoenix Park, which is close by. It is one of the largest enclosed parks in the world within a city limit, covering an area of 1,752 acres, with a seven-mile wall circumventing it. The name is derived from the Irish Páirc an Fhionnuisce, meaning 'Park of the Clear Water'.

Originally formed as a royal hunting park in the seventeenth century, it was opened to the public in 1747. A large herd of fallow deer still roam the park today. As well as the Phoenix Park Visitor Centre, the park is home to many other places of interest, including Áras an Uachtaráin, the American Embassy, Farmleigh House (the official Irish State guest house), the Wellington Testimonial, Ashtown Castle and the Zoological Gardens.

My walk has a rural feel to it now, as I become distanced from houses and traffic. It has become gradually more secluded and enjoyable, with a scattering of young deciduous trees by the towpath. The leafless trees on the pathless far bank, come right down to the water, and are interlaced with the green of ivy.

Through a gap in the trees I have a rear view of the splendid Victorian Italianate Ashton House, built circa 1830, whose grounds back onto the canal, while its front overlooks the Tolka River to the north.

On a hillock above the trees, a little north of the 10th Lock, I get a clear view of the dome of Dunsink Observatory, the former residence and place of work of Sir William Rowan Hamilton. It opened in 1785 as the observatory attached to Trinity College Dublin, and is the oldest purpose-built scientific research centre in Ireland.

In the 1880s, the local mean time at Dunsink Observatory became the legal time for all of Ireland, just as Greenwich Mean Time was for all of England. The offset at that point between both was approximately 25 minutes, 21 seconds. Summer Time was introduced in 1916 to save energy during the First World War. When Summer Time ended on 1 October 1916, clocks in Ireland were adjusted and set for Greenwich Mean Time, thus ending the official use of our own Dunsink Time.

There are a number of references to Dunsink time in James Joyce's acclaimed novel *Ulysses*, set in Dublin on 6 June 1904. In the Circe episode of *Ulysses* where Leopold Bloom is on trial, Mrs Yelverton Barry, indicating Bloom, says:

> *Arrest him, constable.... He made improper overtures to me to misconduct myself at half past four p.m. on the following Thursday, Dunsink Time.*

Dunsink Observatory

Dunsink Observatory

Dunsink was never a good site for observational astronomy because of Ireland's weather. In recent times this has been compounded by light pollution, which increasingly makes our sky less dark. It is famous instead mainly for the theoretical and mathematical work that has been carried out there.

The city starts to intrude on my tranquility once again, as I continue westward, with a noticeable increase in traffic noise. I pass St. Brigid's GAA Club, from where the air is brought to life with the enthusiastic sounds of energetic sports activity and cheering. Soon after, the high walls and building of Navan Road Parkway Train Station come into view, which caters mainly for residents of new apartments built on the old Phoenix Park Racecourse.

The rural once again envelops me as the skeletal silhouettes of trees in the still water surpass any prized painting. It lifts my heart as I walk briskly on.

The 11th Lock is double-chambered and there is an old lockkeeper's cottage on the far bank, painted a dazzling white, with a bicycle parked by the wooden fence. A magnificent spruce fir stands nearby, displaying its long, brown, cylindrical cones. Its regular shape and conical top presents as a harbinger of Christmas, even though that season is long past.

The folk group The Dubliners recorded a song called 'The Zoological Gardens'. I suspect that the lock referred to in the verse below is in fact the 11th Lock as it is on the outskirts of Castleknock.

> *We went out there by Castleknock*
> *Says she to me 'Sure we'll court on the lock'*
> *Then I knew she was one of the rare old stock*
> *From outside the Zoological Gardens.*

Over the years I'm sure this quiet secluded spot has attracted many courting couples.

My journey continues along the tarmac path until I eventually arrive at a series of bridges associated with the Blanchardstown Interchange. This enormous behemoth of modern engineering incorporates an aqueduct for the canal, while also accommodating the Dublin-Sligo train line. It is affectionately known as Spaghetti Junction. Despite the

11th Lock

11th Lock looking east

graffiti and ivy, the old Ranelagh Bridge, dwarfed by this enormous construction, still looks as sturdy and beautiful as ever. The towpath continues beneath it, allowing me to skirt under it. The M50 put paid to this bridge as a thoroughfare for cars, but it remains an important historical landmark.

Immediately after it lies the aqueduct which carries the Royal Canal over the M50 Motorway. As I stroll across its towpath by the clear water, I stop to look around and take in this amazing piece of modern engineering. I am surrounded by a network of bridges. There is traffic to the left of me, traffic to the right of me and traffic below me, yet I am safe on this isolated path, by the still water of the Royal Canal. There is something almost surreal about walking its bank with traffic whizzing all around me, the endless colours looping and swirling in all directions. However, I am quite happy to leave this strange display of continuous motion behind me and set off westward.

On the short stroll to the next canal bridge I am stopped by a grandmother pushing a small child in a buggy.

'Excuse me,' she says, 'did you notice if there are any swans along this stretch.'

Royal Canal Aqueduct at M50 interchange

'No,' I answer, 'I haven't seen any since the far side of the Blanchardstown bypass. However I did notice some ducks.'

She looks down lovingly at the little girl. 'Sorry love,' she says, 'No swans today. Will we look at more ducks?'

The little girl, glancing at me shyly, nods her head.

'Thanks,' says the grandmother, looking up at me with a gracious smile, 'I guess the ducks will have to do so.'

A few paces more and I am at Talbot Bridge, Blanchardstown, and the double-chambered 12th Lock. This marks the beginning of a 12 kilometre stretch of canal devoid of locks, ending at the 13th Lock beyond Leixlip. The whole area about here is very clean and charming, with the exception of a large, black water pipe that crosses the underside of the bridge. However, immediately beyond the bridge, there is a grassy strip between the towpath and the lock chamber, planted with shrubs and bordered by a series of bollards linked by chains. Stone steps lead up from the chamber to the footboards and breast gates at the upper level, on both sides of the canal.

A man strolls leisurely towards me. Guessing he is local, I take the opportunity to ask him about the large buildings on the far bank, which were built with varying shades of brown, white and grey stone.

'Oh,' he says, 'you're looking at the site of the former Blanchardstown Mill, an old woollen mill dating back to the early nineteenth century. It served a number of uses over the years, until it was finally demolished in 1994, having been damaged by fire.'

'So what is the present building used for?' I ask.

'They are actually apartments, built on the original mill site. In fact, some stone was recovered from the rubble of the old building and used in their construction.'

There is a friendly silence before another question enters my head.

'I noticed a culvert on my approach to the bridge, feeding into the canal from beneath the road. Was that connected with the mill?'

'Indeed, it was actually the end of the tailrace associated with it.'

I thank him kindly, delighted with this information, before I head off leaving the lock behind.

Strolling by a jetty, I examine some narrowboats and barges which are tied up to the mooring posts. They add to the allure of this quarter with a variety of brightly painted exteriors, windows with curtains or blinds, and in some cases floral displays.

The main types of boats I encountered along the length of the Royal Canal were barges, narrowboats and cabin cruisers.

A barge was a general term for a work boat. They were normally flat-bottomed vessels used for carrying cargo. Boats and barges that were specifically built for the Grand and Royal Canals were usually referred to as canal boats, the oldest form of industrial transport in Ireland. Originally horse-drawn, they eventually became motorised. Some have now been converted for leisure use, as have imported craft such as Dutch Barges. Barges are usually between 10 feet (3.05 metres) and 13 feet (3.96 metres) wide and can be up to 60 feet (18.28 metres) in length.

Old mill converted to apartments

A narrow boat is a type of craft designed specifically for the smallest canals in the British Canal System, where the lock width can be as narrow as seven feet (2.13 metres). Thus narrow boats have a beam or width of six feet, ten inches (2.08 metres) or less. They come in a variety of styles and in lengths up to 72 feet (21.94 metres). Narrow boats normally have engines. A peculiarity of the boat's spelling is that *narrow boat*, written in two words, denotes a historic craft, that is, ex-working craft. However, *narrowboat*, all one word, denotes a modern build.

Modern cabin cruisers are power boats and are used purely for leisure. Such craft are increasingly used by owners for pleasure activities, including exploring the inland waterways. They vary in length from 20 feet (6.09 metres) to 45 feet (13.7 metres).

Regardless of the choice of transport on the Royal Canal, the boat must be capable of passing through the smallest lock safely. This is lock No. 18 and its dimensions are:

Broombridge to Blanchardstown

Length: *75 feet (22.9 metres)*
Breadth: *13.3 feet (4.0 metres)*
Depth of cill: *4.7 feet (1.4 metres)*

I carry on westward by more colourful boats, reflecting on what life must be like for these canal dwellers. Storage boxes are stacked along the bank, keeping surplus possessions dry from the elements. Bins too, are close to each boat. Deck gardens adorn many of the vessels. Each occupier has made their boat their home and has settled into, what seems like, a tight-knit community along the canal bank. There is always the option to travel up and down the waterway at their choosing. It is becoming more and more an appealing way of life.

Boats at the 12th Lock

6.

BLANCHARDSTOWN TO CONFEY

Gunpowder, Tragedy, Castles and a Priory

After a short amble beyond the 12th Lock, I arrive at Granard Bridge on the Castleknock Road. Walking beneath its cut stone arch, I continue along the towpath.

Interestingly, some of the houses on the far bank have their gardens extended beyond their boundaries, right down to the canal. Most of them have a fence close to the water's edge for safety. It is strange to see wooden decking with chairs, a glasshouse, a beehive, stored wood, a ladder and even a lifebuoy in these gardens. In some cases these extended sections are being used efficiently for composting. It demonstrates the ingenuity of these residents, making the most of their enlarged property while not encroaching on anyone else's space.

My towpath is quickly transforming into a narrow muddy channel, as the canal cuts through what a sign tells me is the Deep Sinking or An Gearradh Domhain. The going gets tougher here with my hiking shoes deeply sinking into mud. However, my reward is the peace and quiet as I leave the M50 behind with the housing estates of Blanchardstown off to my right and those of Castleknock to my left. All about me are wood pigeons cooing, robins pticing and magpies chakk-kackking.

There is a rather unusual looking Waterways Ireland boat up ahead and when I reach it I discover two men on board. I address the one closest to the bank.

'Are you cutting back the trees?'

Approaching Granard Bridge

'Yes,' he answers, 'we have been working all winter, not only cutting back trees, but also clearing the canal bed.'

'Tell me this,' I say. 'I'm fascinated by the two metal arms stretching out from your boat with a tyre on each end. What are they for?'

'That arrangement is for balance and allows us to work safely. See the long mechanical arm over there,' he says, pointing, 'the one with the grab on the end. Well that's used to clear the canal bed.' The puzzle of the long arms solved, I bid them goodbye as I leave.

The name Deep Sinking is soon understood, as the walls of this 4.5 kilometres long cutting fall deeper and deeper below the towpath. The more northerly route originally proposed for the Royal Canal would have been less costly. It would have avoided the Carpenterstown quarries, necessitating time and gunpowder to construct this deep channel through the hard, black, calcareous stone. There are places along here where the solid wall of rock can be clearly seen extending down from the canal bank and into the water.

Walking this section requires some care, especially in wet weather. The path is narrow at times and the steep drop to the water below can be as much as 9 metres in places, where it resembles a gorge. Some ash saplings are growing down the sharp descent, but a well-established parent is hanging precariously by its roots, close to the top of the drop.

Deep Sinking sign

Deep Sinking towpath heading toward Kirkpatrick Bridge

The cutting through the Deep Sinking is also very narrow so that during those early days, when there was a lot of traffic on the canal, it was impossible for two boats to pass through it safely. A horn was sounded as a warning that a boat was about to enter this narrow channel. If there was no reply the boatman could proceed. However, if he heard an answering call, he waited for the other boat to pass him before entering the Deep Sinking.

My personal experience of passing through this cutting on the water was indeed thrilling. The charming Jenny Wren offers trips along this waterway aboard her canal barge, the *Shalakabooky*. Her enchanting boat is painted in bright colours, and the deck is ablaze with a variety of potted flowering plants. Its neat interior contains every modern convenience in miniature. My wife and I joined Captain Jenny on one such trip on a day in summer, and what a glorious experience it was.

Entering the Deep Sinking, the walls of rock rose sharply to the banks high above, with trees overhanging on both sides, their branches intertwining above the water, forming a tunnel of greenery for us to pass under. I was struck by how perfectly still everything was on that calm balmy day. It would take a leap of the imagination for anyone to convince themselves that they were actually passing so close to the suburbs of Dublin City. The only signs of life were the woodpigeons and collared doves cooing in the overhead foliage, swallows dipping and diving over the water in search of food, and charms of chaffinches entertaining us with their flight.

As the barge idled its way through this rocky passage, Jenny talked to us about the terrible tragedy that occurred in the Deep Sinking in 1845, when the evening passenger boat en route from Dublin to Longford struck a rock on the side of the canal and capsized, with the loss of sixteen lives.

From our vantage point, it became clear how such a disaster was magnified by the sheer rock walls flanking the waterway. Jenny spoke with passion about the accident, and about the people on board. She took out her guitar and began to play a song she wrote, a fictional reimagining about a nurse called Nora who met her death that fateful

Tom and Helen on Jenny Wren's barge

Solid Rock of Deep Sinking

day. Her beautiful voice filled the air of the Deep Sinking, as her notes relayed the story of Nora's tragic end. She had entertained Dick Warner when he travelled the Royal Canal by barge for his RTÉ documentary. We felt very special sharing the same experience.

Jenny then pointed out an old well with a brass pipe at its base on the south bank, and the remains of stone steps which provided access to it. A brass handrail ran along by the steps for ease of descent to the precious water. However, the well is now stagnant and no longer in use. None of this is visible from the path above, but is clearly seen from the waterway below.

As I make my way carefully along the towpath, I pass by a burst of yellow gorse glowing with a rustic glory, blending with the silence of this short-lived seclusion. In Dublin, we called this shrub furze, and in the west of Ireland it is called whin. It blooms generally from February up till at least May. In some locations it can bloom all year round, bringing to mind Irish botanist Zoe Devlin's reference to a well-known country saying:

'When gorse is out of blossom, kissing's out of fashion.'

It is a welcome floral reprieve before reaching the busy Kirkpatrick Bridge in Carpenterstown, over which traffic is carried along the Coolmine/Carpenterstown Road. Beyond it, I am still in the Deep Sinking and the path remains soft and slippy.

This muddy trek continues under the modern Dr. Troy Bridge, also known as the Diswellstown Road overpass, connecting Diswellstown Road in Clonsilla to Porterstown Link Road. The street art and graffiti are interesting, with a mix of cartoon characters and fancy lettering. While the self-expression of street art is image-based, graffiti is word-based. Street art is usually legal and in fact often commissioned. Graffiti, on the other hand, tends to be illegal, unwanted and disapproved of. In my experience there are good and bad exponents of both.

Setting off again, I squelch along the 200 metres to Kennan Bridge, Porterstown. As it is not possible to pass under it, I must cross carefully over the Porterstown Road to pick up the towpath again which has switched over to the north bank. I notice a wreath mounted on the bridge wall with a plaque beside it confirming Jenny's story:

> *In memory of the sixteen people who lost their lives when the*
> *Dublin to Longford passenger boat sank here*
> *25 November 1845.*
>
> *Erected by R.C.A.G. 25 Nov. 1995.*

Those who died have not been forgotten, as the Royal Canal Amenity Group chose the 150th anniversary of the tragedy to erect the memorial.

A tall, odd gothic building on the north bank close to Kennan Bridge has an unusual triangular-shaped window just below the apex. Most of the other windows are boarded up and the building is partially clad in ivy. However, it is fenced off to the public and there are signs of possible restoration in progress. A bright clump of lesser celandine close by adds some colour to its dilapidated yet curious exterior.

Jenny Wren related an interesting story about the Porterstown National School, opened in 1854 and subsequently closed in 1963.

According to civic lore, the local priest, Father Dungan, approached Lord Annally of Luttrellstown Castle and asked him if he would donate to the building of the Catholic school. When Lord Annally told him 'to go to hell', the priest retorted with these cutting words, 'I will build the school in spite of you and it will be a visible reminder to you wherever you go.' Hence the tall primary school building resulted. Some say that the priest then put a curse on Luttrellstown Estate, 'that a crow would never build, a ewe would never lamb and a hare would never run on the land.' Since then, the school has been referred to by the local community as 'The School of Spite'.

When I have walked more than half way along the Deep Sinking the path widens a little and has a tarmac surface. Ivy has snaked its way up the bare branches of leafless trees and its reflection in the water produces an eerie atmosphere that seems to settle on all of nature.

Towpath just after Callaghan Bridge

However, I am soon struck by the vibrant whiteness and strong pungent scent of wild garlic, which is a pleasant surprise. After a few short steps I see, rising up along the railway embankment, a dense carpet of winter heliotrope, whose large and wonderful kidney-shaped leaves outdo its smaller flowers.

I am now entering a corridor of trees filled with the pleasant chirping of birds, which takes me all the way to Callaghan Bridge in Clonsilla. My path continues under it and there is a footbridge adjacent to it serving Clonsilla Train Station. From the road I take a photo of the still functional railway signal box, with its classic construction of wood and red brick. The name CLONSILLA is proudly displayed on the upper section.

Clonsilla railway signal box

I descend the steps to the towpath, sitting down on them to enjoy lunch. Clonsilla has its own wealth of heritage sites well worth a visit.

The nearby Luttrellstown Castle can be traced back to Geoffrey Luttrell of Norman origin, a member of a royal commission appointed by King John in 1204. The Luttrell family held the castle and estate for over 300 years until 1811.

In the mid-nineteenth century it passed to Lord Annaly. In the early twentieth century Arthur Ernest Guinness, brother of Lord Iveagh, became owner. He made a present of the house to his daughter Aileen on her marriage to an airman, Brinsley Plunkett.

In 1953, the estate and castle were used in the film *The Knights of the Round Table* starring Robert Taylor and Ava Gardner. There have been many famous visitors to Luttrellstown over the years, including President Regan and Prince Rainier and Princess Grace of Monaco. In 1999, David and Victoria Beckham were married here.

In 2006, the castle was sold to its present owners, J.P. McManus and John Magnier. Luttrellstown Castle Resort is available for private residential bookings, family celebrations, weddings, sporting events and corporate occasions. The 567 acres of private parkland also incorporate a championship golf course.

After lunch I stroll a short distance to the nearby Saint Mary's Church of Ireland which dates from 1846. It is an impressive limestone building with a Gothic arched door and a castellated bell tower. The church grounds and graveyard are well kept, with interspersed yew trees. Inside, there is a stained glass window by the world famous Evie Hone, installed in 1935. It depicts St. Fiacre, who is the patron saint of gardeners and cab drivers, and whose feast day is 1 September.

Evie Hone was born in Dublin, in 1894, and was crippled from an early age. She pursued her artistic interests with great determination, studying in both London and Paris. On her return to Ireland in 1927 she first made a reputation as an abstract painter. Within a few years, she was working with stained glass and had joined An Túr Gloine (the Tower of Glass), a stained glass co-operative established by Sarah Purser.

Evie was commissioned to design the glass of the great East Window in Eton College Chapel which many consider to be her masterpiece. Unfortunately, St. Mary's is closed now so I shall have to wait to view Evie's stained glass another day.

Recommencing my towpath walk, I am soon reminded that the nesting and breeding season is fast approaching. Raucous rooks fly overhead, drowning out any other bird song that might be present. I approach the Railway Bridge, constructed from enormous metal shafts secured to the concrete by large nuts and bolts. It carries the Dunboyne railway branch over the canal after it leaves Hansfield Station, serving the transport needs of the communities in this recently developed area.

The Deep Sinking ends here. A sign just beyond the bridge alerts boaters coming from the west that they are entering this narrow channel. Sweeter birdsong now fills the air as I leave the rook colony behind.

I arrive at Pakenham Bridge, Barberstown, and pass beneath the endearing cut stone to find a barge changing direction at a conveniently wide turning point. The hedgerow is high and dense along the towpath. However, due to the scantiness of the vegetation on the far bank, the railway line is visible, running close to the canal. The grassy towpath shows muddy ruts from tractor tyres that stay with me all along the two kilometre section of canal to the next bridge. This is the first sign I have seen of farming activity. However, during the rest of my journey I will encounter evidence of agriculture throughout the hinterland of the Royal Canal.

The hedgerow becomes less and less dense as I carry on, and the rural aura of my surroundings starts to envelop me. I see field after field of flat land stretching out for a great distance. Black plastic bales of silage are laid out in a neat row in one green field. Another has been ploughed and recently planted, so that green shoots are beginning to emerge from the brown soil. Walking through this agricultural land, by farmhouse and barn, is a stark contrast to my journey along the urban towpaths, where I passed so many houses and factories.

The quiet is suddenly broken by a swish then a click, and it takes a second to register that I am close to the golf course at the Garda Sports and Conference Centre at Westmanstown.

Further on, there are some metal markers for fishing. The stretch of the Royal Canal between the 12th Lock at Castleknock and the 13th Lock at Deey Bridge, Collinstown, Leixlip, has four permanently pegged match sections and over the years has hosted international fishing competitions. The canal is well stocked with coarse fish, whose quantity and health are regularly monitored. Roach, perch, tench and pike are most commonly caught here but bream and rudd have also been known to reward the avid angler. Carp are stocked but not easily caught.

A male and female mallard grace the water, while rooks and grey crows fill up the air with discordant throaty sounds in the tall trees along the boundaries of nearby fields.

Towpath after Pakenham Bridge

Just a stone's throw further on, my eye is drawn to the rear view of a house with a distinctive character. A smaller building in the foreground with a fancy wooden canopy seems to serve as a shelter of sorts. Jenny Wren informed me that both structures were part of the original railway station for this area, before Clonsilla or Louisa Bridge stations were built.

Collins Bridge, its name intact and legible, forms a backdrop to it, incorporating an arch for the canal and another for the railway line. Walking the peaceful section beyond it brings back some wonderful memories of our barge trip, with dragonflies of various colours swarming above the water. We ducked and resisted their determined flight as they were absorbed in competition with others of their species, disregarding any obstacles in their path. Their size was impressive, as their translucent wings surged them forward in their endless frenzied pursuit of females and food.

Approaching Collins Bridge

'Some of the dragonflies are almost as big as small birds,' Jenny remarked, amused, as she watched me duck low to avoid a winged devil darting towards me.

However, the exquisite damselflies stole the show as they flew close to the water's surface, sometimes landing on lily pads to rest. We observed a male and female flying across the water together, wrapped in a 'mating wheel' embrace, or more appropriately in a 'mating heart' embrace, as this is how it presents itself to the world. All the while they are on the lookout for suitable plants on which to lay their eggs. We were truly immersed in nature's plan for survival with such an abundance of entomology making the most of that sunny summer's day.

Jenny's barge glided close to a stationary heron perched on some flattened reed. After waiting for us to pass, it then rose, spreading its enormous wings and flew past within a metre of us as we watched in awe. I looked carefully at how it flew with its neck retracted as if to make it more compact. However, with a wingspan of well over 1.5 metres, its efforts to streamline itself seemed futile. Jenny was familiar with this heron and the pattern of its behaviour. She predicted that when it reached Collins Bridge it would turn and fly back to its original perch of reeds. So we were rewarded with another close-up of this magnificent bird in flight as it returned to its roost.

I am now north of the townland Coldblow. It takes me along a towpath of grass and mud, overshadowed by silvery-grey beech twigs bearing pointed brown buds, to Cope Bridge, almost two kilometres away. Coldblow lives up to its name. Wide open to the elements, I struggle against a strong southwesterly to keep my cap on.

The award-winning St. Catherine's Park is just across the railway track. Its origins can be traced back to the Norman conquest of Ireland. It still contains the ruins of a thirteenth century priory, as well as the twelfth century St. Catherine's Church. Around 1798 a fine new house designed by the architect Francis Johnston was built in the park and is now Leixlip Manor Hotel and Gardens.

The land for the park was purchased in 1996 on behalf of the State by Michael D. Higgins, who was Minister for Art and Heritage at the time. St. Catherine's Park was officially opened in 2012. Today this magnificent amenity has football pitches, a beautiful playground and a BMX Track, while still managing to conserve the secluded woodland walks which overlook the River Liffey. An area of the park is devoted to an expanse of golden daffodils which delight us in springtime. Throughout the park, strategically planted wildflower meadows contribute to biodiversity, where flowers such as cowslips and poppies bloom.

About one kilometre further along this path, I arrive at the Confey Amenity area and boat slip, which marks the Fingal-Kildare county boundary. I feel a sense of achievement as I cross it, leaving Dublin behind and with the plains of Kildare and Royal Meath ahead of me. The Royal Canal Amenity Group (RCAG) has a large green building with a corrugated roof near the boat slip. There are at least half a dozen barges tied up to the mooring posts.

The housing estates of Confey are beginning to appear over to the south. Leixlip, as a town, is in fact cut in two by the Rye Water and the Liffey. North of the Liffey and east of the Rye is the ancient Irish stronghold of Confey. West of the Rye is regarded as Leixlip, while the whole town bears this placename. Consequently, with the town split in two, each area has duplication in terms of parishes, secondary schools, GAA clubs and soccer clubs.

I pass by a section of hedgerow where ivy has covered a large clump of trees and shrubs, providing concealment for nesting birds. Plants in woodland need light to survive. Most achieve this by the growth of woody stems that grow upward, thus using up much needed energy. The clever ivy piggy-backs these plants, using little energy to reach the canopy where it absorbs the light to make food. Another survival trick of the ivy is to produce its flowers in late autumn unlike most plants. Flies and wasps visit them for their nectar, being the only flowers left at that time. Unusually, it produces its black berries in spring. At a time of year when food is scarce, its swollen berries provide nourishment

Royal Canal Amenity Group

for birds such as woodpigeon, thrush and robins. This in turn ensures that the ivy seeds are widely spread for propagation.

Across a ploughed field I notice an old, stone farmhouse with two large barns nearby. Shortly after this, the small Sileachain stream runs down from north to south and is tunnelled beneath the canal, to flow through the housing estates of Leixlip and on into the River Liffey. The Sileachain Valley is an area of natural biodiversity with thirty-four bird species and more than ninety different plant species identified within it.

Just beyond here are the premises of Confey GAA Club. Its grounds butt back to the road over the double-arched Cope Bridge, which takes the traffic over the canal and railway, towards Dunboyne, Clonee and Lucan.

I have decided to take a short walk to Confey Cemetery where I can view some nearby ruins of interest. At the back of the graveyard the ruins of St. Columba's Church are nestled amongst a copse of yew trees. A plaque mounted on the front wall, with a skilfully crafted inscription, reads:

CONFEY CHURCH, DATED C. 1200,
RESTORED 2000-2001
BY KILDARE COUNTY COUNCIL.

Ruins of St Columba's Church

Confey Castle and heifers

Although roofless and invaded by creeping plants, it is possible to walk inside to admire the arched doors and windows, and to take a close look at the various headstones within. Along with the ruins of Confey Castle, which lie in a field to the far side of the graveyard, it forms the remains of a medieval village.

I climb the metre high wall at the back of the graveyard, keen to explore the castle ruins. On the far side, the drop is twice as deep. However, my descent is helped by an old palette leaning against a sturdy tree. Entering the nearby field, I discover that the castle is barely visible from under its cloak of ivy, and it is guarded by an advancing army of sixteen heifers. I get two snaps in quick succession and stop to assess the situation. One brave girl starts to run towards me. I accept the challenge, advancing in her direction with a loud shout. She momentarily jumps away in fright.

However, my confidence is short lived as soon the herd regroup. Alarmingly, the charge begins, so I turn about and break into a dash. They cut me off on my right-hand side. With one final spurt I dart to the wall, jump up on the palette and land in the safety of the graveyard. I never envisaged this exploration would be so challenging. It certainly has used up my last reserves of energy.

When I have sufficiently recovered I make my way back to Cope Bridge. Feeling tired but well exercised, I look forward to a shower and a nourishing meal to revive me. As I stroll to my nearby home, I ponder on the hidden gems that can be found tucked away in fields, bridges, towpaths and laneways.

View from Jenny Wren's barge

7.

Confey to Leixlip

An Aqueduct, a Spa, a Brewery and a Writer

Cope Bridge is a brisk 10 minute walk from my house in the townland of Confey in Leixlip, so shanks mare will suffice to get me started this morning. The third day of my walk begins here in late March, taking me from Confey to Kilcock. Although the temperature is just 8 degrees and the sky is overcast, at least it is dry. I set off at a fast pace, buoyed by the thoughts of today's adventure.

William Cope's name was immortalised when the bridge was named after him. He was a director of the Royal Canal Company from its inauguration until 1802. An interesting aspect to this bridge is that

Towrope marks on Cope Bridge

if you walk beneath it, you can see in the stone wall the indents left by the ropes which were used by the horses to pull the barges. This of course happened over many years of wear.

The north bank of the towpath skirts around a turning circle for barges. A large turf market developed at Mullingar, and a smaller one here at Cope Bridge, in the early part of the nineteenth century when turf was transported by barge to Dublin from the Bog of Allen and the Bog of Cappagh. The transport of turf by road was slow and expensive. The canal proved a quicker and cheaper alternative, becoming a major source of revenue for the Royal Canal Company. The annual quantities of turf carried rose to a high of almost 83,000 tons in 1839. Yards for selling and distributing turf developed in Dublin. The largest, at Broadstone, was run by the Irish Turf Company. Sometimes live animals and potatoes were part of the cargo. Manure was carried in the opposite direction from Dublin to places such as Leixlip.

Limestone was plentiful throughout County Meath and the contractors, Henry, Mullins & MacMahon, had a large base near Leixlip which used the canal exclusively for the transport of building materials. Bernard Mullins, of this firm, became a director on the board of the Royal Canal Company.

Confey railway station is just across the waterway. Space is tight and the pedestrian bridge that crosses the rail line juts out over the canal in a cantilever design. The canal circumvents the housing estates of Confey, as does the railway, forming a boundary to these residential areas.

Next I am on a familiar path of rough shale heading west and the houses have disappeared. Trees are reflected in the still water and the image is perfect and stunning. It makes

Trees reflected in water near Cope Bridge

me feel like time has stopped, leaving space for a long, slow inhalation of breath and a moment of elation and reflection.

I pass by grazing sheep close to a farmhouse. Further on, a large area of tilled farmland has attracted grey crows and woodpigeons. These guys can readily zone in on prime foraging locations. What an incongruous scene lies before me of sheep, birds and a farmhouse, dwarfed by the towering pylons dispatching their load to the nearby technological giant Intel!

The hedgerow is full of blackthorn in partial flower. The occasional horse chestnut tree is displaying large sticky buds, just waiting to open and spread their five fingers. The soft-grey branches of the ash are tipped with black buds, eager to open and display their leaves, while a solitary willow shows off her yellow-grey catkins.

Blackthorn (top) and primroses (bottom)

Suddenly, bursting out beyond a vast cloak of ivy, a clump of primroses brightens up the dark green hedge cover, proclaiming that spring has definitely arrived. The name primrose means first rose. I love its delicate, pale yellow flower and the contrast with its sturdy, bright-green, crinkled leaves.

The canal now takes a wide sweep gradually turning southwest. Along the arc of its surface, the stems of dead reeds have gathered on the bend, breaking up the reflection of the trees in the water. The railway has taken a more gradual sweep in the same direction, so that the ellipse left between them is now a wasteland of trees and shrubs, creating the perfect bird sanctuary. Small birds are flitting from tree to tree, the song of each species intermingling to form a superb avian orchestra. Meanwhile, on the water mallards, moorhens and swans are in abundance and appear to be happy in each other's company.

I arrive at a point where the towpath is formed of large concrete slabs for a distance of a few metres. Below them is an adjustable weir through which the overflow from the canal can escape. This creates a man-made

Canal at Confey

waterfall, which gushes into the valley below. Beyond the weir, the railway meets up with the canal once again.

Just before Louisa Bridge, I arrive at the Rye Water Aqueduct, built in 1791, which is approximately 270 metres long. Taking almost six years to complete, it was built to carry the canal across the Rye Water, which flows beneath the sturdy arch 30 metres below.

The choice of this route was a costly one, involving the excavation of the Deep Sinking and the construction of the massive earth embankment above the Rye Water at Leixlip. It has been suggested, although there are no records to support it, that this diversion took place at the instigation of William FitzGerald, the second Duke of Leinster, who was a director of the canal company. True or false, it certainly resulted in the canal passing by his home at Carton Demesne and through the village of Maynooth, which he owned.

Beginning of Rye Water Aqueduct

As I walk along the aqueduct, I arrive at an old building whose door and windows are infilled with concrete. However, it has been thoroughly rejuvenated visually. The artist has created a door frame and door, as well as window frames and curtains. The walls have been painted white, with a garden superimposed at the lower level and a young girl busy with a watering can, while a horse and dog look on.

The guide to the Royal Canal tells me that this derelict house was once occupied by the lengthsman, who was responsible for this section of canal. Information signs inform us it was the fare collector's house or watchman's house. It is likely that the person in question had multiple duties and that all terms were valid. I walk down the steps to the back of this house, which is at a lower level than the front. This lower story was used as a stable for canal horses.

I follow the steep path down to the valley far below the aqueduct, which leads me to the base of the waterfall. I watch in awe as it cascades from the overflow weir on the canal 30 metres above. A stream flows from it, and as I follow its course I pass a sea of butterbur, with their long maroon flower clusters that will later turn to pink. Soon after, the stream joins the larger body of water, the Rye Water, which in turn will soon join the River Liffey at Leixlip. As I stare at the aqueduct towering high above me, I am in awe at just how enormous this piece of engineering was for its time.

Back on the towpath, I approach Louisa Bridge and its adjacent train station, passing a path that leads down to Leixlip Spa. During the canal's construction, a hot spring was uncovered by workmen

Collector's house near the aqueduct

building the embankment for the aqueduct. This warm mineral spring was then piped to a Romanesque bath nearby. The Right Honourable Thomas Conolly MP, of Castletown, intended to build a pump-room and a hotel here, but after his death the project was never realised. It was also a most picturesque location, as the waterfall could be seen from the spa. The Royal Canal passenger terminal in Leixlip was situated close to the spa.

The benefits of the minerals in the water resulted in it becoming a fashionable tourist attraction for day trippers from Dublin during the late eighteenth century. Among the modes of transport used were coach, jaunting car, horseback and on foot. They would drink as much of the mineral water as they could and bottle some more to take home. The water from the spring was tinged red. One account by Casear Otway, the Protestant curate of Leixlip, recorded in the *Parliamentary Gazette* in 1845, attributed this not to the presence of iron but to 'a very little red worm' and claimed that drinking this water was a certain cure for a hangover:

Romanesque bath

Let anyone who had drank over night from fifteen to twenty tumblers of punch, and whose head is so hot that it makes the water fizz into which it is plunged. Let him, I say, but take a quart or two of the water of this spring, on the following morning, and he will lose all his whiskey fever, and walk home as cool as a cucumber.

By the late nineteenth century the spa's use declined and it became overgrown. In 1975, the bath was uncovered from its blanket of grass and weeds by the Leixlip Boy Scouts group and local members of An Taisce, The National Trust for Ireland. Shortly after the spa's rediscovery, work commenced on its restoration.

Across the water, two Waterways Ireland dredging vessels are moored. Standing on the far side of the railway is the old train station house, built in 1924, which is now a residential property.

A few more paces and I am standing on Louisa Bridge which was built in 1794 and named after Lady Louisa Conolly. The name and year of the bridge's construction are still visible on the stone plate. Louisa was reared at Carton House, situated between Leixlip and Maynooth. However, she was not a member of the FitzGerald family but one of the four Lennox sisters who were great-granddaughters of Charles

II. She moved to Castletown House, Celbridge, after her marriage to the Right Honourable Thomas Conolly. The author Maria Edgeworth visited Castletown circa 1815, and in a letter said she found Louisa at seventy to be charming and perceptive, with no ostentation whatsoever.

Wild marjoram

Leixlip's story stretches very far back in time. It has recently been discovered that it was inhabited 5,500 years ago by stone-age man on the bank of the Liffey in Cooldrinagh, on the southeast side of the town.

The Viking invaders arrived in AD 795. They gave Leixlip its name from the Old Norse Lax Hlaup, meaning salmon leap. The Irish name Léim an Bhradáin is a direct translation of this. The site of the salmon leaping was said to be near the confluence of the Liffey and the Rye Water. Battles raged back and forth between the Irish and the Vikings until Brian Boru's definitive victory at Clontarf in AD 1014.

The Anglo-Norman invasion of Ireland began in the twelfth century. Leixlip castle was built strategically on a rock at the confluence of the two rivers in AD 1172 by Adam de Hereford, a follower of Strongbow. In 1958, the founders of the Irish Georgian Society, Desmond Guinness and his wife Mariga, bought the castle and Desmond lived there until his death in 2020. Many famous guests stayed over that period, including Mick Jagger and Jerry Hall.

Leixlip also has connections with other famous people. There is a plaque on a house on Main Street commemorating the Fenian William Roantree, who lived there. Another reads *Here Arthur and Richard Guinness leased a brewery in 1756.*

The tall building at the end of Main Street, known locally as Shingled House, was built in 1740. In 1934 the property became the home of

Guinness plaque

the Shackleton family, descendants of the famous Antarctic explorer Ernest Shackleton. This family have connections with the Royal Canal, spreading far beyond Leixlip. They were also former owners of Shackleton Mill on the Strawberry Beds. In more recent times the Bewley family, known far and wide for their coffee, lived at Shingled House.

Samuel Beckett's mother, May Roe, was born in the locality and lived at what was then Cooldrinagh House and Demesne. This house became Beckett's Hotel, which unfortunately closed during the Covid epidemic and never reopened.

The writer Leland Bardwell grew up in Leixlip. Her father, Pat Hone, came from a line that included two notable painters, Nathaniel Hone the Elder and Younger, as well as the stained glass artist Evie Hone, whose work Leland greatly admired. Leland herself was an accomplished writer over a number of genres that included poetry, novels, short stories, plays and memoir. She died in 2016, age ninety-four, survived by her six children. Leland's well-crafted and original work, which often deals with those wounded in life in an affectionate and witty manner, earned her membership of Aosdána.

Engrossed in the history and the famous people who inhabited this small town over the centuries, I set off to continue my journey along the banks of the Royal Canal.

8.

LEIXLIP TO MAYNOOTH

Spooks, Follies, Dukes and Seminarians

The sun is appearing intermittently from behind clouds as I resume today's walk towards Maynooth and on to Kilcock. Strolling along the north bank, I can feel and hear the crunch of gravel beneath my feet.

On the outskirts of Leixlip, a short walk from the canal, lies the Wonderful Barn, now a world heritage site. Over the entrance door is a mural tablet bearing the inscription:

1743

EXECUT'D

BY JOHN GLIN

It was built on the instruction of Katherine Conolly of Castletown House, the then widow of William Speaker Conolly. It is generally considered to have been a famine relief project, providing employment for the poor, after the Great Frost followed by the Great Famine of 1740–1741, a century before the Great Irish Famine of the 1840s.

The barn is quite an unusual structure; it deserves the name wonderful as it resembles a tower from a fairy tale. This grain store's five storeys rise to a height of 73 feet (just over 22 metres) in a tapering cone. A flight of 94 steps wind their way round the exterior to the crow's nest viewing gallery, commanding an excellent view of the surrounding countryside. There is a spacious haggard below, with two dovecotes of similar design though smaller than the barn.

The Wonderful Barn

I am soon approaching Collinstown Bridge, passing beneath an ESB 110kv Power Line that connects Corduff Transmission Station to the one at Maynooth. There is a spur off this line, feeding the large Intel Production Plant, which is close by on the Maynooth Road.

Intel has been continuously expanding from the time it began operations in Leixlip back in 1989. Since then, the company has invested over €30 billion in turning the 360-acre former stud farm into one of the most technologically advanced manufacturing locations in Europe. This is the largest private investment ever made in the history of the Irish State. The semiconductor wafer fabrication facility plays a central role within Intel's global manufacturing network. It currently employs 4,900 workers and thousands of jobs were created in the building trade during the various stages of its construction.

The road crossing Collinstown Bridge connects Leixlip to the M4 motorway. There is a plaque beneath it on the graffiti-covered wall displaying the bridge number 16A and the year of construction, 2003. It is also known as the Matt Goff Bridge, dedicated to that local gentleman who was born in Leixlip in 1901. Matt was a Gaelic footballer on the Kildare and Leinster teams, which is interesting as there are no provincial teams nowadays. He played in six All-Ireland finals between 1926 and 1935, winning an unprecedented six Leinster titles in succession, as well as two All-Ireland medals with the Kildare team. This team was the first ever to be presented with the Sam Maguire Cup. When he died in 1956, GAA players from all over Ireland formed a guard of honour at his funeral. A Celtic cross was unveiled at Matt Goff's grave in 1958.

The following is part of a poem that P.J. O'Connor of Kells wrote in praise of Mattie.

> *A sportsman and a gentleman*
> *On the field and off*
> *Kildare will find it hard to field*
> *Another Mattie Goff*

Moving on, I pass an old wall covered in ivy which appears to be the boundary wall of the grounds that would have been associated with Collinstown House. In the eighteenth century this house was the home of Daniel Simmonds, who for around twenty-five years was secretary to the Turnpike Commissioners. The ruinous state of the protected structure of Collinstown House stands in grim contrast to the newly constructed Intel factory nearby.

A gap in the old wall leads me through what may have been a gateway once. I find myself exploring a narrow stretch of mature holly and beech. The floor of the wood is an alluring blue with its carpet of wild violets. To the ancient Greeks violets were the symbol of virginity and were used to embellish the nuptial bed. The Greeks also used violets to make perfume, and the Romans used them to flavour wine.

Back on the towpath, the crunch of beech shells underfoot makes a pleasant change to the grating of gravel. As I walk along, my footsteps evoke a harmonious percussion, reminiscent of a peaceful mantra. A scattering of oak leaves signals this mighty stalwart of our native woods. A vision of beauty turns me breathless as a small tortoiseshell butterfly floats by, the first I have spotted this spring.

My eye catches a patch of green alkanet in bloom, its blue flowers questioning its name. It is thought that it was originally a source of red

The 13th Lock

dye, which comes from its roots. The bees are very fond of it, however due to its prolific nature it is an unwelcome species in a garden.

I approach Deey Bridge and the 13th Lock, the first since the 12th Lock at Blanchardstown. During the heyday of the canal, this location was not a place the boatmen would choose to tie up for the night. It was said that it went through the site of a graveyard, causing unrest among the corpses buried there. Others claimed it was unpopular due simply to the unlucky number thirteen. Whatever the reason for its avoidance, our famous politician and writer Arthur Griffith, who founded and later led Sinn Féin, was moved to write a witty poem about this, which he called 'The Spooks of the Thirteenth Lock'. He begins:

> *Every night of the year about twelve of the clock*
> *The spirits and spooks of the dread thirteenth lock*
> *Sit winging their bodies a-this and that way*
> *And singing in chorus, Ri tooril li lay.*

The poem tells the story of a gallant captain who mocks the ghosts as they sing. As a result, when asked a question he can only answer 'Ri tooril li lay', first to his wife as to what he'll have for dinner, then to his

Entering the 13th Lock

manager regarding the ship's log, and as a consequence was sacked from his job. Taking to his bed, the perplexed doctor treating him exclaims in the penultimate verse:

> *There's no such disease in the Pharmacopay*
> *That I ever heard tell of as, Ri tooril li lay.*

In the last verse, as the poor man lies dying, he tries to pray, but the only words that come from his lips are, yes, you've guessed it ...

The Spook of the Thirteenth Lock is also the name of an Irish band who took their name from Griffith's poem. They combine trad Irish folk music with modern experimental rock, producing a very original and interesting sound. Their 2018 concept album, in four movements, called *Lockout* deals with the 1913 lockout and the battle against exploitative working conditions, led by Jim Larkin and James Connolly. The album's intensity is gripping, partly due to the slow-mounting and effective crescendos.

The old lockhouse associated with the 13th Lock has its door and windows boarded up, though the slate roof looks sound. Next to it, a recessed house has a long, elaborate pigeon loft in front of it. The feathered occupants are visible, looking eager for flight. To my disappointment, on a revisit in 2020 I found that the loft had been demolished. However, I have learned since that it was merely disassembled by the owners and reassembled at their new home.

A second trip aboard Jenny Wren's barge took my wife Helen and I from Cope Bridge to Carton Wharf. There was another female crew member on board this time to assist in passing through the 13th lock. It also required the help of a Waterways Ireland employee.

Jenny's assistant steered the barge into the lock chamber. With our skipper on one side of the lock and the Waterways Ireland employee on the other, they closed the tailgates as we sat on the deck enthralled, encapsulated by the steep walls of the lock. They resembled childhood images of the Hanging Gardens of Babylon, with a variety of vegetation clinging to the crevices in the huge blocks of limestone, and trailing along the walls. Green ivy and the small pink-purple flowers of Herb-Robert, as well as clusters of a larger white flower were amongst them. We marvelled as the water slowly began to rise, covering this vibrant vegetation as we rose likewise. When the water reached the

Tom and Helen on Jenny Wren's barge

Jenny Wren

higher level of the canal above, our lock operators, like clockwork, opened the breast gates. We could now view the new level that we had ascended to, allowing us to proceed. Viewing this coordinated operation step by step from a barge was thrilling.

After the 13th Lock, there is a lightness in my step as I pass a row of tall majestic Scots Pine. The lower branches of this tree die off early, leaving the lower trunk bare. The bark is a beautiful rich orange-pink, most noticeable higher up the trunk. The needle-slender leaves, which are two to four inches long, are grouped in pairs. In former times, the resinous wood of this tree was used for making torches, which burned with a bright light.

Through a scattering of spring branches I can make out a traditional stone farmhouse on the far side of the road, and the outline of outhouses and cattle in the adjacent fields. It is, in fact, Hedsor House, on the lands of the farmer Thomas Reid, whose family have worked this farm for over a century.

In 2013, Reid lost his challenge in the High Court against the IDA's compulsory purchase of his farm for potential new development. His land is sandwiched in between Carton House Estate and the Intel site

Canal as seen from the barge

in Leixlip. The judge at the hearing said that the national interest must outweigh the interests of the individual. However, in November, 2015, Reid won his appeal to the Supreme Court by a unanimous judicial decision. It was ruled that Section 16 of the 1986 Act does not confer any power on the IDA to acquire lands not required for immediate use, but which might be utilised at some future time.

Reid's attachment to the farm is evident in the hand-written protest signs on the gateway to his house, regarding the vulnerability of his house and lands. The documentary film maker, Fergal Ward, on noticing these signs, visited him in 2015, and over a two and a half year period made a film entitled *The Lonely Battle of Thomas Reid*. It received the Dublin Film Critics Circle Best Irish Film award at the Dublin International Film Festival in 2019 and has been screened in many countries.

A magnificence blaze of Alexanders in the hedgerow, with their greenish-yellow umbels standing out against the dark green leaves, diverts my focus back to the towpath.

Out on the water, there are bubbles rising, and I can see a shoal of tiny young minnows close to the surface. Through a gap in a row of young ash trees, I have an open view of the traffic whizzing by on the Leixlip/Maynooth road.

The far bank is about three metres above the water, supporting trees which tower above the canal, in contrast to the bank on my side, which is close to the water.

The wall of Carton Estate comes into view across the road and it stretches all the way to Maynooth. The Rye Water flows through the historic estate and passes under the aqueduct before reaching Leixlip.

Thomas Reid's farm

The white flowers of the blackthorn brighten up the hedgerow. A lovely clump of wild strawberries, with large-toothed trifoliate leaves and white flowers tinged with green, add to the display. The traffic noise in my right ear is balanced by the quiet of the waterway in my left.

Across pastures with occasional clumps of trees, I see The Obelisk, also known as Connolly's Folly, which was designed by Richard Cassels. Standing 140 feet (42.6 metres) high, it is composed of several arches and is adorned with stone eagles, urns and pineapples. The latter represented affluence and this exotic fruit was much sought after at that time.

Like the Wonderful Barn, The Obelisk was also built under the instruction of Katherine Conolly, after the Great Frost followed by the Great Famine of 1740–1741. Its construction provided employment for the local poor who were paid a halfpenny per day. It cost £400 to

Donaghmore church and graveyard

complete. Originally, The Obelisk served as a rear entrance gateway to Castletown Estate. It was restored by the Georgian Society in the 1960s.

In the middle of a field, on my approach to Pike Bridge, I see a cluster of yew trees surrounded by the stone wall that is said to contain the remains of an early monastic site, consisting of a medieval church and a graveyard in the area of Donaghmore, also known as Grangewilliam. On investigation I discover a style that gives me access to the field and another to the site.

Half-concealed, fallen headstones, covered by a variety of creeping plants, create an uneven surface underfoot. The atmosphere within is steeped in antiquity. Very little of the church ruins are visible, however the west gable rises defiantly from the overgrowth.

Of the many graves, the oldest I discover is 1747, though some are too worn and weathered to read. The graveyard was also the original location of an Ogham stone, which is now safely housed in the National Museum of Ireland. A wooden altar is erected here for annual ceremonies. This is certainly an ecclesiastical oasis surrounded by green fields.

I return to the canal arriving at Carton Wharf and Pike Bridge. The name and date 1793 are chiselled into the stone, and a large display of berry-laden ivy hangs over its wall. Though pretty, it cannot compete with the bright yellow flowers of the nearby forsythia. Like the blackthorn, in early spring this shrub produces flowers before the leaves appear. It is named after the Scottish botanist William Forsyth, who lived in the eighteenthth century and who was gardener to King George II.

The harbour here was discovered during renovation of the canal. It was built to serve Carton Estate, owned by the FitzGerald family. The location of the harbour further supports the suggestion that the second Duke of Leinster used his influence to advocate this more costly diversion in order to serve his residence at Carton.

One of three public gate entrances to the estate is just across the road. Our experience resting in this wide harbour on board the stationary *Shalakabooky* was wonderful, as we sipped Jenny's homemade

Entrance to Carton estate from Pike Harbour

lemonade. We discussed the various boats moored here and their owners, and discovered that there is still a barge maker manufacturing such craft in Dunboyne. Jenny told us how the Second Duke of Leinster deemed the Royal Canal to be very special. He decided that all boats on this canal should be of a certain length, so as to only fit into locks of the Royal Canal and not those of its competitor, the Grand Canal.

As I leave Pike Bridge, two mallards fly in to land in a graceful manoeuvre, with feet raised to skim and brake on water. It moved me to write a haiku:

> *a mallard skims*
> *into his reflection*
> *becoming himself*

As I crunch along the undulating gravel path, the hedgerow is predominantly blackthorn and ivy, with the occasional hawthorn breaking through. The vigorous elder is still obvious within this rising tangle of thorn and leaf, surviving easily within. The hedge has been perceptively cut back before the birds begin nesting, ensuring safe habitats for them.

The road has gradually distanced itself from the canal, allowing the atmosphere to become quiet again. The crab apple tree I pass will flower in a few weeks, when its white petals will be tinted with pink. Pockets of gorse stand like beacons along the way on this overcast afternoon.

As tired legs and pangs of hunger slow me, the tall spire rising from the College Chapel in St. Patrick's College suddenly comes into view, heralding my approach to Maynooth.

The college was founded in 1795 and the spire was added in 1902 to commemorate the first centenary of the College in 1895. It rises to a height of 273 feet (83.2 metres), thus making it the tallest spire in Leinster.

The green fields are soon replaced by houses and an enormous Tesco store on the outskirts of the town. A Waterways Ireland sign announces Maynooth, with some black and white mooring posts leading me to the Mullen Bridges, named after the canal director Joseph Denis Mullen. The newer of the two bridges spans both the canal and rail line and is made of stone, blending in tastefully with the older structure. Beige-coloured lichen forms endless shapes on the cut stone, a common characteristic of the canal's built heritage.

Lichens are dual organisms, consisting of a fungus and one or more algae. The fungus provides a structural form that protects the algae from extremes of light and temperature. On the other hand, by providing sugars produced through photosynthesis, the algae help the fungus to grow and reproduce. Thus this symbiotic arrangement is mutually beneficial. Lichens have a long lifespan, some living for hundreds of years. Being sensitive organisms, they are important indicators of changes in the environment and of pollution. Lichen classification is difficult to the untrained eye as there are many similar species. The patterns formed by lichen can be fascinating and I spend a few moments absorbing this natural evolving canvas.

Mullen Bridges

The towpath leads me to the splendid Maynooth Harbour that widens out off the main canal route. There is a delightful island in the centre of Dukes Harbour as it is locally known. Voluntary community groups planted native trees of silver birch and weeping willow on the island and along with grasses and reeds, they form the perfect sanctuary for the vast range of bird life nesting along the canal.

Lunch on a bench here is a real treat. My seat is recessed into the boundary wall, behind which a long row of daffodils are ablaze. Just in front of me, mallards leave their footprint on the water, as they rise gracefully to the air, while others stand on the edge contemplating a plunge. A couple of scrawny rooks forage for tit-bits on the wall by the daffodils. On the far bank, a colourful children's playground is alive with various forms of activity. Children love birds and I'm sure they enjoy coming here to watch the antics of the ducks.

Maynooth is a booming college and commuter town 24 kilometres west of Dublin, just 40 minutes by train from the capital. Leinster Street, named after the Dukes of Leinster, stretches from the harbour as far as Main Street, close to St. Patrick's College and Seminary.

Maynooth Harbour boat slip

The college was founded in 1795 by the Irish Parliament and over 11,000 priests have been ordained here since. The Seminary set out to educate young men for the priesthood in Ireland rather than France, a move aided by the slow dismantling of the Penal Laws in Ireland, giving more freedom to the church. However, since the 1970s, vocations have seen a steep decline, with only twenty-one studying for the priesthood in 2024.

The labouring classes of Maynooth derived great advantage from the seminary's proximity. It employed tailors, shoemakers, seamstresses and washerwomen, and also required the skills of local builders, upholsterers, cooks and victuallers.

In 1914, St. Patrick's College, Maynooth became a recognised college of the National University of Ireland in perpetuity, while remaining a Pontifical University. It was not until 1966 that lay students were admitted.

A Jesuit, Father Michael Mac Greil, lectured in Sociology for two and a half decades at Maynooth College, from 1971 to 1996. He championed many causes, including prison reform, the Irish Language and Traveller rights. In 2014, he published his memoir, *The Ongoing Present,* in which he brings his analytical and balanced observations to bear on diverse subjects, from his upbringing in Mayo to the history of the Irish State, with economics, religion, politics and social change woven through it.

Father Mac Greil highlights the fact that over the years, the humanities have been devoured by the growing appetite of economics, with the Irish educational syllabus being oriented more and more to serve the needs of industry. On the challenge of getting the balance right, he suggests:

> *an obligatory foundation in arts and humanities for all third-level students of science and technology*
>
> *so that it*
>
> *would be a check on the excesses of the monopoly of economic interests.*

The John Hume building is named after one of its most famous alumni. John Hume is the only recipient of all three major peace awards: The Nobel Peace Prize, the Gandhi Peace Prize and the Martin Luther King Award. John passed away in August 2020 and tributes to him came from many world leaders.

Maynooth's importance extends even further back in history. At the gateway to St. Patrick's College and Seminary are the keep and ruins of a Norman FitzGerald castle, built around 1200. Norman keeps were usually massive square towers, the strongest portion of the castle's fortification, to which the occupants would retire during a siege. It typically contained a well, living quarters and service rooms. A chapel was part of the castle complex and dates back to 1248. It still stands as St. Mary's Church of Ireland, within the outer wall of St. Patrick's College.

The name FitzGerald has had an important and long standing association with the town of Maynooth. The FitzGerald's came from Wales to Ireland during the Anglo-Norman invasion in 1169 under Richard de Clare, more commonly known as Strongbow, who granted land in County Kildare, including Maynooth, to Maurice FitzGerald.

The FitzGeralds became one of the most important Anglo-Norman families in Ireland, and by the early fourteenth century they had been raised to the title of Earls of Kildare.

Under Garret Mór and Garret Óg, the castle became the centre-point of Kildare's influence and innovation. However, in 1535, when Silken Thomas rebelled against Henry VIII, it was successfully besieged and extensively damaged. Though eventually restored, it was largely ruined after Cromwell's arrival in 1649.

The FitzGeralds subsequently left their ancient family seat and eventually made Carton their home. A tree-lined avenue extends from the gates at the east end of the town for one kilometre through the estate.

In 1739, Robert FitzGerald, 19th Earl of Kildare, embarked on the enlargement of the surrounding park at Carton. He commissioned renowned architect Richard Cassels, also responsible for designing the earl's Dublin residence, Leinster House, now Dáil Éireann, to remodel and extend the old house into a three-storey Palladian mansion. A charming boathouse, with bargeboard gables, is located close to a five-arched limestone bridge crossing the Rye Water.

One of Lady Emily FitzGerald's children was the famous Irish patriot Lord Edward FitzGerald, leader of the 1798 rebellion. During the uprising Carton was about to be burned by the rebels when the Lady of the House brought a portrait of Lord Edward to their attention, thus saving Carton House from ruin.

In 1766, the FitzGeralds had their title changed to that of Dukes of Leinster. During the twentieth century, the 7th Duke of Leinster, Edward FitzGerald, developed a gambling habit, eventually losing Carton. The Irish government came under pressure to buy this beautiful mansion, but decided not to. It is now a luxury hotel with two golf courses.

Bridge over Rye in Carton

Carton Boathouse

Its forest walks and facilities can be enjoyed by all. However, in a small, secluded graveyard, surrounded by yew trees, hidden from public view, headstones mark the resting place of FitzGerald family members.

This magnificent house was used in the making of many films, including Stanley Kubrick's *Barry Lyndon* in 1975. A TV mini-series, based on Stella Tillyard's book *The Aristocrats* (1999), subtitled, *Caroline, Emily, Louisa and Sarah Lennox, 1740-1832*, was set here and relates part of the fascinating history of Carton House and Estate. The four Lennox sisters were great-granddaughters of Charles II, King of England. Emily Lennox married James FitzGerald the 20th Earl of Kildare in 1744. She bore him nineteen children during their marriage. In 1751, after the deaths of their parents, three of her sisters, Louisa, Sarah and Cecilia, were taken to Ireland to live at Carton with Emily. Louisa, who gave her name to Louisa Bridge, later married the Right Honourable Thomas Conolly of Castletown House.

Maynooth Castle ruins

Lost in thoughts of adventurous celluloid, I leave Duke's Harbour and this busy university town. My mind is awash with stories of the rise and fall of one of Ireland's most famous families, and the college that educated so much of our clergy, and how this all impacted on a small town and the local community through which the Royal Canal flows.

9.

MAYNOOTH TO KILCOCK

Water Polo, Markets, Accordions and Missionaries

Heading westward, away from the hustle and bustle of a thriving university town, I look forward to being enveloped in the tranquility of a serene rural landscape once again.

The path soon leads me beneath the newly constructed Bond Bridge. The engineers incorporated the date of its original construction, 1795, on the east face and the date of the reconstruction for road widening, 2006, on the west face, marrying old and new.

A bottle-green barge, heading west, emerges from beneath the bridge, cutting a figure of grace through the water. I wave to the three individuals on board and my salute is reciprocated, as I watch the craft pass by.

The water close to Bond Bridge is alive with fish, creating concentric circles as they approach the surface and arcs when they dive below. As the sun has come out, the movement of these circles and arcs is reflected and displayed on the underneath of the arched roof of the bridge in full black and white, phantoms of the real thing.

The solid, capped boundary wall of St. Patrick's College and Seminary begins beyond the bridge and continues for some distance, showing the extent of the expansive college grounds. Horse chestnut trees tower above it. The graffiti on the old stone depicts mostly faces, but the number seventeen, written in large Roman numerals, stands out

Seminary wall covered in ivy

like something from an old Latin text. I ponder what aspect of divine nature it might refer to, settling eventually for the mystery.

There is an outline, still discernible, of an old archway in the wall, now bricked up. Back in those days, when trade was the canal's raison d'être, it is almost certain that this arch accommodated the delivery of goods to the college, in particular the supply of coal.

With the housing estates of Maynooth behind me, the dwellings I pass all have their own large plots of land, with greater separation from their neighbours. Behind the college wall, the foliage of beech, and occasional ash, has replaced the horse chestnut. Eventually, the wall comes to an end.

The grass either side of the towpath is freshly cut and its strong aromatic smell fills the air. A line of native oak and holly form a dramatic backdrop to a struggling fence. The hedgerow is shocking pink with Japanese rose beside a rather lost-looking yew sapling.

Passing another yew tree, I begin to wonder if there is perhaps a graveyard in the vicinity. The reason for planting yew trees in churchyards has never been satisfactorily explained. Some believe it is because they were regarded as being symbolic of the resurrection of the body. Others hold the opinion that it encourages farmers to

Gushing water at 14th Lock

keep their grazing animals away from churchyards and from the highly toxic leaves, bark, wood and seeds of the yew.

Out on the canal, mallards colour the water while a furtive moorhen seeks cover by the far bank. The Lyreen River is tunnelled beneath the canal at this point, and I can see it emerging down below the towpath. It flows into Maynooth, where it joins the Rye Water, part of a network of tributaries that eventually join the Liffey.

As I approach Jackson Bridge, I am excited by the welcome roar of falling water bursting into life from the 14th Lock, my first lock since the ghostly 13th Lock at Leixlip. This cut stone bridge is a magnificent five arch structure, serving the canal, the railway and a small stream. The fourth is an accommodation arch and the fifth a towpath arch, the second only of its kind on this canal. The plaque on Jackson Bridge displays its name, along with the lock name, accrediting Rd. Evans Engineer, for this amazing structure.

I head westward again, my nostrils full of smells from local farms as I look across onto cultivated farmland, with trimmed hedges bordering outhouses and fields of grazing cattle. The air is alive with the songs of blackbirds, audible above the din of traffic on the nearby road.

I come across the remains of a campfire in a small clearing, overseen by a bright, refreshing clump of primroses. An arable field nearby is sown with cereal and the old stone farmhouse sits comfortably at its edge, framed by a variety of maturing trees.

Bailey's Accommodation Bridge comes into view, spanning both the railway and canal. Such bridges were built by the canal company to

Five Arched Jackson Bridge

accommodate land-owners and farmers, whose lands were severed by the building of the canal. Accommodation bridges tend to be narrow cut stone arched structures. However, precast concrete has replaced the old bridge here, with the original cut stone pillars supporting it.

My passage beyond is brightened by a shiny cluster of lesser celandine, a flower with eight to twelve narrow petals, forming a golden star. A true herald of spring, they were a favourite of Wordsworth, who had the following to say about them in his poem 'To the Small Celandine':

> *Ere a leaf is on a bush,*
> *In the time before the thrush*
> *Has a thought about her nest,*
> *Thou wilt come with half a call,*
> *Spreading out thy glossy breast*
> *Like a careless Prodigal;*
> *Telling tales about the sun,*
> *When we've little warmth, or none.*

I am gliding on auto pilot, lost in a tranquil dream, when a collared dove bursts from the foliage overhead and wakes me from my reverie.

Ivy again covers the trees and shrubs of the hedgerow, a perfect hideaway for larger birds to nest in camouflage. The ghostly forms of trees in the shimmering water are a changing cycle of images as I walk past, yet the sun's reflection among them is constant.

I am now in the townland of The Maws, passing the sports grounds and buildings of the North Kildare Club. I notice a burrow in the bank rising from the towpath. The clever animal had started digging, and having come up against an obstacle, began again lower down, thus creating a safe haven for itself.

A miniature arched cut stone outlet is built into the far bank. A delicate stream of water flows from it feeding the canal, while beyond it towers Chamber's Bridge. The date 1793 is inscribed here, as is the familiar name, Richard Evans.

The 15th Lock is immediately after it. The cottage beside the lock is modern, not resembling the regular lockkeeper's cottage. Close to the lock wall, the pink-purple flowers of the red dead-nettle are starting to bloom. It has a passing resemblance to a nettle, yet cannot sting as it has no stinging hairs. The red refers to its dark-red stems.

15th Lock

The canal opens out after the 15th Lock, and there is a towpath on the south bank also, which gives access to half a dozen colourful boats moored there. The canal bank grasses are nicely mown and the gardens of the pretty white cottages nearby have seen the touch of a loving hand, making it a pleasant place to pause and take in the view. County Meath is within stepping distance as the county boundary runs just north of the canal, before skirting around Kilcock.

Swallows are feeding on the wing, sweeping down occasionally to the abundance of insects just above water. It is my first sighting of this acrobatic bird since the year began. Swallows are mainly blue-black on top, with a black breast band, whitish belly and a long forked tail. Their arrival is always welcome, as they are a sign that summer is not too far off. These seasonal visitors usually arrive from Africa by mid-March or April. They return to Africa in early autumn, gathering in large groups on overhead wires, preparing for departure.

On my approach to Kilcock, the hedgerow disappears and the grassy towpath becomes exposed to the public road that leads to the town. Along the bank, I encounter an endless row of blossoms, as daffodils and narcissi greet me. I can smell their fragrance and can almost taste their butter-yellowness on my tongue. Their vibrancy and jollity touch me as they dance in the breeze. I can almost hear them sing.

The path leads me to the expansive, welcoming harbour at Kilcock. Its transformation into a wonderful amenity area is due to the Kilcock Branch of the Royal Canal Amenity Group, which was formed in 1982. On the far bank is the home of Kilcock Canoe Polo Club, founded in 1998. It hosted the European Canoe Polo Championship in 2003.

As I draw near to Shaw's Bridge and the double-chambered 16th Lock, I notice an attractive block of old terraced buildings across the street, all brightly painted. The bridge was rebuilt in the 1990s.

The place name Kilcock derives from the Irish Cill Coca, the Church or Cell of Coca. Saint Coca is said to have founded the first church here sometime in the sixth century. It

A row of golden daffodils

Kilcock Canoe Polo Club

was built on high ground on the southern bank of the Rye Water, close to a well of pagan religious significance.

St. Coca's Catholic Church, built circa 1865, is a beautiful example of Gothic Revival architecture. It is adorned with stained glass windows, a timber gallery and carved timber altar furniture. Its 30 metre tower, with cast-iron clocks, is prominent on the skyline.

Close to the church stands the Presentation Convent, built as a novitiate for the foreign missions. It was established in 1879 by three sisters who came from San Francisco. Local nuns and teachers tell how those nuns brought the sapling of a redwood tree with them, which they planted on the convent grounds. It is now an enormous sturdy tree, a striking presence in the surrounding landscape.

Bríd Dáibhís (Bridie Davis) studied Irish Literature at Maynooth College and entered the Presentation Novitiate in 1947. On profession she was assigned to Kilcock Presentation Convent. As Sister Fintan, she taught in the adjoining Scoil Coca Naofa, where she was a great inspiration to her pupils, particularly in Irish language and culture.

Bríd was an accomplished writer in Irish and English. She chaired the local Irish Language organisation Glór na nGael and was a founder of Comhaltas Ceoltóirí Éireann. Spirituality and nature are recurring

Kilcock Harbour and Shaw's Bridge

themes in her writing. In the poem 'Dún Laoghaire', from her 1989 publication *Cosán na Gréine*, she was inspired by the divine in the harbour.

Nár mhéanar dom	*Wasn't I fortunate*
I nDún Laoghaire na long	*In Dún Laoghaire of the ships*
Tráthnóna lán de sheolta!	*An evening full of sails!*
An ghrian ina cailís	*The sun is a chalice*
Ar dhromchla an chuain;	*On the crest of the harbour;*
Pobal an tSamhraidh	*The Summer congregation*
In ómós ag siúl;	*Walking in reverence;*
Na bádóirí ina sagairt	*The boatmen priests*
Faoi sheol.	*Under sail.*
Cuan beo.	*A living harbour.*
Cuan draíochta	*A magic harbour.*
Cuan Dé.	*Harbour of God.*

Bríd Dáibhís died in 2017.

The square in the town is on the site of an old market place, laid out by the Normans in the twelfthth century. During the early fifteenth century there were two weekly markets held in the square, on Wednesdays for corn and Saturdays for meat.

Another view of Kilcock Harbour

By the early nineteenth century, there were nine fairs held annually in the Fair-Green. They were big events and a great day out could be had forging new friendships, completing land deals and agreeing marriages. Many of the business deals were transacted in the local hostelries. A reflection of the importance of Kilcock as a commercial centre in the general area in the seventeenth century is evidenced by the use of a measurement all over North Kildare called A Barrel of Oats Kilcock Measure.

Business in the town was served well by convenient transport, first as a stopping post for the stagecoach, then later by passenger boats on the Royal Canal. However, trade declined after 1847 due to the arrival of the railway. The last Kilcock Fair was in the late 1950s, ending an era of extensive commercial activity. The old, bustling market square is now a car park.

However two industries in the town, Kelly's Bakery and the Leaf Factory, continued to provide much needed local business for decades afterwards. But now the waft of fresh bread and the sweet sugary smell of chewing gum have also disappeared. The enormous Musgrave's warehouse at the edge of town has replaced them as a new source of badly needed employment.

Cox of Kilcock were renowned for the sale of German musical instruments made by Hohner. The autobiography *A Tig Na Tit Orm* by Maidhc Dainín Ó Sé, father of the TV personality Daithí Ó Sé, has been translated from the Irish as *House Don't Fall on Me*. Maidhc was a keen accordion player. He remembers a favourite weekly radio programme of ballads and traditional music, sponsored by Cox of Kilcock. He got his first accordion through the post from Cox's shop. Accordions came to Ireland not only from Germany, but from England, Scotland and America, when a returning family member often brought one home with them.

Today, Kilcock is mainly a commuter town for people travelling to work in Dublin and elsewhere, yet it still has an agricultural hinterland.

Having rambled around the nooks and crannies, through the network of small streets laid out like spokes in a wheel from the FairGreen, I board the next scheduled bus after just a short wait. It takes me to Lucan, from where I walk home through St. Catherine's Park, as I ponder with pleasure my forthcoming return to Kilcock to continue my journey westward.

10.

KILCOCK TO ENFIELD

Sustainability, Reeds, Buzzards and Conversations

Almost a month after my last canal walk I park in what was once the busy market square in Kilcock. I step out into the dazzling late April sunshine to begin the fourth day of my canal adventure, travelling further inland as far as Enfield.

I join the Royal Canal on its north bank, after Shaw's Bridge, at the double-chambered 16th Lock. A small harbour, with some mooring posts, lies beyond it. From the wooden jetty on the south bank a young man is dangling his bare legs with his feet in the water. The secluded, grassy towpath skirts the town, which is almost hidden from view by willow trees and a tangle of bushes.

Allen Bridge, known locally as Spin Bridge, is on the outskirts of Kilcock. It was extensively renovated and widened circa 1960. Passing beneath it, I am under the original arch, a preserved hidden gem. Strolling along the grassy towpath, the townland of Kilglin is to the north in County Meath and Boycetown and Pitchfordstown are to the south in County Kildare. I hear the bleating of sheep and see their white specks in a far off field through a gap in the thorny hedge.

The band of vegetation along the water's edge is known as the reed fringe. The plants here have their roots anchored in the mud of the canal bed, while their leaves and flowers rise above the water. This fringe of growth is important for the healthy survival of the canal: it provides food, shelter and breeding sites for birds and other aquatic animals; prevents the growth of algae; and protects the canal banks from erosion by absorbing the wave energy from the wash of boats.

Close up of Burnet Rose

The reed fringe is dominated by grass-like plants, which all look quite similar, such as reeds and sedges. The common reed is the tallest of these and can be recognised by its large, purple flower-heads in early autumn. The bulrush, or reedmace as it was formerly known, is also quite distinctive, with its near cylindrical spike of brown and yellow flowers in mid-summer, on a sturdy, erect stem. Other plants, such as bogbean and marsh marigold, are also present.

As I quicken my pace, the humble dandelion continues to catch my eye, with a goodly amount of these yellow flowers adding to the colour of the towpath and surrounding fields. They take the April sunlight and transform it into a radiant glow that shines deep within me. So the dandelion becomes my golden emblem for today. Over seventy species of dandelion have been recorded in Ireland. However, they are so alike that individual identification is almost impossible.

Dandelion is a member of the daisy family and the name dandelion derives from the Latin *dens leonis*, meaning lion's tooth. The diuretic properties of the plant, promoting the flow of urine, led to the expressions piss-the-bed and wet-the-bed. In fact, the dandelion has been used in a wide variety of herbal cures for coughs, warts and as a blood cleanser. The young leaves can be eaten as a salad, while the roots can be dried and roasted to make a palatable coffee substitute. Dandelions are a valuable food source for bees, providing them with nectar and pollen, especially in early spring when other sources of food are scarce.

Growing up in Dublin, we called the dandelion in seed a Jinnyjoe. Jinnyjoes provided us with innocent forms of amusement. Most involved blowing at the seed head while singing a rhyme, and counting the number of puffs it took to dislodge all the seeds.

I am now close to the Kildare-Meath county boundary. There will be three more crossings back and forth over this border today as far as Cloncurry Bridge, with the canal marking the boundary for some of this time.

The black and white forms of grazing cattle dot a nearby field. A group of their brown brothers are scattered about another. It is evident along here that the richness of the land can support the substantial amount of farming activity taking place along the canal.

As I saunter along, my mind ponders on food production and its consequences. Food eaten by developed countries is often imported to excite the palate with an increasing variety of texture and taste. Yet the carbon footprint associated with importing food from every corner of the planet is an environmental problem. It begs the question if such exotic dining is sustainable. Hence, the Green Movement encourages the practice of eating what is locally produced and seasonal.

The ash trees along here tower above the elders, while two large willows display their grey catkins. The stems of the common reed rise along the far bank, waving their feathery seed heads in the mild breeze, looking like an army of dishevelled, sand-coloured troops reeling from action. Summer will add colour and straighten their resolve.

Magnificent blooming hawthorn

The relative silence is broken by a high flying jet, the third since leaving Kilcock behind. I surmise that there is a transatlantic flight path overhead as I observe the white contrails streaking the blue sky.

Suddenly I am rewarded with my first flash of the hawthorn blossom, and as I come under the spell of this sturdy tree, its long arms covered in white gloves seem to reach out, as if to embrace me. Hawthorn is associated with magical powers. The fairies were said to be especially fond of this tree and cutting them down was thought to incur the wrath of the little people. A hawthorn tree was often planted near a holy well that was known for its healing properties. People placed rags and other objects on the tree and prayed.

I am now almost four kilometres west of Kilcock, with the townland of Ferrans to the north. Approaching McLoughlin's Bridge, I see an angler in full camouflage casting his line from a little jetty below the towpath. On reaching the bridge, I notice its name chiselled out on the stone plaque with the date 1797 and R. Evans acknowledged again. Just below is the double-chambered 17th Lock, which is also known as Fern's or Ferrans Lock.

Consulting my guide, I notice that the Rye water feeder enters the canal close by. Two men are leaning on the west side of the bridge chatting. Approaching them, I enquire if they know its location.

'Just across the way,' the shorter of the two indicates, pointing east with a lively wave of his hand.

I cross the bridge in the direction indicated and notice, built into the canal north bank, a concrete outlet through which a feed from the Rye's precious water source replenishes the canal's water. I retrace my steps to the friendly locals on the bridge, who are still in deep conversation, oblivious of time.

'So are you out for a bit of a stroll on this lovely day?' the shorter man asks.

'Well, I'm actually walking the canal in stages, from the Liffey to the Shannon,' I answer, 'and I'm taking down a few notes along the way.'

Rye water feeder looking east from McLoughlin Bridge

'That's great,' he says. 'The walks along the canal about here are beautiful and I'm sure it's just as lovely all the way to the Shannon. I would advise you to sit down every evening and write down everything you can remember about that day.'

His wise words reinforce in me the need to keep a careful record of each day's walk, so I tell him I will follow his advice. This seemed to be a good opportunity to enquire about the summit level, a term I wished to understand better.

'It starts this side of Mullingar at the 25th Lock,' he explains. 'The summit level, which is the highest level the canal rises to, is approximately 25 kilometres long, with Mullingar roughly at its midpoint. There are no locks along it, as you might guess.'

Still leaning on the bridge wall, he gazes briefly down the long stretch of water ahead and then adds:

'Another thing you'll notice is that the balance beams of the lock's breast gates and tail gates will be facing the opposite

A closer look at the Rye water feeder

direction after the summit level, because the canal's descent will now be towards the Shannon.'

Bidding them goodbye and thanking them for such an interesting conversation, I continue on my way with a greater understanding of the canal from an engineering perspective.

After McLoughlin's Bridge, the towpath changes to the south bank. To the north I notice a field dominated by rooks. Their collective name, a clamour of rooks, is a perfect description of the racket they are managing to create.

There are no locks over the next 32 kilometres which has become known as the Long Level. The stretch from Fern's Lock to Enfield passes through the Cappagh Bog. During the canal's construction, major problems were encountered here, such as the sides slipping and the bottom swelling up due to the boggy nature of the terrain.

In addition, they faced the requirement for another 'deep sinking' between Cloncurry Bridge and Enfield in order to maintain the canal at a constant level, thus avoiding the need for locks. As a consequence, the work became very labour intensive and the company found itself in financial difficulty once again. This shortage of working capital became a problem for the Royal Canal Company during the 1790s. Several attempts to raise money from parliament and subscribers helped continue the staggered progress of this project.

In 1800, a parliamentary enquiry resulted in the responsibility for government financing of inland navigation being placed in the hands of a new body, known as the Directors General of Inland Navigation. The sum of £500,000 was made available to the canal directors, finally increasing the possibility of the project being completed.

The presence of the Royal Canal transport system through the Cappagh Bog resulted in the development of turf-cutting there on a large scale. So despite the structural and financial problems encountered, it was the area around Kilcock and the Bog of Cappagh that eventually derived the most benefit from the sale of turf. Between 1 May 1821 and 28 January 1822, forty-three boat loads were sent to

Canal lock mechanism

Dublin, at an average of 90 tons per load. Transporting turf provided the Royal Canal Company with a major source of revenue, so the financial benefit was mutual.

Over on the far bank, I see two sturdy pillars supporting large decorative cast-iron gates, giving access to a long avenue. This is a back entrance into the 686 acres that make up Ferrans Stud Farm, which is owned by the award-winning Juddmonte Farms Ireland.

This section, stretching from McLoughlin's Bridge to Cloncurry Bridge, is almost six kilometres long. A beautiful corridor of trees lines my way and the silence is heavenly.

I hear the subdued hum of a cabin cruiser engine, which soon comes into view, towing a smaller boat with an outboard motor. There are two men in the cabin, one with his leg sticking out the door. He gives a friendly wave.

'How are yah?' he shouts.

'Grand,' I shout back. 'What a glorious day!'

Then he disappears from view, the chugging of his engine dimming into the silence.

After a straight stretch, I am approaching a bend. I notice a historic milestone and can decipher the number 23 inscribed on it. Such stones, of which few remain, were erected to indicate to boatmen their distance from Broadstone Harbour. In this case, 23 miles or 37 kilometres.

Cruiser passing by

A large bird of prey soars high above. From its broad wingspan and fan-like tail I can tell it is a buzzard. The species was absent in Ireland from the late nineteenth century until 1933, when a pair bred in County Antrim. Since then, these raptors have spread slowly south and have become widespread in recent times. Their diet consists of a wide variety of prey, including, small mammals, birds, rabbits, insects, earthworms and amphibians. Its talons help to catch its prey and its short, hooked bill is perfect for eating meat.

The growth of trees along here, on both sides of the canal, is so dense that I feel as if I am walking through a wood. Further along the way, afforestation is evident to the north, with trees of mainly beech and Sitka spruce.

The bleating of sheep alerts me to a farm behind the high hedgerow. Further on, there is a tractor on the far bank, which gives access to a farm from Cloncurry Bridge. There is a steel silo close to a barn, most likely storing fodder for animals. However, steel silos can also be used to store grain safely by use of temperature control and ventilation systems. They also prevent vermin from contaminating the grain.

I soon find myself in the townland of Kilbrook, the birthplace of the poet Teresa Brayton. Teresa wrote 'The Old Bog Road', which refers to a nearby road running south from the canal. It was later set to music by Madeline King O'Farrelly of Rochfordbridge and has since been recorded by many singers.

Teresa Cora Boylan was born into a nationalist family in 1868 and emigrated to America at the age of twenty-seven where she married Richard Brayton, a French Canadian. In 1932, aged sixty-four, she returned to Ireland permanently. She spent the last three years of her life in the room where she was born. She died in 1943 and is buried in nearby Cloncurry graveyard. In 1959, President Éamon de Valera, whom she had admired, unveiled a memorial cross over her grave.

Nature and nationalism are recurring themes in Teresa's poetry. However, her most famous poem, 'The Old Bog Road', examines an exile's nostalgia for his homeland, a theme she was well placed to write about:

And what's the whole world to a man when no one speaks his name

Later in the song she describes his sad thoughts on missing his mother's wake and funeral.

Old Bog Road sign

And here was I on Broadway with building bricks for load

When they carried out her coffin from the Old Bog Road.

My journey continues through the western reaches of the Bog of Cappagh. A magnificent display of hawthorn appears before me, spilling over into the canal in all its floral glory, its reflection in the water adding to the brilliance of its presence.

I embrace my uplifting company, the wind in my ears and the choral sound of overlapping bird songs. A stationary heron comes under my radar. As I approach within 20 metres, it takes a short flight west, placing a safe 300 metres between us. Mallards paddle leisurely on the water. The only man-made sound, barely perceptible, is the hum of traffic on some road I had long forgotten.

I almost jump with fright when I disturb a collared dove, which is startled into sudden flight. The speed of its beating wings is fascinating, ploughing through the foliage to head skyward.

Approaching Cloncurry Bridge, on the fringes of the Bog of Cappagh, the land becomes waterlogged and boggy, which accounts for the predominance of sallies, rushes and reeds now making their appearance. Bulrushes, in the reed fringe, have died back a light brown colour through winter and have yet to flower this year. They stand erect, with last year's fluffy seed heads, like tanned candy floss on a stick.

A large metal gate blocks most of the towpath. However, an old metal swing gate leads to a stone wall, the perfect place to set up for lunch. Under a blue sky, I enjoy my cheese roll and coffee. Feeling refreshed, I walk up onto Cloncurry Bridge. There is a sign here that reads Rathcore Text Alert Area, reminding the relaxed traveller that even among all this calm and beauty there is always the possibility of danger. I take to the towpath again, which has now switched back to the north bank and has become a road, allowing access to some houses along the canal.

Marshy ground approaching Cloncurry Bridge

Cloncurry Bridge

In a field off the far bank, I notice a church tower cloaked in greenery, with a graveyard surrounding it. The church is marked on my map and the mound is identified as a motte. Whatever structure was originally present on that motte is long gone and replaced by a tree, so I call it One Tree Hill.

Cloncurry was mentioned in the *Annals of the Four Masters* as far back as the sixth century. Strongbow was once Lord of Cloncurry. When he died in 1176, his daughter made a grant of the land in this area to Adam de Hereford. These early Norman settlers were constantly under attack from those unconquered Irish west of Cloncurry. To guard themselves against surprise attacks they built a motte and bailey here.

When the tarmacked access road eventually swings away to the right, I tread on a soft grassy path by the canal bank again. As I stop to observe a solitary swan, a female jogger flashes by at high speed, jolting me back to reality. I am in dandelion territory once again. Their vibrant glow is still alive to me, serving me well as today's emblem.

A wooden bench on the canal bank offers me a welcome rest and a moment's contemplation before continuing. I listen to the wind whispering through the reeds and rushes, mingling with the sweet tweeting of birds, and the calmness of this earthly haven descends upon me.

Motte with tree

The steep drop to the canal water becomes evident after this, as I encounter that second costly 'deep sinking'. I am approximately 8 kilometres along the Long Level when I realise I have not heard the rhythmic and soothing fall of water through a lock for some time.

Enfield Train Station marks the end of today's walk. I continue on past it and finally reach Enfield Bridge, which carries the old Kilcock to Kinnegad road over the railway and canal.

On the main thoroughfare a low hedge has been skilfully clipped into the placename ENFIELD, offering the traveller a warm welcome to the town. The Irish name for Enfield is An Bóthar Buí, which means The Yellow Road. There are two theories as to the origin of this name. The first is that during rainy weather the wheels of the stage coaches churned up the soil and left yellow mud. The second is that it derived its name from the yellow ragwort that lined the road.

In the days before so many of Ireland's small towns were bypassed by motorways, villages like Enfield were the perfect place to stop for refreshments on the long journey to the midlands or further west.

During the eighteenth and into the nineteenth century, the area was known as New Inn or Innfield, after the original Royal Oak Inn, believed to have been situated on the site of the nearby Bridge House Bar and Restaurant. Towards the end of the nineteenth century a new

A topiary of the placename Enfield

postmaster was appointed, who came from the district of Enfield in London and he decided to use this name as the placename for his new work location. However, the name Innfield still appears on some maps as the official name of the town.

Back at the station, I stop to admire the attractive stone building which, I decide, must have been the original ticket office. There are curtains on the windows and it now seems to be the home of some lucky family. Taking a seat to wait for the train, I notice that the old signal box is still standing on the opposite side near the disused platform. An old rusted water tower stands close by from the days of steam trains.

At last I am boarding the train bound for Dublin. I alight at Kilcock Station, locate my car and drive home, satisfied with my peaceful trek over a variety of terrains, crossing and re-crossing county boundaries in the process.

11.

ENFIELD TO THE HILL OF DOWN

Bealtaine, Ribbonism, Herons and a Missing Hill

On a dry, overcast, mid-May morning I set out on the fifth day of my journey, leading me deeper inland through some small villages, avoiding the bustle and business of towns.

Parking at Enfield train station, I enter the Royal Canal Way from the bridge onto the south bank. 'Harvest Walk' is written on a signpost, a fitting name in a town that holds an annual 'Harvest Festival'.

This gravel towpath is bordered by mown grass. Behind a wooden fence, a variety of shrubs in a mixture of subtle yellows and greens are being cultivated. Soon I am passing a line of well-established trees, growing on the sloping bank that falls to the water below.

A burst of bluebells light up this dull morning, their stems and flowers drooping gracefully, as if bowing before some unseen lord. After drinking in such delicious blueness, my feet take me off on a lively jaunt.

I pass beneath the Enfield Inner Relief Road to where the towpath becomes a corridor, flanked by a variety of tall native trees. Beneath the lower, leafless branches some blossoming soul has planted narcissi, a splash of white and yellow brightening up the grass borders.

An enclosure for cattle extends down to the water's edge, providing access for them to drinking water. The canal meanders out of Enfield, but the railway line follows a more direct course westward, with the two never far apart.

At one point, the canal bank is flanked on both sides by a wall of limestone blocks, suggesting that there were once stop gates here. Stop gates were used in an emergency, such as a breach in the canal bank, to prevent the water in the entire section from flowing out. They were also useful when draining a canal section for repair work.

May, or Bealtaine in Irish, is certainly putting on a magnificent floral display today. The ancient Festival of Bealtaine was celebrated on the first of May to welcome the summer months during which the Druids lit the Baal-Tinne, the holy, goodly fire of Baal, the Sun-god. They drove cattle on a path between two fires, singeing them or burning the blood as a sacred offering to Baal.

Other customs included dancing around the decorated May Bush, leaving yellow flowers on neighbours' windowsills to offer protection and good luck to the house and choosing the Queen of the May from among the young local girls.

The Christian feast of Easter slowly replaced the Baal festival after St. Patrick lit his paschal fire on top of the Hill of Slane in defiance of the pagan High King, Laoghaire.

Eventually, the practice of choosing the Queen of the May was overtaken by devotion to the Blessed Virgin Mary and Marian processions became common throughout Ireland. The well-known hymn 'Queen of the May' celebrates the crowning of Our Lady with blossoms. It begins:

> *Bring flowers of the rarest*
> *bring blossoms the fairest*
> *from garden and woodland and hillside and dale.*

A pretty clump of cowslips in full bloom appears before me. These yellow flowers hang drooping to one side in a cluster. They have orange markings on the inside, with tight, green skirts on the outside, narrowing to stalks that attach to the main stem.

According to the naturalist and nature writer Marcus Woodward, in his book *How to Enjoy Wild Flowers* (1927), 'the cowslip is Venus's flower, and those wishing to preserve beauty need but bathe their faces in a cowslip wash.'

Two barns peep above the shrubs, which open out on fields of grazing animals. The only sign of human life is a farmhand, with a chainsaw and face protection, cutting up a fallen tree. He has no hope of detecting me above the visceral, staccato-revving of the engine.

I soon arrive at the Blackwater aqueduct, which carries the Royal Canal over the River Blackwater, flowing about 10 metres below.

Cowslips

There are two tributaries of the River Boyne called The Blackwater. This one is called the Enfield Blackwater or Kildare Blackwater, which rises north of the village Prosperous in County Kildare, flows northwest and eventually enters the Boyne at Donore.

The second Blackwater, called the Leinster or Kells Blackwater, rises near Bailieborough in County Cavan and flows southeast through Virginia, before joining the Boyne at Navan.

As I pass the quaint, unmarked Kilmore Bridge, I can feel the remoteness of this area in the luscious gleam of the greenery and the absence of man-made sound. Beyond it, the Royal Canal Way switches to the north bank, and proceeds to head in a northwesterly direction.

The path soon narrows to a beautiful meadowy walk. A row of hazel trees behind the hedgerow stretch on and on, creating a linear wood alongside me. The hazel is a symbol of, among other things, fertility, wisdom and poetic inspiration. I feel their ancient magic as I pass and am reminded of the W.B. Yeats poem 'The Song of Wandering Aengus', which begins:

River Blackwater Aqueduct

I went out to the hazel wood,
Because a fire was in my head,
And cut and peeled a hazel wand,
And hooked a berry to a thread ...

The wood of the hazel has been used in making furniture, fencing and in wickerwork. Its large leaves tend to curl and are more round than oval. In a few months it will produce the most succulent hazelnuts, an important food source in Ireland from earliest times.

Wildflowers adorn the canal bank and hedgerow. Amongst them is germander speedwell, a little flower with four bright blue petals and a white centre, considered a good luck charm for the traveller. Tufted vetch, with its bluish purple flowers and narrow, oblong leaves, climbs through the undergrowth. There is still space, nevertheless, for the daisy, dandelion, celandine and primrose to shine across at an infantry of bulrushes along the water's edge.

As the line of hazel finally ends, the hedgerow is again filled with blackthorn and laden with the creamy blossoms of the hawthorn.

Hazel tree with nuts

I encounter the smooth leaves of the snowberry hanging from red stems. This bush will soon burst into bloom, with tiny pink flowers. In autumn, it will produce eye-catching, white, plump berries, poisonous to humans, though pheasants are known to eat them.

Overhanging beech have left thousands of nuts on the path below and for a while I am lost in a blissful reverie as I crunch along. As traffic comes within earshot again, I am soon jolted back to reality. A farm-style gate with a turnstile to its right leads to the Moyvalley bridges. The first one is modern and carries the new road section over the canal and railway, bypassing the small village of Moyvalley. Beyond it is the old arched canal bridge which, interestingly, has a pedestrian refuge at road level, a place for pedestrians to stand in safety while traffic passes. I step onto the grassy floor of the tiny walled recess, soaking up the greenery and colour along the waterway.

There was once a fine canal hotel at Moyvalley but the ruins were demolished in 1977 to make way for the approach road to the new bridge.

Just off the canal's north bank, facing out onto the old bypassed road, stands Furey's Select Bar. This quirky establishment has an old-world charm, with the front facade constructed of white, diagonal wooden laths and the sides of white, corrugated tin. In contrast, the windows, doors and edgings are painted a deep maroon. Old advertisements for Wills cigarettes, both 'Gold Flake' and 'Wild Woodbine' adorn it, which were mounted in days long before the smoking ban.

From the old bridge I look down on a series of barges moored in a row, with not a single ripple lapping the bows in this world of quiet calm. The May sunshine has left me in a hot sweat. Peeling off one layer of clothes, I lose my precious pen from my shirt pocket. I search frantically in the maze of grasses, but to no avail. I set my sights on Furey's pub. It is midday as I enter the premises and I find that I am alone with the barman.

'Excuse me,' I say, 'I've lost my pen and I'm wondering if there is anywhere around here I might buy one?'

'Do you just mean, like, a normal biro kind of pen?' he says to me, as he begins to rummage around behind the bar, shifting items aside.

Furey's pub

'The very thing,' I say, with a sense of hope. 'Anything at all that I can write with will do fine. I'll pay you for it of course.'

'No you won't,' says he, as he places a biro firmly in my hand. I am grateful for his understanding and thank him for his generosity.

Armed with my invaluable writing implement, I press on along a gravel path that soon turns to grass. An old lady is walking dogs that are splashing into the water and climbing out again, really enjoying the ritual. Then a cyclist comes whizzing by, whom I pass again later, as she retraces her spokes. A gentle breeze has sprung up, sending silky ripples along the water surface.

After 15 minutes, I come to the Ribbontail Footbridge, which has been restored by the Longwood Branch of the RCAG and which was originally erected to facilitate people crossing the canal to a nearby church. It is not clear how this bridge received its name. Ribbontail suggests a connection with the Ribbonmen, who are said to have congregated around the bridge when they were active in the area. The name 'Ribbonmen' is said to derive from their custom of wearing a green ribbon in their buttonholes.

On a national level, Ribbonism supported the nationalist movement and worked to repeal the Act of Union. On a local level, their aim was to protect the interests of the working class and the rights of tenants, who may have been in danger of exploitation or eviction by unscrupulous landlords and agents.

As I make my way to the back of the bridge I become aware of a heron that lands and perches on the opposite canal wall close by. Reasonably well hidden, I stay still and observe. To my delight it does not fly off but stares into the water mesmerised. I realise it is eyeing the concentric circles below, contemplating a delectable meal, its silhouette on the water within easy reach of the tasty fish. I watch and watch hoping this bird will dive. Suddenly the loud, staccato screech of its mate comes upstream on the wind. The transfixed male suddenly comes to life, and abandoning its lucky prey flies off downstream, dutifully returning to the heronry.

Ribbontail footbridge and stop gates

The grey heron is Ireland's tallest bird, standing at almost a metre high. As its name suggests, it is predominantly grey, though its head is white with a black crest. The neck is also white but with black stripes on the foreneck. The heron hunts alone, standing like a sentry by the river, ready to make a swift, fatal strike. Yet despite the solitary nature of their hunting, they nest in tall trees in sometimes huge communal heronries. They were often hunted during the Royal Hunt, being a favourite dish among royalty, as much esteemed for their taste as pheasant and peacock. Herons have been symbolic of many things including contemplation, vigilance and divine wisdom.

In his poem 'Heron', the Enniskillen poet Francis Harvey captures the fascinating take off and flight of this extraordinary bird.

> *He creaks into flight. The wind buffers him, gives him*
> *a bumpy ride: it seems he must somehow end up*
> *in a twisted heap of canvas and struts on the mountainside.*
> *But no: he tacks into weathers with a prow that rises*
>   *and falls in the swell.*
> *The ghost of the pterodactyl haunts him in every cell.*

I carry on with a sprightly step, crossing the county boundary once again into Meath, from where I see houses on the outskirts of Longwood.

There are two young boys fishing on the approach to Longwood Harbour.

'Did you catch anything?' I ask.

'Yes, a perch and a tench,' says the older lad.

'Wow, well done. Do you have them there?'

'No, you're not allowed, so we put them back into the canal.'

'Ah, good lads! Well you must be good fishermen; I hope your luck continues.'

Heron

Soon I am standing where the canal spreads out in a semicircle to form Longwood Harbour. There is a sturdy stone building here with a red door, and close by an outhouse of similar construction. These buildings are the home of the Ribbontail Paddlers Canoe Club.

Longwood village, historically called Moydervy, lies about 1.5 kilometres northeast of here. The twenty-first century saw an increase in its population, with a number of new housing estates springing up, turning it into a busy, bustling little village. Just beyond the harbour, I cross over the Longwood Road aqueduct.

Soon after, I arrive at the River Boyne aqueduct 250 metres further on, with its three impressive arches. The Royal Canal Company faced financial problems during its construction. It is judged to be one of the finest stone aqueducts in Ireland, and is best viewed from below, with the railway viaduct a short distance away.

Leaning on its wall, I gaze at two swans gliding peacefully in the water far below. The River Boyne and the River Blackwater have been designated Special Areas of Conservation (SAC) by the National Parks & Wildlife Service (NPWS), because of specific habitats and species,

Longwood Harbour

which are listed as Alkaline Fens, Alluvial Forests, River Lamprey, Atlantic Salmon and Otter.

The Boyne is quite a small waterway at this point in its course. Rising at Trinity Well near Carbury, County Kildare, it flows west through Edenderry in County Offaly, then turning northeast it follows its course through counties Meath and Louth, growing in volume along the way, until it eventually enters the sea just below Drogheda. The Boyne is 112 kilometres long, but at this point it has only travelled approximately 20 kilometres. I notice a border of trees and shrubs along its banks, which plot the route of the river through the landscape, as I follow it as far as the eye can see. Many sites along its course are steeped in history, myth, legend and fact, dating from ancient times to the present century. Two are of particular importance.

Brú na Bóinne is a major tourist attraction. It has been a World Heritage Site since 1993, containing the important Neolithic passage tombs at Newgrange, Dowth and Knowth, built around 5,000 years ago, making them older than Stonehenge and the Great Pyramids of Giza.

The other site of significance is the Battle of the Boyne, fought in 1690 between the Protestant King William III (of Orange) and his Catholic father-in law, King James II, whom William had deposed in 1688.

William's victory ensured the continuation of Protestant ascendancy in Ireland, which is celebrated on July 12 each year, particularly in Northern Ireland. Its lasting consequences still affect Northern Irish politics.

Crossing this well-constructed aqueduct and the Boyne, I resume my journey along this peaceful towpath. My eye is drawn to a Japanese rose bush, whose pretty pink flower will soon be in bloom and whose red hips appear in autumn. I stroll on past ash and beech, and as the towpath suddenly becomes narrower, I am led through a row of vivid hawthorn blossom, followed by a yellow corridor of gorse, a heavenly delight of seclusion and beauty.

River Boyne

Before I know it, I have arrived at Blackshade Bridge. Its Irish name is An Scáth Dubh. Beyond it, a series of green pastures surround me, with cattle feeding from bathtubs transformed into troughs. Having passed a small wood of alder and chestnut, a dredger appears, travelling towards me. The operator is lost in concentration on the job at hand, as weeds trundle up along the conveyor belt of his machine, which he empties onto the canal bank for collection later.

The grassy path turns to gravel approaching the Hill of Down or Killyon Bridge. As this is yet another unmarked bridge, I decide to check my exact location. Seeing an elderly lady about to enter a house I look for her assistance.

'I'm sorry to bother you.' I say. 'I just want to get my bearings right and I thought maybe you could help.'

She greets me in a cordial manner. 'I'll do my best', she says.

Narrow path lined with gorse

'I'm trying to identify each bridge as I come across them. Is that Killyon Bridge below on the canal, which is also referred to as the Hill of Down in my guide book?'

'Yes, indeed it is. They're one and the same.' Her friendly face lights up a shade as she answers.

'Well, that's cleared that up for me.' I say. 'Thanks so much for your help.'

'Well thank God you're on the right track now.'

As I leave this helpful woman, the overcast sky sheds its rain at last. Quickly putting on my raingear, I walk back to the shelter of the bridge, where I enjoy my well-deserved lunch protected from the downpour.

There is a small harbour here, with some moored boats. Both banks are ablaze with a magnificent variety of colourful shrubs and flowers. Even a kayak and a miniature rowboat have been florally decorated. The gorgeous erect tulips with their sturdy leaves are my favourite.

The canal and railway bridges at the Hill of Down are adjacent to each other. An old dilapidated house close by, almost obscured by foliage, was most likely associated with the canal or railway.

As the rain continues to fall I take a stroll over to a pub on the far bank. A sign hanging from a pole at the bridge points towards The Hill, Lounge Bar, Shop and Post Office, Moran's, about 50 metres away.

Entering Moran's shop, the owners greet me in a friendly manner.

'It's a right wet spell we're getting,' remarks the woman as she nods towards the rain drumming on the window pane.

'Unfortunately, it is. Hopefully it will clear soon,' I answer. 'Have you been running these premises for long?'

'We have been the proprietors here for fifty years now,' the man confirms. 'However, the building is much older and at one time was associated with the railway.'

'I noticed a small hill in the distance as I approached the bridge,' I remark, 'and wondered if it is the Hill of Down.'

This brought a smile to his face. 'No,' he replies. 'The Hill of Down is the name of the townland but curiously, there is no hill associated with it.'

Great Willowherb

'Well that's a strange one, indeed!' I answer, smiling too. I decide to make a small purchase in acknowledgement of their helpfulness.

'You can stay a while and shelter till the rain eases, if you wish', he says, as I pay him.

'Well thanks very much for the kind offer,' I reply. 'However, I aim to walk as far as Killucan today. I'm only half way there with 10 kilometres to go, so I better keep moving.'

'So you've walked 10 kilometres already,' says the woman. 'That's a good trek.'

Hill of Down or Killyon Bridge

'Yes, it sure is. Well thanks very much for all that local information.' We bid our goodbyes and I continue on my way.

The people of this townland have proved to be very helpful and friendly to the passing traveller. I am determined to reach Killucan today, despite the rain. Fortified by lunch and with an uplifted heart, I return to the towpath to press on with my walk west.

12.

HILL OF DOWN TO KILLUCAN

Eskers, Old Inns, Deep Space and Camillians

West of the Hill of Down, I am journeying through a lowland region called the Central Plain, which stretches from Dublin to East Galway. The shapes and forms on this terrain evolved over two million years, when a series of ice ages killed off all animal and plant life, reshaping the landscape.

Eskers, ridges of sand and gravel, evolved when deposits were laid by rivers flowing under the vast sheets of ice. They became exposed at the end of the last ice age approximately 10,000 years ago when the ice melted. Eiscir Riada, which runs through the central plain, was thus formed. As I make my way along the towpath, I consider the first humans who arrived during the early Stone Age around 9,000 years ago. About 2,000 years later the midlands became covered by sphagnum bogs. Eskers provided an invaluable dry route through these bogs for early inhabitants.

When Tara was the seat of the High Kings, the *Book of the Dun Cow* records five great roads radiating from it, the most important being the Slí Mór. It led from Tara, joining the Eiscir Riada near Clonard and continued to Galway. Today, this important esker lies devastated from many years of excavation of its sand and gravel for the construction industry. So as I cross this terrain I will watch for signs of unusual embankments and ridges which have been shaped over time.

As I ramble on, I am suddenly overcome with an uncanny feeling that I am being spied on. Looking across the waterway, I find myself face to face with cows of different colours, black, white and brown, standing, staring at this stranger on the far side, contemplating who I might be, or if I am the provider of food. Further on, the grace of three white horses emanates from a field. Bindweed has wound its way through the other plants along the verge, so that its pretty white flowers appear to belong to another species.

When I arrive at Ballasport Bridge, I discover that there is a turning circle on the west side, similar to the one at Confey. Beyond the bridge, the towpath has switched to the south bank, and I am led onto a rough gravel surface. There is a long stretch now, of almost four kilometres, with no canal crossing.

The canal widens somewhat and the reed fringe extends three metres out into the water. Eventually the reeds die down, exposing a beautiful display of white water lilies floating on the surface, spreading out from the bank in all their aquatic glory. Unfortunately, they only open in full sunshine, so on this dull day it is left to me to imagine the golden yellow stamens at the centre of the virgin white petals. They are

White water lilies

a fine contrast to the yellow variety that I have seen so often. Beyond here, an abundance of reeds extend out into the water once again.

The canal is so still, a broad ribbon of reflection running into the distance, mirroring everything along its route, from trees to bridges, cattle pens, and the many varied grasses of the canal's reed bed.

Horsetails are growing along here in abundance. This is the Field Horsetail. The branches grow out from the stem like spokes on a wheel. I find it extraordinary that horsetails are the sole survivor of a line of plants going back 300 million years. Yet here it is today, standing erect and healthy. Horsetails reproduce from spores rather than seeds and have an extensive root system. They were uses in folk remedies, for many different ailments, including kidney and bladder trouble, arthritis, bleeding ulcers and tuberculosis. Horsetail supplements can still be bought to this day. However, the plant can be highly invasive and is resistant to herbicides.

A fabulous row of sturdy beech trees, rising from the hedgerow on the far bank, marks the boundary of Hyde Park Stud. It is on a tract of land formerly owned by the D'Arcy family, who came to England during the Norman Conquest.

Hyde Park

By the late seventeenth century, the former D'Arcy lands had fallen into the hands of the FitzGerald family. This situation, however, was short-lived. Under the Penal Laws, if a Protestant discoverer could prove a Catholic landowner had evaded a law, their lands became forfeit to the Crown, with up to a quarter share going to the discoverer. In 1717, Mathew Palin, a lieutenant in the army of King William III, gained ownership of Hyde Park when he brought a successful case against Henry FitzGerald, who was convicted of high treason.

Hyde Park estate later passed to Joshua Palin. Dying without an heir, he left the estate to his niece, Martha Grierson, who married James D'Arcy. Through this marriage the lands at Hyde Park estate eventually passed from the Palin family back to the D'Arcy family in 1777, an amazing turn of fate.

The D'Arcy family name was notable in Ireland right through to the twentieth century before the estate became the stud farm that it is today.

D'Arcy's Bridge

A rough tarmac surface on both sides of the waterway provides a thoroughfare for the various properties along the canal banks. These paths stretch all the way to D'Arcy's Bridge, honouring the D'Arcy name.

Enjoying expansive vistas across spacious fields, I soon arrive at the large rectangular cut stone structure that is Thomastown Harbour, where a bright display of shrubs on both banks greets the visitor. There is one barge berthed here at present and I am excited to see No. 3 painted in black on a white background on its green hull. This must be the Killucan Barge, also known as the No. 3 Float, which was purchased by the Royal Canal Amenity Group from CIE for £10 in the 1990s.

For many years this old barge lay semi-submerged and rusted. It was restored over time with funding from the then Minister for the Arts, Culture and the Gaeltacht, Michael D. Higgins, and later by Waterways Ireland. It is a living, floating memorial to all who worked on the restoration of the Royal Canal. On the reopening of the canal's main line on Friday, 1 October 2010, the Killucan Barge No. 3 Float led a flotilla of boats into Richmond Harbour, Cloondara, County Longford to rapturous applause.

Riverstown Feeder

The Riverstown Feeder runs along the edge of the car park here and is carried, via a culvert, into the canal. A slipway for boats was constructed in 1985 when the harbour was restored by the Killucan Branch of the RCAG.

To the right of the slipway stands Nanny Quinn's Bar and Restaurant, a bright attractive hostelry, painted magnolia, with its name in red lettering. My curiosity entices me to stop for a coffee so I can take a peek inside.

Nanny Quinn's Thomastown Harbour

The traditional bar has a welcoming wood burning stove and a solid wood counter. I take a seat on one of the barstools. The rest of these premises are laid out with tables and chairs for dining. Some photographs of local people on the wall tell stories of times past. Some are farm scenes and there is one of Nanny Quinn herself, processing a payment at the till. The bright walls of the dining room offer a nice backdrop to paintings of pastoral scenes, which are an interesting contrast to a large painting of a rugby team in action.

As I sip my coffee, the lady from behind the bar approaches in my direction.

'Excuse me,' I enquire. 'I'm intrigued by the name Nanny Quinn. I saw her photograph and wondered if she's still alive?'

'Oh God, no,' she replies. 'Poor Nanny is long gone.'

'So who runs the place now?' I ask.

'Actually, it's me. I'm currently leasing the bar,' she says.

'Do you know how old this establishment is?' I ask.

'Well,' she replies, 'when I was a little girl, thirty-five years ago, Nanny Quinn was eighty years old, so the pub could be early twentieth century perhaps.'

As I leave, I thank her kindly for sharing her past memories about this local hostelry.

From Thomastown Bridge, I can see down onto the 18th Lock. The canal now begins a steep climb over three kilometres up to the summit level. This is achieved through a series of eight locks, spaced out at approximately 400 metre intervals, which looks like a staircase ahead of me. The water level has to be equalised in the lock chamber before a craft can ascend to the next level. It must have been a frustrating section for barge operators with so many lock gates to open and close over such a short distance. I'm sure progress was extremely slow then, and must still be for leisure craft today.

On the far towpath, just beyond the lock, there is an unnamed modern building. On trying the door, I find with a burst of excitement that it opens.

'Excuse me,' I say to the man I encounter inside. 'I hope I'm not intruding but my curiosity got the better of me as to what purpose this building serves.'

'No bother,' he says. 'You're actually now standing in a Waterways Ireland Maintenance Depot.'

'Very interesting,' I reply. 'So what do you do here?'

'Well,' says he, 'the Office of Public Works took on responsibility for the canal back around 1994. However, ownership fell to Waterways Ireland in 2000 after the Good Friday Agreement. Since 2008, this depot has been responsible for maintenance of the canal, and we now have a staff of eighteen.'

This friendly man is full of information about what is involved in the maintenance work as he continues to enlighten me.

'Occasionally, if there is an unusually hot spell during the summer months, the water level in Lough Owel, which feeds the canal, can become very low. This results in the canal water falling to a worrying level, affecting the whole eco system. To prevent vegetation drying up, which would have a devastating effect on the animal, fish and insect life that depend on this water, the maintenance team use generators and 15 centimetre pipes to pump water into the canal, from sources such as the River Boyne.'

'That's fascinating,' I say. 'I've seen those pipes and generators during summer on a couple of occasions and wondered what they were for.'

'Well there you go, now you've got it.'

As I leave the depot, I express my gratitude to this friendly, informative staff member. I cross the lock to the south bank and continue my walk.

Within 25 leisurely minutes, I have passed by the closely spaced 19th, 20th and 21st Locks, each with a small jetty. Unlike a boatman's frustration in equalising water levels, for me there is great novelty in passing one lock after the other in quick succession. This stroll is over relatively flat ground, except for a very obvious rise on the approach to each tail gate, giving me a definite impression that I am climbing, moving closer to the summit, as if through a series of well-spaced steps. It takes me through the sheep-dotted townlands of Cushinstown and Grehanstown, enjoying the sights and sounds of this rural environment.

Rambling along, I consider how Killucan is 2.4 kilometres to the north of here. Along with its neighbouring village of Rathwire, the combined population is 1,682, according to the 2011 census. In the past the area's fertile land, along with the arrival of the Royal Canal and later the Midland Great Western Railway, ensured its prosperity. In 1961 the canal finally closed to navigation and Killucan Railway Station closed only two years later. There was a lull in the fortune of these villages for a while. However, in recent decades as infrastructure improved and house prices in Dublin spiralled, they became popular with commuters. Their population almost quadrupled in only 15 years.

The Order of St. Camillus has three communities in Ireland, with their motherhouse in Killucan. Camillus de Lellis was born in Italy in 1550. At age seventeen he became a mercenary soldier, travelling with his father and fighting many battles. Camillus had a bad temper and

Cows drinking

was prone to violence. He was addicted to gambling and at the end of one game literally lost the shirt off his back. He developed a leg wound that stayed with him for the rest of his life.

Like Matt Talbot, he had a sudden epiphany when he became overwhelmed by his violent and sinful life. At age twenty-five, he joined the Capuchins. On a visit to Rome to seek treatment for his wound, he realised that God was calling him to care for the sick. Unable to do this alone, he managed to gather a following from which the roots of the order were nourished. Many Camillians died as a result of treating and caring for the sick, contracting the diseases of their patients. Camillus died in 1614, age sixty-four. He was canonised a saint in 1746 by Pope Benedict XIV. The Camillians in Killucan run a nursing centre that cares for the sick to this day.

Killucan and its environs have produced people of talent and genius. Laurence O'Rourke of Riverstown, Killucan, excelled in the field of engineering and became involved in a type of travel that was far beyond the realm of canal or railway.

My fascination with space travel since I was a young boy was fed by adventure classics, enraptured by kidnappings, piracy, chasing whales and being stranded on desert islands. Then I discovered Jules Verne who took me on a *Journey to the Centre of the Earth* and later carried me *From the Earth to the Moon*. Such science fiction seemed incredible at that time until the Americans landed a man on the moon in 1969. But something even more remarkable was afoot in the early years of the twenty-first century and it was called the Rosetta Mission, named after the Rosetta stone, found in 1799, which provided the key to an ancient civilization.

Back in 2004, the European Space Agency launched the Rosetta Spacecraft, with the lander Philae on board. Laurence O'Rourke of Riverstown was the Lander System Engineer for this ten-year mission and one of its two science operations coordinators. Rosetta's mission was to chase, orbit and land on one of the Jupiter-family comets. It was thought that studying this comet might answer key questions regarding the origin and formation of our Solar System over 4.6 billion years ago.

Rosetta was the first spacecraft to orbit a comet, quite an achievement considering this comet is over 500 million kilometres from Earth. Its Philae probe made the first successful landing on the surface of a comet. Discoveries made by Rosetta and Philae suggest that comets could have helped bring about life on earth, by seeding our planet with the necessary raw materials.

My thoughts on Killucan are suddenly interrupted by my arrival at Riverstown Bridge and the 22nd Lock, my finishing point for today. I am delighted to see that the old Killucan signal box, part of our railway heritage of redbrick and wood, is still standing here beside the main Dublin-Sligo railway line.

The rain, which had eased off for a while, is now becoming heavy again. I had noticed an advertisement along the canal that said:

Cunningham's
The Hideout Pub
150 metres Left

With time to while away before my lift arrives, I decide a reviving cup of coffee would provide a great excuse to get in out of the rain.

Cunningham's Hideout Pub and Shop

The entrance to the Hideout Pub is through a shop that seems to sell everything the sign had indicated: 'Groceries, Petrol and Diesel, Light Hardware, Fishing Tackle and Tea and Coffee.'

I am greeted by a cheerful woman and a young girl who are behind a wooden counter.

'Dreadful weather isn't it?' says the woman.

'It certainly is,' I reply.

'What can we do for you?' she enquires.

'Oh, I'd love a cup of coffee and a chocolate bar, if that's possible,' I answer.

'No problem,' she says, 'if you take a seat in the bar next door I'll bring it to you.'

As I enter, I noticed three men seated on high stools at the bar, deep in conversation over their pints. I decide to sit at a nearby table and I begin to write up notes.

I obviously aroused the curiosity of the locals, as minutes later the oldest of the three turns cordially to me and says, 'Tell me now, where are you from yourself?'

'Leixlip,' I reply. 'But I'm walking the Royal all the way to the Shannon, which is why I'm here. Are ye locals yourselves?'

'Well more or less,' he says. 'I'm from The Downs.'

'You must have seen some big changes along the canal over the years,' I say.

'I have for sure,' he replies. 'There's been a huge increase in the amount of people walking and cycling the towpaths.'

At this stage my coffee and chocolate arrive and I discover the woman's name is Paula. When she returns to the shop my friend continues to further my knowledge of Royal Canal lore.

'You know, I remember Guinness being transported along this canal. In fact, if you look carefully as you pass under Down's Bridge, you will notice the imprint left by the constant rubbing over time of the ropes fastened to the horses, as they pulled the heavy barges along the water.'

'That's really interesting,' I say. 'I have seen similar marks at Cope Bridge in Leixlip.'

'Well, look out for the ones at Down's Bridge and, who knows, you might find some more along the trail. My cottage is one kilometre beyond that, beside the footbridge.'

'I'll watch out for that so.'

I discover that the proprietor, Paula Cunningham, runs the shop and pub with help from her daughter. On re-entering the shop, I strike up a conversation with Paula about the premises.

'Originally, it was a hotel three storeys high,' she informs me. 'The kitchen was in the basement, the dining room on the ground floor, and the sitting room on the first.'

'And would the hotel have had close connections with business on the canal?' I venture to ask.

Old cottage and outhouse

'It did for sure,' she answers. 'At the back of the premises there are lots of old sheds and outhouses, a good sign of how busy it was here in the past. Those outbuildings would have been used for storage and as stables for barge horses. Workers transporting cattle and other goods would stay in the hotel. Such goods were often moved between the canal and the adjacent railway or vice-versa.'

It is interesting to note that the last bye-trader operating on the canal, Leech of Killucan, ceased to operate in 1951.

'And how long have the Cunninghams been the owners?' I then ask Paula.

'Well, my grandfather bought the building in 1917. Then in the 1960s my father extended it, creating a nice lounge area. The dance floor was clad with the wood salvaged from Palmerstown House Pub in Dublin. He also used to sell motorbikes from a building he rented beside the railway station, just across the road from the bar and shop.'

I ponder on what a resourceful man he was, keeping such a variety of businesses afloat all at the one time. Paula then informs me of her own recent business venture.

'I have some rooms upstairs,' she says, 'which I have had newly decorated and I hope to advertise them as Airbnb as soon as they are fully refurbished.'

'Well that's wonderful,' I say. 'It's a good location to stay for anyone walking or cycling the canal. I could have availed of them myself if they had been ready.'

I reflect on how good it is to see such continuity in the hospitality business passing from grandfather to father to daughter. The enterprising gene in this family keeps adapting to the changing needs of society.

My transport home has just arrived at Riverstown and I am reasonably dry once again, so I bid Paula and her daughter goodbye. A short text secures a quick transfer from Cunningham's Hideout Pub to the car, through the now driving rain. As I close the car door, I acknowledge my wife's effort in travelling so far to ferry me home.

As we make our way back to Leixlip, I recount incidents and sightings on today's most interesting walk. I also share the many conversations I enjoyed with local people in canal-side hostelries, closely linked to the story of the Royal Canal.

13.

Killucan to Mullingar

The Summit, Squirrels, Pipers and Lilliputians

Enthusiasm grips me as I set out on the sixth day of my walk, which will take me to the highest point on the Royal Canal before its slow descent to the Shannon.

It is three weeks since I left the towpath at the 22nd Lock. The weather has improved over that period and this June day is delightfully sunny and warm. I rejoin the towpath for walkers and cyclists on the north bank at Riverstown Bridge. From here, I will continue my ascent of the staircase of locks that will bring me to the start of the 24 kilometres-long summit level.

Just beyond the 22nd Lock, I encounter the unusual sight of a pair of geese and a pair of ganders on the water as I stop briefly to observe their antics.

At the 23rd Lock, I search in vain for one of the few milestones left along the towpaths, which is mentioned in my Guide Book, indicating that it is 43 statute miles from here to Broadstone Harbour.

I come across my first clump of yellow iris, standing almost a metre high, with one flower fully open. This solitary beauty is followed by a whole row of spectacular golden-yellow blossoms. I could only gaze and gaze at this intricate flower, whose delicate form is a marvel to behold.

This plant is also known as yellow flag. It has three, erect upper petals and three larger, downward-curved petals, marked with red-purple lines, forming an oval shape. The flowers of the yellow iris can

Yellow Iris

be in bloom from May to August, the exact period being weather-dependent.

It is no wonder that in Irish myth yellow flag is a symbol of beauty. In the legend 'Midhir and Étaín', the beautiful maiden Étaín is described as having hair like yellow flags in summer, or like red gold after it is rubbed. The grey-green leaves are shaped like a sword. In the past, they were used for thatching or bedding and as a cure for diarrhoea, toothache, colds, sore throats and jaundice.

During the feast of Corpus Christi, country people traditionally placed leaves of the yellow iris on benches outside their houses, where the old people sat telling stories to the young. I remember in my youth, walking in a procession along our suburban streets behind the priest, with the Blessed Sacrament displayed in a monstrance, before Benediction of the Blessed Sacrament back in the church.

I am soon ascending yet again, this time to the 24th Lock. Before I know it, I am rising to the 25th Lock and have now arrived at the start of the summit level. This continues as far as Coolnahay Harbour and the 26th Lock, a distance of just under 25 kilometres, over which no locks are required. Recalling my conversation with those two friendly men at McLoughlin's Bridge, I see that the V shape of the closed breast gates and tail gates are pointing west, so I will expect them to change and point eastward after this long 25 kilometre stretch. What a wonderful sense of achievement I feel arriving at the summit, not quite like reaching a trig point on a mountain, but the summit none the less, despite the fact that I am just less than 100 metres above sea level. Even the hillocks around here are low.

As I continue along the Central Plain, I see a cottage on the far bank with smoke curling from its chimney. Some sheds close by are constructed from mostly recycled materials. Two concrete walls offer some support, but the others are made from old wooden planks, pallets, old doors and sheets of corrugated tin, which are also used for the roofs. My father-in-law, surely before his time, built sheds in the same manner. Nothing was wasted back then, when a second use was found for most objects, long before the Green Movement existed. One of these structures serves as a henhouse, as a sign reads:

Fresh Eggs For Sale.

Beyond the 25th Lock, the cycle friendly path I am on veers off to the right but the walkers' towpath is now a cushioned grassy path that continues, as I do, under the old Footy's Bridge. Soon after I am aware of two cyclists swishing by on their path above. Both paths converge after approximately 500 metres, as I rejoin the tarmac once again.

Soon my nostrils are welcoming the aromatic scent of meadowsweet, even before its creamy white flowers appear before me. This plant was used to flavour such drinks as mead, beer and wine. In fact, the name, meadowsweet, comes from the Anglo-Saxon *meodu-swete*,

Footy's Bridge

Meadowsweet

which means mead sweetener. It was traditionally strewn amongst rushes on the floor of rooms, to keep them fresh and pleasant smelling, acting as a natural air freshener.

Meadowsweet contains salicylate, which has a similar effect to aspirin and was widely used in Ireland and Britain to cure fevers, colds, sore throats and other pains.

A pink variety of hawthorn emerges from the hedgerow, whose subtle, pale colour is just about discernible in the bright sunshine. Meanwhile the canal meanders on, flanked by relatively low lying shrubs.

The sturdy pillars of the elaborate N4 Road Bridge come into view. Built in 1975 to take the heavy traffic off the old McNead's Bridge, it spans the canal and railway and the road to Coralstown, which sweeps beneath it. Original plans did not include full navigational clearance. However, following representations from the Inland Waterways Association of Ireland (IWAI), the Minister for Local Government at the time, Jim Tully, intervened and Westmeath County Council agreed to his request to alter the plans. This was a welcome turning point in the campaign for the restoration of the canal. Since then, permission for non-navigable bridges has been refused, preserving the Royal Canal's original purpose as a waterway for boats and barges.

At the small harbour, I read a plaque telling me that an oak tree has been planted here in memory of Joe Maguire, founder member of Mullingar RCAG, a fitting commemoration to a man dedicated to the canal's restoration.

Mary Lynch's Bar

I follow the towpath under the new bridge, then cross the old McNead's bridge 50 metres beyond, and arrive at a well-known hostelry, Mary Lynch's Bar, Restaurant and B&B. On its beige and wine exterior, the name Mary Lynch is prominently displayed as a Family Grocer and Wine Merchant. My curiosity gets the better of me so I take a look inside.

A wooden bar is located in one corner of the pub. Advertisements hang on the walls, harking back to bygone days. One reads Players Please and another reads White May and Royal Standard BP Lamp Oils. The proprietor appears which presents me with an opportunity to chat with him.

'These premises look as if they're steeped in history,' I remark.

'Mary Lynch's dates from the 1900s,' he informs me. 'Mary's father had bought it and then Mary, who never married, took it over until 1985.'

'So are you a Lynch yourself?' I ask.

'No,' he answers. 'I'm a Moriarity. We subsequently bought the premises and are still running it.'

'And was it connected with the canal in the past?' I enquire.

'Yes it was,' he informs me. 'Way back, it had been a little shop and pub, with sheds at the rear for canal horses. Both canal workers and boat people used to stay here.'

It was informative to hear the story behind this old inn and how similar its function was to Cunningham's shop and bar at Riverstown.

Leaving Mary Lynch's pub, I pick up the towpath again on the south bank, where there is a sign that reads:

> *Mullingar Cycle Network –*
> *Boardstown to Meath County Boundary*

It was officially opened on 15 April 2014 by Alan Kelly, T.D., being funded by his department and Westmeath County Council. There are also information signs here for the Royal Canal Greenway and the Royal Canal Blueway.

Bank falls off both sides

Nearby, roofed with vegetation, a forlorn, ghostly ruin with gaping doors and windows fights for survival. The towpath is like an embankment along this section, with the canal dropping below me on one side, while on the other fields stretch down to the railway, with a forest beyond. Three thoroughfares are visible now, with the canal flowing along in the centre, as it heads west, while the rail line is to its south and the N4 to its north.

I pass a field, with a series of ditches and drains for channelling the excess surface water off the land. On the opposite bank, are two six-inch plastic pipes shooting water into the canal, pumped from a stream that is ducted under it, just as the man in the Waterways Ireland depot described.

Soon after, my nose detects the delightful scent of strongly aromatic yarrow, with its dark green feathery leaves. It shines, with disc

Yarrow

florets of yellowish-cream, surrounded by white ray florets, along the towpath verge. In Irish Folklore, advice was offered for safe travel:

> *Pull ten leaves of the yarrow and throw one leaf away, then put the nine others in a white cloth and tie it with a string around your neck. If this is done, anyone that is going on a journey will return safe and won't have any accident or see any evil spirits.*

As my trip is well and truly on its way, I'll have to forego this advice and take my chances.

Yarrow was known by the Romans as *herba militaris*, the military herb, for its value on the battlefield. Achilles, the Greek warrior, was reputed to have applied it to the wounds of his soldiers in battle in order to staunch the flow of blood.

Approaching the lifting bridge

The towpath now starts to fall from the raised level, bringing it closer to its surroundings. I can see the lifting accommodation bridge up ahead, the only one of its type that I encountered on this trip, allowing access to and from farms. The crossing platform that straddles the canal is wooden, and the metal frame supporting the working parts is large enough to allow farm machinery to pass beneath it. A handle operates the complex arrangement of chains and pulleys involved in the lifting. Both farmers and boaters operate this bridge and it should always be left in the lowered position.

It is in the up position now and there is a cruiser attempting to navigate through the narrow channel beneath it. By the time I arrive, the boat

Lifting bridge

has managed to pass through. Two women are on the bank turning the handle, attempting to lower the bridge, but it is not shifting. One of them points out that a steel wire cable is loosening, but the bridge is not budging. I suggest winding it up again to see if it will free things up. Just then, one of the two men from the boat arrives to assist in the unsuccessful manoeuvre. All of a sudden a car pulls up with two farm workers. The younger one, with curly black hair and a wild beard, steps up and, with his hands, pushes the bridge downwards without any fuss. With a sigh of relief, they thank him and he drives on over this fragile structure without having uttered a word.

'Local knowledge,' says our boatman, 'you can't beat it.'

I couldn't agree with him more.

As I stroll along enjoying the June sunshine, lost in my own thoughts, I am slowly lulled back to my surroundings, by the hum of a tractor ahead of me. It has an attachment for cutting the wild growth along the canal bank. I wave to the operator as I pass.

Now another row of yellow iris lights up the bank across the water, a colourful foreground to a substantial farmstead. These large farms demand continuous daily activity. Feeding animals, supplying them with vast amounts of drinking water, making hay and silage and many other chores besides are all part of a farmer's daily routine. To a city dweller like me, it would seem as if the work never stops.

A rustle in the hedgerow disturbs my thoughts and I am just in time to spot a red squirrel disappearing through the foliage of a beech tree. He emerges soon after and starts to climb. I follow him patiently with my eye and I am rewarded with the most dexterous display of acrobatics I have ever seen, as he moves from branch to branch and tree to tree, sometimes catching a branch with his tail. He is certainly in his element among the high branches. This beautiful native squirrel had declined in number since a one-off introduction of the grey squirrel in County Longford in 1911.

Red squirrel

The American grey, whose numbers in Ireland are now higher than the native squirrel, is more aggressive than its red cousin. Unlike the red squirrel, the grey squirrel strips young saplings of their bark, digs up flowers, raids birds' nests and generally has a detrimental effect on native woodland. Tragically, the greys are a carrier of the deadly squirrel parapox virus, and while not harmful to themselves, if picked up by the reds it will cause the infected animal terrible suffering and certain death within weeks.

However, recent studies have shown that the red squirrels are increasing in number in some parts of Ireland. This would appear to be due to the recovery of another native species, the pine martin, whose numbers had dwindled over time due to hunting and deforestation. It has been a protected species since the 1970s. The grey squirrel, unlike the great acrobat I have just witnessed, is not as agile and tends to forage more on the ground. As a consequence, it becomes an easier target for its predator, the pine martin.

Reluctantly I leave this theatrical scene and recommence my journey. I notice in the forest that row after row of hazel trees have been planted. Not only are they more beautiful than endless forests of non-native evergreens, but they are also important for biodiversity. Squirrels are very fond of hazelnuts.

On the opposite bank, I see a large heap of silage, almost as high and as broad as a house, covered in black plastic and secured with rubber tyres.

I now arrive at Downs Bridge, in the townland called The Downs, or Na Dúnta in Irish. As I pass under it, I discover the rope marks on the side of the walls as described to me in the Hideout Bar. I have a vision of two horses, one in front of the other, with heads bent to the task, their heaving lungs filling the air with the vapour of their labour, as they pull their load underneath the bridge.

Beyond it is a stop gate, which is the perfect sheltered place to sit and have lunch. I sip my coffee and dine in style, taking in the surrounding view. A row of black mooring posts, with their tops painted

Downs Bridge stop gate

white, are mounted along the trimmed grass bank, where a barge and two smaller craft are moored.

Rope marks on Downs Bridge

Fully refreshed, I set off again through what seems like an endless patchwork of rolling farmland. The canal soon turns west once more. The N4 comes into view again and an extensive footbridge crosses it, providing local access over this treacherous thoroughfare.

Two springer spaniels approach me on the towpath. Though these animals are old and slow on their feet, they still have a beautiful well-groomed appearance. Their male owner, of a ripe old age as well, is sitting in his car, reading a newspaper. I pass him and wave, as he looks up with a curious expression on his face.

Now I have arrived at the old footbridge, constructed of precast concrete, skirted around the edges by steel safety railings. It is covered by a large, bushy coat of ivy and the steps are carpeted with moss. I grab the handrail and begin to ascend, with a mild sense of trepidation. From the top, looking west, the canal is flanked to the north by the main Sligo road and to the south by a cottage with a corrugated roof, followed by endless fields of large shrubs and trees.

When I descend, I immediately pass the cottage belonging to the gentleman I spoke to in the Hideout Bar at Riverstown. I smile at knowing the identity of the owner. His self-sufficiency is evident from the vegetables growing in the garden and the hens visible in the henhouse foraging for food.

Just beyond here, the canal widens momentarily and its bank's green verge is lit up a luscious yellow by a cluster of meadow buttercups. The land all around has become decidedly boggier now, with heather and gorse growing in the damp fields.

Just off the towpath I discover a milestone, with the number 48 visibly etched on it, indicating 48 miles to Broadstone Harbour. These old milestones are gems, helping to map my progress towards the Shannon.

The canal winds its way past the farms of the Central Plain. On the far bank, a herd of cattle are strolling along westward, keeping me company as if they too had just discovered this marvellous walk.

There are many bird boxes erected along here, which I soon discover are part of a biodiversity project. Cumulus clouds are scattered like floating candy floss across the sunlit sky on this glorious day.

Mooring posts appear that lead me to Baltrasna Bridge. I've come across this name in County Meath also. The Irish name is An Baile Trasna, which translates as the Town of the Crossing. The craftsmanship of the wonderful stone arch sits well amongst the luscious vegetation that lines the course of this waterway.

An information sign close by indicates the High Bank Walk, which is up above the north towpath. It is a semi-wild route, described as

Information about the High Bank Path

having a reduced mowing scheme, for experienced walkers, who can enjoy discovering such flowers as the pyramidal orchid and devil's-bit scabious, as well as pollinating bees and butterflies. Biodiversity is in action here, with bug hotels and bird boxes in place.

As I continue onward, a cyclist emerges from the west and we pass each other with a wave. After Baltrasna Bridge I pass a row of young ash trees, whose grey bark glimmers a silvery hue in the sunshine. Along the verge, a cuckooflower, commonly known as lady's smock, manages to catch my eye, almost undetectable among the tall grasses. It stands on its upright stem, displaying white petals, though pink petals are more common on this plant.

Cuckooflower

The towpath is now six metres above the canal, with the water far below me. Ferns grow down the slope, all the way to the water, covering the bank and slope with their luscious, feathery greenness.

I bid good day to an elderly lady walking two dogs and we stop to talk. 'Yes, I'm walking the canal today from Killucan to Mullingar,' I say, in answer to her question.

'Ah, what a lovely walk,' she replies. 'You must look out for the prayer garden and the holy well, which are not too far up ahead.'

'That sounds very interesting, I certainly will.'

'There is also a Norman castle off to the south of here,' she adds.

'Well that would be a bit out of my way for today,' I tell her. 'However, I would love to investigate it at a later date.'

Bidding each other goodbye, I continue on my way, pondering the strong religious connection with the canal along here.

Within minutes, I come across a partially overgrown path that leads me up the slope of a steep embankment, where I discover the secluded prayer garden. There is an air of solemnity about it, tucked away up here in this quiet space overlooking the canal. Descending to the towpath, I keep an eye out for the holy well, but I have no success in finding it.

Along here, the canal wall displays a rocky surface, indicating that the builders, once again, had to blast through it to produce the cutting. During construction of the canal, work on the summit level was slow and costly due to this same hard rock. For boat users, good judgement is required through this narrow channel, as well as awareness of a silt bar which builds up along the floor of the canal, requiring regular dredging to maintain a navigable depth.

Having meandered between the N4 and the railway, the canal now meets up, once more, with the train tracks. Shortly afterwards, I arrive at Boardstown Bridge which carries traffic on the N52 across the waterway.

The canal now turns northwest onto a straight stretch towards Mullingar. After a short distance, a heron almost distracts me from the discovery of a particularly interesting feeder with twin stone culverts, just above the canal waters, known locally and aptly as the Pig's Nostril.

Pig's Nostril

At this point, I am almost half way along the summit level, without a lock in sight. As a city boy the locks were always a great attraction, whether as a short cut or for swimming. Back then, I was totally unaware of the necessity for these locks and how they facilitated boats, travelling from sea level upward from the city. I move along, pondering those far off memories.

As I soak up the June sunshine I draw closer to the provincial market town of Mullingar, the county town of Westmeath with a population of 20,000. Like so many settlements in Ireland, Mullingar was founded by the Normans over 800 years ago. It is built on the River Brosna and is surrounded by many lakes, whose waters and shores are overflowing with history and legend.

I arrive at Saunders Bridge on the town's outskirts. The canal now takes a great loop north around the town, before continuing on its meandering journey westward. The railway, on the other hand, takes a shorter loop through Mullingar, with both meeting up again at the far side of the town.

A row of cultivated cotoneasters and laurel lead me to a Waterways Ireland sign that reads Mullingar, and beneath it An Muileann gCearr.

Piper's Boreen Harbour

The name is derived from the wry or left-handed mill, the rotation of whose millstone was said to be miraculously reversed by the seventh century saint Colmán of Lynn. Thus, as noted by Mullingar historian Ruth Illingworth, it is probably the only town in Ireland to be named after a miracle. In the town centre there is a sculpture incorporating a large millwheel that commemorates the famine locally.

The sign on the towpath is positioned at a harbour on the canal known as Piper's Boreen. It is said that pipers and other musicians played here, sometimes enhanced by local dancing, for people embarking and disembarking from the boats. During the years of the Great Famine they also played a final farewell to many emigrants passing through Mullingar along the canal banks on their long trek to Dublin.

I am reminded of the harsh reality of more recent forced emigration, as the

Plaque at Piper's Boreen

Lough Owel feeder

song 'The Reason I Left Mullingar' comes to mind. Written by Pat Cooksey in 1980 and recorded by the Furey Brothers, it was dedicated to all those Irish building workers who left home in the 1970s to work in London, many of whom never returned home. Their homesickness and loneliness was often washed down with drink and their week's wages spent in the pub.

Beyond Piper's Boreen Harbour, the canal bridges come in quick succession because of the network of streets criss-crossing the waterway through this vibrant town. Within minutes, I am approaching Moran's Bridge where there is a small harbour with some mooring posts. I am soon passing over the sturdy Springfield Tunnel aqueduct. A new pedestrian tunnel passes beneath the canal, with the River Brosna, the third largest tributary of the River Shannon, running beneath that again.

Half way around the loop that skirts the town, a small stone bridge on the far bank marks the point where the Lough Owel feeder enters the canal. The bridge is reflected beautifully in the water, a perfect symmetry being denied only by the refraction of the incident light. Just beyond it is Mullingar Harbour which is effectively split in two by Scanlan's Bridge.

As Lough Owel lies about four kilometres north of Mullingar, so Lough Ennell lies approximately the same distance south of the town. The fully restored Belvedere House and Gardens, which comprises 160 acres of maintained estate, a sensuous Victorian walled garden, and several impressive follies stand on its northeastern shore. A tour of the house tells of its chequered history.

Mullingar Harbour

Belvedere House

The Jealous Wall

It was built by Robert Rochfort, Lord Belfield, in 1740. His cruel treatment of his wife earned him the title of The Wicked Earl. When his brother George built his home, nearby, with its back facing Belvedere House, Robert was infuriated. He built The Jealous Wall to block his view of his sibling's house. It still stands 300 years later, and remains the largest folly in Ireland.

George Rochford, the father of Robert and George, resided at Gaulstown House. He was a close friend of the famous writer Dean Jonathan Swift, who stayed as a guest there on occasion. Local lore has it that one day Swift was out in a boat on Lough Ennell when, looking towards Nure, also known by its ancient name of Lilliputa, he noticed a number of walkers. He remarked on how tiny these people in the distance looked from where he was. Thus the idea of the Lilliputians emerged. After the success of his novel *Gulliver's Travels*, published in 1726, the locals began to refer to the area as Lilliput, in preference to Nure.

Today, on the south shores of Lough Ennell, is the Jonathan Swift Park. Besides the beautiful woodland walks, there is an adventure centre where one can hire a boat, swim, fish, or play par 3 golf.

Not far beyond Mullingar Harbour, I pass a stone plaque, with a Celtic cross and an inscription that reads:

Bealach an Aifrinn
The Mass Path
Anno Domino 2000 Year of the Great Jubilee

A turnstile in the wall opposite the plaque leads up a leafy path to the Cathedral of Christ the King.

I finally arrive at the Green Bridge, which will mark my finishing point for today. The train station is just across the road from here. However, with time to spare, I will explore Mullingar before catching a train home later.

Walking into the open Market Square I find myself visualising a nineteenth century scene on a busy market day, with cattle bellowing and drovers trying to keep them in check. It brings to mind the well-known expression, 'Beef to the heels like a Mullingar heifer'. It is a complimentary phrase commenting on the high quality of Mullingar beef.

The impressive Joe Dolan memorial sculpture stands prominently in the square outside the Market House. While the hippies were singing of free love, Joe was singing 'Love of the Common People'. Some of Joe's other recordings include 'Tar and Cement' and 'You're Such a Good Looking Woman'. Many of his songs were international successes and Joe Dolan and the Drifters toured extensively worldwide. He had an amazing range in his voice, powerful yet controlled, and he was charismatic on stage, bursting with energy. That charisma comes across in the sculpture through Joe's trademark smile, as he holds a mike in one hand, with the other outstretched to the crowd in joyous salutation. Joe died in 2007 at the age of 68.

Plaque at Fagan's

I take a short stroll to the Greville Arms Hotel on Pearse Street. Upstairs, there are a number of items on display. For me the most exciting item here is a sculpture of a very dapper James Joyce. The face is actually made from Joyce's death mask, and I feel as though I am meeting the great man in person. Mullingar is the only part of Ireland, outside Dublin, where Joyce ever spent time.

Joyce came to work in Mullingar in the summers of 1900 and 1901, when his father was assigned by Westmeath County Council to bring the electoral roles up to date. While working here, James is purported to have stayed in Phil Shaw's Photographers shop and sub-post office. In *Ulysses*, he places Bloom's daughter Milly working at Shaw's. A plaque on the wall of this building, now Fagan's Office Supplies, quotes from Episode 4, Calypso, 'Getting on swimming in the photo business.'

Other references to Mullingar in his novels include the Greville Arms Hotel, the *Westmeath Examiner*, the railway station and the Royal Canal, while his first novel Stephen Hero has a chapter set here.

Joyce's experimental use of language and exploration of new literary forms became a major influence on novelists in the twentieth century, and *Ulysses*, despite being initially banned in many countries for being deemed obscene, has come to be accepted as a masterpiece. Mullingar proudly celebrates its association with this great writer on Bloomsday each year with readings and tours.

James Joyce also visited the eighteenth century Levington Park Country House, which overlooks Lough Owel, while staying in Mullingar. The US-born writer J.P. Donleavy was later to become the owner of this fine estate and farm of 200 acres. His most famous book, *The*

Ginger Man, was initially banned in Ireland, France and Australia for much the same reason as Joyce's *Ulysses*. The ban was eventually lifted and it was translated into dozens of languages. With sales topping 45 million, he amassed a fortune that enabled him to buy this beautiful home outside Mullingar, where he lived until his death in 2017.

Vintage car outside Greville Arms celebrating Blooomsday

Leaving the Greville Arms, I walk briskly back to the nineteenth century train station, pass the ticket office and into a spacious waiting room. Back then it was the only station in the country, outside of Dublin, with an underpass. In addition, it had electricity, which was uncommon in the days before the ESB took control of the electricity supply.

The disused Mullingar-Athlone rail line runs southwest of here, with grass threatening to cover it from sight. Devoid of human presence, pigeons have moved into the old buildings there. They flutter about from one dilapidated structure to the next, quite at home in these surroundings.

However, there had been plans afoot since 2014 to convert this old line into a 42 kilometre greenway stretching from Mullingar to Athlone, and indeed it has opened since, with many access points along the way. It shouldn't disturb the pigeons though, as the Old Rail Trail, as it is being called, begins west of the station, over one kilometre away.

The provincial town of Mullingar swells with character. Its impressive architecture and notable associations make it a unique place to visit. I'm glad I had the opportunity to delve into its mysteries. As I sit on the train heading home, I feel relaxed and fulfilled after this long, enjoyable day.

14.

MULLINGAR TO COOLNAHAY

Studs, Genealogy, Local Lore and a Teahouse

On a sunny morning with occasional cloud, I hop on the Sligo train at Maynooth to begin the seventh day of my canal walk. I disembark at Mullingar station, a little past Green Bridge, and rejoin the Royal Canal towpath where I had left it nine days ago.

As I head west, I find that the towpath is busy with some people walking dogs, others cycling, and one girl using a piece of gym equipment installed here. Out on the water, two swans create the perfect liquid art, concentric circles bisecting each other, a beautiful ephemeral display.

The canal swings southwest now and I soon arrive at the relatively new Grange Bridge, which is busy with traffic. Beyond it, I finally find myself on the outskirts of Mullingar. The far towpath is now a road, which leads from Grange Bridge to Kilpatrick Bridge.

Neat, white-fenced paddocks trimmed and manicured for grazing and galloping become conspicuous. Ireland's midlands are widely known for the breeding and racing of thoroughbred horses. As I wander along, I notice that well-groomed horses, stud farms and riding stables are now as common as dairy farms and farm animals had been.

I can see Charlestown Stud just off the far bank. It is one of the best known training yards in the region, which had been run by Dot Love along with Ciaran Murphy. Dot played a big part in Michael O'Leary's Gigginstown House Stud Farm by breaking in and pre-training young

Swans on the Royal

horses. In the 2013 Irish Grand National, Liberty Counsel, who was trained at her stud, was a surprise 50-1 winner. Dot, originally from Denmark, retired in January 2021 and had a great exit from her career with two winners, namely, Betty Zane at Cork and Flindt at Fairyhouse. Ciaran Murphy has now taken over the licence and continues to train at Charlestown.

Westmeath is also home to Kilbeggan racecourse, one of Ireland's most popular, with average attendances of around 5,000 for each of its eight fixtures.

The horse industry plays a big part in the economy of the Midlands, helping to boost tourism. It provides a vast amount of jobs for trainers, stable staff, vets and farriers, as well as boosting the local economy with horse sales. The local community also benefits from race days, when purse strings are loosened on food and drink, betting and entertainment, transport and accommodation. There are a number of riding centres in this area, such as Mullingar Equestrian Centre.

I stop along the towpath to observe a cob and pen foraging by the shallow edge of the canal, while a hungry cygnet looks on. In a field nearby the black calves there look new to this world, heads bent grazing.

Kilpatrick Bridge

A small, welcoming cluster of yellow water lilies are in bloom approaching Kilpatrick Bridge. I walk up onto it, taking time to soak up the rural tranquility from this higher vantage point. Just beyond the bridge I am surprised to find a lifebuoy mounted by the hedgerow, far too rare a sight.

Newly cut grass

Soon I am looking across at a newly mown field, sloping above the far bank, with three houses at the top of the rise. The grass is laid out in zig zag lines of contrasting green, with the darker heaped lines ready to be packed in black plastic for silage. Black specks of avaricious crows have landed for the feast, feeding in the tightly cut grass.

I am momentarily spellbound at the sight of three spectacular white and brown piebald horses, all in placid repose. Two cows come into view, grazing on the far bank, one black and the other predominantly white, with black spots and patches, resembling an overgrown and overweight Dalmation dog.

I stop now at the sight of another milestone which reads 55, the approximate distance in miles to Broadstone Harbour. This equates to 88.5 kilometres, indicating I am well past the halfway mark of my journey to the Shannon, a realisation that propels me on my way.

Over on the opposite bank are the grounds and clubhouse of Shandonagh GAA, with its blue and white club-coloured flags blowing in the wind. Beyond it, a row of spruce tower above all else.

The remains of an old wall lead me up onto Belmont Bridge. From it, I take in the view. I notice a dog owner watching his dog having a swim, both of them in playful spirits.

Pressing on, the towpath has now switched to the north bank. The south bank is overgrown with trees, leaning out beyond the water's edge, casting a shadow from whose shelter a family of mallards now emerge. These colourful ducks brighten up this long shaded section, along with a small flotation of water lilies. The atmosphere is pleasantly quiet, the only sound being the hum of a tractor in the distance.

From a tangle of grasses, the flowers of Herb-Robert raise their tiny pink blossoms high on their red stems, emerging from their lobed, decorative leaves. In *How to Enjoy Wild Flowers*, Marcus Woodward tells us

Piebald horses

And black and white cows

Approaching Belmont Bridge

that it was so named from a legend that it cured a disease called Robert's-plague, named after Robert, Duke of Normandy. But he states that the Church also claims the flower, associating it with St. Robert.

I arrive at the Ballinea Bridges, where the new bridge has been constructed just beyond the old one, carrying traffic from Mullingar to Athlone. It is an ideal place to stop for lunch and pangs of hunger affirm it. The canal widens here into an open harbour, with the slipway running down to a turning point for boats. Two cars pull up into the car park with a woman in each. They emerge and go walking in opposite directions, one with a dog and the other alone.

The whole harbour is a lovely, well-maintained amenity area, with the occasional sycamore providing shade. A solitary swan treads the water. A wooden bench has the poignant inscription *Dia a thug dúinn Í Dia a thóg úainn Í*. It translates as God gave her to us, God took her from us.

There are apparently only two skew bridges on the Royal Canal, the one here at Ballinea and another back at Ballasport Bridge. There are engineering difficulties in designing the courses of skew humpback bridges. Although these problems were most likely overcome by the Romans, the early canal engineers usually took the easy way out and realigned the roads to cross the canal at right angles. Although the original bridge at Ballinea has now been bypassed and the road realigned, it is great to see that the old skew bridge remains as a historic landmark in this area.

There is a plaque on the bridge to the memory of the priest and Celtic Scholar, Father Paul Walsh (1885-1941), who was from Ballinea. He was a prolific writer and his works are still highly regarded in academic circles. Father Paul had an intimate knowledge of Irish genealogy and of Gaelic manuscripts. In his book *Irish Men of Learning*, he traces the fates of a number of learned families, such as the O Duigenans and the Mac an Bhairds. In the same book he writes a critical analysis of some of the most famous Irish manuscripts, such as the *Great Book of Lecan* and the *Book of the Dun Cow*.

Revitalised after a nourishing lunch in this little gem of a harbour, I set off afresh and discover that the towpath has now switched to the south bank again. It takes me under the cut stone skew bridge and follows on under the new bridge. Soon after, the canal and the old rail line part company as the rail turns south towards Athlone, and I follow the waterway in a northwesterly direction towards Ballynacargy.

I pass a row of ash trees growing by the water's edge. In the past, propelled keys from the parent tree must have been carried by the wind to propagate here. Across the water is a charming homestead, with flower baskets mounted on the pillars of the wooden gate.

Plaque in memory of Father Paul Walsh

Row of golden buttercups

The wild grass verge is radiant with the yellow of buttercups as far as the eye can see. The white flowers of the field rose now get their turn to dominate the hedgerow, followed by the lower lying burnet rose, with its cream flowers. White and pink hawthorn blossom and the flowers of the humble bramble adorn the hedgerows, while out on the water the yellow water lily displays its beauty. I examine the hawthorn closely. It has many small bunched, white flowers, each with five petals, and many stamens with black anthers, giving the flower a speckled appearance. The reeds now rise about a metre above water and over their feathery tips I notice a field, dotted with black cattle, on an incline in the townland of Ballynaclin.

Hawthorn blossoms

Mullingar to Coolnahay

As I walk along savouring the solitude, I become conscious of a gentle sound, growing in volume, until the trickling water of a stream appears below me through a tangle of hedge.

Along this stretch of the canal, my view of the surrounding area is hampered by embankments, steep inclines noticeable in what has been a fairly level terrain. I begin to wonder if they are moraines, usually composed of soil and rock that were formed millennia ago by moving glaciers. I pass by another old milestone, marking 57 miles from Broadstone.

On approaching the Shandonagh Bridges, a Waterways Ireland employee emerges from his car, boards a dredger and starts up the engine. The new functional bridge has an awkward asymmetrical appearance, with a west to east gradient, while the older bridge behind it is a solid piece of architectural delight. Sadly, it just wasn't wide enough for modern traffic requirements.

In a field just beyond these bridges, there is an old, wooden CIÉ rail carriage with its red paint peeling, yet the company logo is still visible. It is decades since I last laid an eye on such a specimen of railway stock.

With the dredger now in the distance, it has become very quiet again, and I am absorbed in birdsong emanating from the hedges. Before me is a picture postcard scene of a herd of black cattle on a drumlin dotted with hawthorn trees.

A long view down an open section of canal reveals reeds by the water's edge hugging both banks. My ears are slowly alerted to a tractor's hum, while in the other direction sheep dot the landscape, my first sighting of these woolly creatures since Mullingar.

Up ahead, a line of mooring posts herald my approach to Coolnahay Harbour and the welcome sight of the 26th Lock, the first one in 25 kilometres. I had missed the soothing sound of water gushing through the lock, from one level to another. This location is a crucial landmark on my journey, not least because this harbour marks the end of the summit level. From here, the canal will make its slow but steady descent to the Shannon.

Coolnahay Harbour

Coolnahay Lockhouse for tea and scones

The V shape of the lock's breast and tail gates are now pointing in the opposite direction, east, as I recall the mantra: 'The V always points towards the summit level, breast gates first, followed by tailgates.'

During the building of the canal, when the construction crew reached Coolnahay in 1809 the company encountered financial problems once again. It was suggested that the canal should terminate here, which probably accounts for this rather large harbour being built. Eventually, the government intervened and in 1813 the Directors General of Inland Navigation took over control of the concern, with instructions to complete the Royal Canal all the way to the Shannon.

This substantial harbour has approximately ten boats moored here at present. Beyond the lock stands Dolan Bridge, with its plaque clearly on display. Interestingly, on a nearby sign adorned with flowers planted at its base, it is referred to as *Coolnahay Bridge* 26. The surrounding area is manicured, with a green and white boat, planted with a delightful display of flowers, adding to the picturesque scene. This welcoming space has picnic tables, the perfect place for a family to spend a sunny afternoon enjoying the canal while savouring a wholesome picnic.

I look across at the sturdy lockhouse on the far bank. It is a beautiful white cottage with an olive green door that matches the windowsills and the picket fence. Flower pots and planters brighten up its surrounds further, with reds, yellows and blues. To the right of the door is an old plaque, *Coolnahay Lockhouse* 26, and outside there is a blackboard advertising tea and scones. It's lovely to see this old lockhouse being used again, serving the locals and canal users with homemade treats and giving the public an excuse to stop and stare.

A rattling noise alerts me to a man opening a gate beside the lockhouse, so I cross over the bridge out of curiosity. A farmer arrives at the gate on a tractor, delivering a bale of hay for the donkeys in the adjacent field. I can hear them braying with excitement, as the sound of the vehicle tells them that grub has arrived. As the farmer leaves, I approach the man, who is now closing the gate, and strike up a conversation.

'Hello,' I say. 'Pleasant day. It's a bit overcast though.'

Looking east from Dolan's Bridge

'Pleasant indeed and no rain, thank God,' he answers.

'Do you live here in the lockhouse?' I ask.

'Yes, I do,' he replies. 'I live here with my wife, whose family have been lockkeepers here for generations.'

I learn that his name is Paddy Crinnigan.

'I noticed the sign for tea and scones,' I venture.

'Ah yes,' he explains, 'my wife Claire bakes the scones.'

'Sorry I can't partake, but I'm not long finished lunch,' I say.

'That's no problem,' he replies. 'She did have a couple in over the lunch period. However, it is most busy along here during the mornings and evenings, with walkers and runners getting in some exercise before and after work. They often stop for a cuppa. The weekends, too, are busy.'

Paddy is a trove of information about the canal in this area and I listen attentively as he generously gives of his time.

'There used to be a large storehouse on the far bank, close to my family home, where timber from Dublin was stored,' he continues. 'There was also a shed for the barge horses. They would tire easily from pulling the heavy barges, and had to be replaced by fresh animals at regular points along the canal.'

'Was turf shipped from here?' I enquire.

'Oh certainly,' he says. 'Turf from the midland bogs was shipped on the canal, from here towards Dublin. Also, during the First World War, when we could get no coal from Britain, coal was transported to here from the Arigna Coal Mines for distribution.'

'It's wonderful to hear all these snippets of information,' I say to him. 'It's like reconstructing a jig-saw puzzle of the past.'

I say goodbye to Paddy, grateful to him for his interesting conversation. Leaving Dolan Bridge and the lovely Coolnahay Harbour, I can't help wondering about old times and present days on the Royal Canal, and how they are linked by people's stories, relating changes they have witnessed over the years.

15.

Coolnahay to Ballynacargy

The Descent, Barrows, Garrisons and a Raffle

Leaving Coolnahay Harbour, I begin my gradual descent towards the Shannon. As with the locks on the rise to the summit, the locks on the fall from it will also be closely spaced, to facilitate the barges' gentle drop downward. Having walked 96 kilometres along this extraordinary waterway since leaving Spencer Dock, I realise I have completed two-thirds of my journey to Richmond Harbour, which propels me along the tarmac path with gusto.

I pass a field with a lovely copse of red and yellow dogwood, before arriving at the 27th Lock, 400 metres westward. The towpath sweeps down from it as I move from the summit towards lower ground.

After just 500 metres, I arrive at the 28th Lock, where there is a sign that reads:

Leave the Lock as You Found It. Breast gate closed and Tail gate open.

Pressing on, the stairway continues to fall from the summit level.

Close by, two Shetland ponies are rubbing heads affectionately. Their beautiful coats display large patches of white and brown, looking like pieces of an enormous jig saw puzzle. They stand between the large clumps of yellow flag, creating a challenge for the finest artist to recreate. In a field beside me, two well-groomed, jet-black horses are chomping on the grass.

Shetland ponies

Jet-black horses

Walsh's Accommodation Bridge, humpbacked and narrow, provides access to and from local farms. There is a brilliant-white, double storey house nearby, and beyond it the canal sweeps northwest.

Walking through the Central Plain of Westmeath, I continue to encounter the occasional hillock on the landscape. From my Ordnance Survey map I discover that there are quite a number of archaeological sites and monuments present in the area, particularly those described as a barrow or mound. They are generally burial sites of earth, or earth and stone, varying in size and having a rounded profile. The classification – burial mound – refers specifically to those that contain burials dating from medieval times onwards.

Walsh's Accommodation Bridge

On the other hand, prehistoric burial mounds are called barrows. These are part of the Bronze Age/Iron Age burial tradition, dating between 2400 BC and AD 400. There are a number of different types of barrows, such as stepped barrows and the circular or oval ring-barrows, which are low to the ground and are a maximum of one metre high. These archaeological monuments are now buried under soil and grass, and their presence is not immediately evident.

I find it interesting to dwell on just how ancient they are, and what may lie within. Some may contain cists, which are box-like structures made of stone slabs in which bodies were buried, either cremated or unburnt. Decorated pottery, either food vessels or urns, are generally found with them.

The rough gravel towpath underfoot is described in a site notice as a cycle path in progress. This has been completed since, and is part of the Royal Canal Greenway.

I appear to be all alone with nature in this paradise, soaking up her sights and sounds. Suddenly, three wood pigeons break from a tree ahead, with a loud flutter, startling me from my peaceful contemplation, as a grey feather floats down before me. The waterway is a linear mirror ahead, before winding its way by a great display of reeds. My ear is enjoying the mingling songs of the many birds and the music of the wind through the leafy trees.

From the old stone Kildallan Bridge I can see three sets of locks, the 29th, 30th and 31st Locks, which are all in close proximity. Each of these has its own distinct lockhouse. The first is whitewashed. The other two have red doors, contrasting nicely with the grey limestone of the buildings. Their doors and windows are recessed and curved at the top, creating an arcade effect at the front.

Coolnahay to Ballynacargy

Embankment and hillocks

It is fascinating to think that a lockhouse was required at every lock, no matter how close the locks were spaced. They now stand as testament to the busy commercial waterway that the Royal Canal once was.

Beside the 29th Lock, a huge limestone slab that was originally part of the old lock wall is lying out of place on the grass. It must weigh a ton and would have required a lot of manpower to lift it. This slab certainly gives some idea of the feat of engineering attached to bringing such enormous blocks of stones to site, back at the end of the eighteenth century, for the building of bridges, locks and lockhouses. Limestone is easily cut and carved, so it was quite suitable for the construction of the stonework associated with the canal. In addition, as this stone is found in every county of Ireland, except Antrim, there was no shortage of supply along the Central Plain.

Within 500 metres I have passed the 30th and 31st Locks, and 0.7 kilometres later I arrive, around a short loop, at the 32nd Lock and Kill Accommodation Bridge. The afternoon sun glares down upon a paddock with an open gate, highlighting its emptiness.

At the 33rd Lock, I almost miss the ruins of the lockhouse, half buried by invasive elder. In the fields, afforestation of young Sitka spruce display a blue hue as they spread out their needle-covered limbs.

Lockhouse at the 30th Lock

Construction of the Royal Canal Greenway is very much in progress on the next straight stretch of over one kilometre, with this dusty gravel path forming the foundation for it.

The Hill of Laragh, off to the southwest, rises gradually to its summit at 123 metres and falls off steeply on the far side, its upper slopes white with sheep. Below the hill, a stone formation in the shape of a chair, which is locally referred to as St. Patrick's Chair, is claimed to cure your back problems if you sit in it.

On a short strip of land by the canal bank, some specimen pieces of old farm machinery are on display, an interesting trip back to erstwhile agricultural methods.

The 34th Lock and Balroe Bridge are another surprise. The lockhouse is in excellent condition, its pebble-dashed walls painted a warm, inviting beige, and it is surrounded by neatly manicured grass. A flower bed has been planted along the bank, with the garden fence as border. Feeling at home here, I decide to take a seat on a mooring post to savour a coffee with a slice of cake, while enjoying the surroundings.

I imagine how life might have been for a lockkeeper back in the nineteenth century, with a nice secluded house, no commuting in heavy traffic and the blackbird's melody to put him to sleep. Yes, that sounds great! Then I remember how it was a 24/7 job, of constant manual labour and that it must have been difficult to balance his demanding work with family life.

The cycle path loops around the lockhouse, until it meets up again with the towpath. There is no path for walkers under the bridge. Instead, they are facilitated by a gap in a wooden fence between the lock and house. Passing through it, I cross a gravel path, before re-joining the towpath, still on the south bank.

The rain that was threatening comes at last, as I head into another long stretch of waterway, so I don my raincoat as I watch the antics of some well-groomed brown horses in the field off the far bank. A murder of crows shoots north from the towpath trees, joining the other darkening clouds overhead. Descending, they land in a field, where their black shapes bestrew the green grass, a dotted graph, now reduced to two dimensions.

Balroe Bridge and 34th Lock

About 500 metres beyond the bridge, two concrete slabs, either side of the towpath, mark the entrance into the canal of the Balroe Feeder, which flows from the southwest.

The reeds must be a metre high along here. Their reflection in the water has upended them, creating the illusion of a row of spears pointing towards the floor of the canal bed. A fish jumping from the centre of the glassy water leaves rippling circles that spread out to the banks.

Onward I plod through these lands of endless husbandry until suddenly I become aware of cottages off to the northeast and I realise, with satisfaction, that I am on the outskirts of Ballynacargy. Partially screened by some trees along the opposite bank, buildings of various shapes and sizes outline the villagescape. Behind them stands a church, with one cross on its apex and another on the bell tower.

A Waterways Ireland Sign welcomes me to Ballynacargy. A few more strides and I am at the 35th Lock. The nearby lockhouse, with boarded up windows, is begging for attention. The larger limestone structure close by, marked 'Royal Canal Hotel-Stores', is in similar condition. However, I'm sure it played an important role during the heyday of the canal. A new building is going up beside it, offering hope that this old structure might be renovated as part of that project.

Reeds along the canal bank

Royal Canal Hotel-Stores in Ballynacargy

Just after the lock lies the expansive, breathtaking Ballynacargy Harbour, complete with slipway. It exudes an overall aura of green and floral neatness, evidence of a lot of work taking place here regularly, with a bench facing the water to absorb it all. A relaxed-looking father and son are fishing together. Beneath the shade of a tree, a picnic table is waiting for a family to enjoy lunch. Ballynacargy Bridge, at the far end of the harbour, is framed by a colourful bed of flowers on both banks. The old engraved name of Smyth Bridge is still legible in the stonework.

I walk along Harbour Street, which is lined with a mixture of small, one storey and two storey houses. The harbour is, in fact, tucked away behind these buildings, invisible from the main thoroughfare, so that this wonderful amenity could be easily missed.

Ballynacargy has an old time appeal to it, partly due to the architecture of the buildings. I enjoy a pleasant stroll along its tree-lined Main Street as far as the Church of the Nativity. There is a large notice on the railing, advertising the local Summer Trad Fest. The recently painted

Ballynacargy Bridge

building has arched, stain glass windows, some modern, and others of a more traditional style. Above the main window is a statue of Our Lady in a recess, with a lamp mounted over it. Higher still is a Star of David, suspended from the cross-bearing apex.

I retrace my steps at a leisurely pace along Main Street. Passing the garage of T.P. Shanley, I notice it appears quiet inside, so I decide to drop in and ask a question that had been puzzling me. The man behind the counter is an approachable and interesting fellow, as it turns out.

'Good afternoon,' I say.

'Good day to yourself,' he answers.

'I'm curious about the two different names for this village that I keep coming across,' I say. 'Perhaps you know their origin?'

'Well, Ballynacargy is the correct name,' he tells me. He continues with a slight resentment in his voice as he says, 'that other name, Ballynacarrigy, was just an anglicised version, not looked upon favourably by the local people.'

'Ballynacargy,' he continues, 'was in fact a garrison town at one time. The evidence can still be seen in the windows of some defence buildings at either end of the village. These windows were built diamond shaped, to allow a soldier, while firing, to have more cover than he would have with the traditional rectangular window. Another thing, the old courthouse and barracks were built beside each other, for speedy imprisonment of offenders.'

'So when were the soldiers stationed here?' I ask him.

'Well, they were certainly here at the end of the eighteenth century, because during the building of the Royal Canal, the army protected the canal supplies from theft.'

'That's a really interesting piece of history,' I reply.

He then continues to further my knowledge of his village with some wonderful stories.

'The former courthouse has been refurbished and the village's vibrant branch of Comhaltas Ceoltóirí Éireann opened its new Teach Ceoil in it, earlier this year. It took a great voluntary effort on the part of this community, which included a number of fundraisers.'

'It must be great to have a venue for the local traditional musicians?' I chirp up.

'Ah sure, it's wonderful,' he answers. 'You know, in the past there was also a Big Hall music venue in Ballynacargy,' continues my new acquaintance. 'Unfortunately, it was bought at a bad time, at the beginning of a recession, and so was not so successful. However, Foster and Allen were among the well-known names that played there back in the 1980s. That was some night!'

My friend then relates to me an interesting story regarding Middleton Park, one of the country's so called Big Houses, which is situated south of here at Castletown Geoghegan. The property sprang to prominence internationally in the 1980s, when its then owner, Barney Curley, decided to raffle it. The legendary owner and trainer of racehorses was originally from County Fermanagh.

With no customers demanding the proprietor's attention, I take the opportunity to enquire further. 'So how did the raffle go?'

'Ah sure, television crews from the BBC and ITV descended on Westmeath for that raffle,' he informs me. 'It was overseen by the sports broadcaster Micheál Ó'Hehir. Apparently the house needed a lot of refurbishment, and the £1 million plus, reportedly made by Curley on the raffle, was more than the house was worth.'

'So he did well out of that venture,' I comment.

'Ah, but it didn't quite end there,' he says. 'A court case ensued and the judge deemed that the raffle was a blatant defiance of the law and must be viewed very seriously. He famously sentenced the gambler to three months in jail, which resulted in him losing his trainer's licence. This would have prevented him from carrying out his next project, to open a racing establishment in Newmarket, England.'

'So how did he fare in jail?' I enquire.

'Well, actually, Curley lodged an appeal,' he tells me. 'His next court appearance was before a different judge, who took a more lenient view of the whole affair. He decided he would waive the sentence and conviction if Mr. Curley paid £5,000 to the St. Vincent de Paul Christmas appeal. Curley wrote a cheque for £10,000 and left court a free man, now able to regain his precious trainer's licence.'

'Wow, that's a fascinating story,' I say. 'Well I had better be off to catch that lift I was promised. I'm really grateful to you for giving me so much of your time.'

'Not at all,' he replies. 'It's been a pleasure.'

Since this most interesting conversation Barney Curley died at the age of 81. Photographs of him appeared in newspapers, magazines and online after his death in May 2021. They all captured him wearing a fedora, a piece of attire he was apparently famous for.

I had popped into the garage to find an answer to one question and found myself regaled with interesting and intriguing stories. Leaving Shanley's, I start to walk towards the village centre. A large information sign on the street tells me that Ballynacargy takes its name from the Gaelic, Baile na Carraige, meaning Town of the Rock. This peaceful village owes much to the arrival of the Royal Canal here in the early part of the nineteenth century. It was an important trading post on the waterway, particularly throughout its first century of operation.

Tree reflected in the water

However, the origins of the village go back much further than that, its first recorded mention being in 1537. It seems likely that the village initially grew and flourished with the decline of nearby Kilbixy, which had been an important town in ancient Meath 500 years ago. Indeed, the parish here is still called Kilbixy and is home to a mausoleum built in 1798 by Lord Sunderlin. He was a director of the Royal Canal Company since its incorporation and he funded the building of the church in Ballynacargy.

The nearby Tristernagh Abbey, sometimes called the priory of Kilbixy, was founded in 1192 by Geoffrey de Constantine. This Augustinian priory achieved a great deal of fame over the years of its existence. Attached to it was a leper hospital, very rare in its time. However, in 1536, the commissioners of Henry VIII, during the dissolution of the monasteries, forced its surrender, ransacked it, and then closed its gates forever. In 1783, Pigot Piers, the 5th Baronet of Tristernagh Abbey, undertook its destruction, leaving only two buildings standing. The ruins of these two buildings can still be seen today.

The abbey was built on the shores of Lough Iron, a lake somewhat inaccessible today. Perhaps that is one of the reasons why it now flourishes as a wildlife sanctuary and as an area of botanical and ornithological interest. It is home to a rich fen community, with rare plant species, and is visited regularly by the Greenland White Fronted Goose and a variety of ducks and waders.

I receive the call for my pick up, grateful to be heading home with another 20 kilometres under my belt. Our journey home is shortened by stories of soldiers, musicians, dance halls and court cases, all part of Ballynacargy's colourful and intriguing history.

Bales of silage

16.

BALLYNACARGY TO ABBEYSHRULE

Secretive Mammals, Planes, Bog Oak and a High Cross

Two weeks later, my accommodating wife drops me at Ballynacargy Bridge, to begin the eight day of my trek. Over the next three days I plan to walk as far as Richmond Harbour and the River Shannon, staying overnight at Ballymahon, Killashee and Cloondara. From there I will walk along the Longford Branch to Longford Town.

I set off westward on a tarmac path, taking delight in the hot humid summer's day. The flowers have departed from the hawthorn trees and the tiny green haws are beginning to appear, leaving me to dwell on nature's eternal cycle. The elder is still holding on to her creamy blossom, which will also soon disappear and will be replaced with black elderberries.

The view opens to rich pastures and low rolling hillocks. Tufted vetch and creeping buttercup line the towpath verge. Their blue and gold colours are appropriate, being the Longford county colours, as I will be crossing the boundary into that county today. Now I see a meadow buttercup, which grows to about twice the height of the creeping variety, yet its flowers are smaller and cup-shaped, though shining with the same bright yellow.

Framed between the high grasses on either bank, four swans glide on the water, two of them young, still displaying dark plumage, perfect depictions of the ugly duckling. A scattered spray of spotted-orchids

Swans gliding on the Royal Canal

raise their pale pink heads up among the greenery, their delicately patterned petals on display and their conical shapes set on erect stems.

Smooth hawk's-beard forms a guard of honour, lining the path to the 36th Lock. At a quick glance one might mistake them for dandelions. However, they grow to twice the height of that species but on branched clusters, and the flower head is smaller. The unnamed accommodation bridge beside the lock is covered with a carpet of grass, dotted with white clover, showing little sign of disturbance. Nearby, a restored white lockhouse has planters filled with red and white flowers decorating its windowsills.

Beneath the bridge, I hear a fish plop, and I see a shoal with vertical stripes darting by. Emerging on the far side, I stop at a wooden jetty to observe a cultivated field in front of a large farmhouse, displaying a job well done.

As I walk along, some young swans, wary of my approach, move from a slow glide to a flutter of wings as they take off upstream. The one adult, who appeared to be foraging with its beak beneath the surface, I realize, is dead. Is it any wonder those poor cygnets were so startled at my presence?

Unnamed accommodation bridge at 36th Lock

Mute swans do not sing, hence the name. But they do communicate in low grunts, and if they perceive a threat, their formidable hissing, accompanied by outstretched wings, is enough to discourage any potential source of danger, whether human or animal. However, danger lurks in the water and overhead. Swans are known to have died from ingesting fishing tackle, especially the lead weights. They have also met their demise from colliding with overhead power lines.

The resident mute swan is Ireland's largest bird and is a common sight, with its all-white plumage and long, elegant, curved neck. The male (cob) is slightly larger than the female (pen) with a larger black knob at the base of his orange-red bill. The cygnets have brownish-grey plumage. In take-off they are laboured. In flight they present a delightful sight, as their powerful wings make a whistling, throbbing sound. The belief that they mate for life is not quite true, though a pair may stay together for a number of seasons. They are frequently seen upending, feeding on the water plants below. Swans were once prized for the table by the rich and powerful. However, nowadays they are a protected species.

The reed bed here is alive with damselflies. They hang like blue flowers from the reed leaves and scatter as I pass. An occasional dragonfly also flits by to delight me. Both of these charming insects are carnivorous and feed on flying insects, from small midges to butterflies. They are the perfect aerial predator, with 360° vision, legs with sharp spines and the ability to detect small movements from a great distance. They can also fly swiftly while changing direction rapidly. Damselflies live from two to four weeks, whereas dragonflies might live up to two months. Dragonflies were among the first flying insects to appear on earth, and fossils of dragonfly-like insects have been found in Carboniferous rocks 350 million years old.

A female meadow brown butterfly flutters by. Each wing is adorned with a black spot surrounded by orange, with dark brown all around the wings' edges. It is a truly beautiful creature, which a red admiral now tries to outdo with its colourful bright red stripes. Soon a large white butterfly joins the parade but who could pick a favourite from so much beauty. I hope they escape the clutches of the dragonfly. This ecosystem is truly a paradise for observing insect life.

I have arrived at the 37th Lock and another unnamed accommodation bridge, with some oxeye daisies sprouting from the joints of the capstones. From on top, I notice a wild rose bush that has scaled the heights of a hawthorn, all the better to display its fine blossoms.

As I descend to the towpath, heading westward, I ponder on the amount of accommodation bridges along this section of the canal. They are certainly testament to the proliferation of farms that use them to move machinery and livestock from one side of the waterway to the other.

There is a lovely view to the north, a layered idyllic scene, the still water with a backdrop of reeds, rising to a green field, then a grey two-storey modern farmhouse topped with a grey-blue sky with hints of cloud. It could be a depiction by the landscape painter John Constable, whose mastery emulated such scenes to perfection.

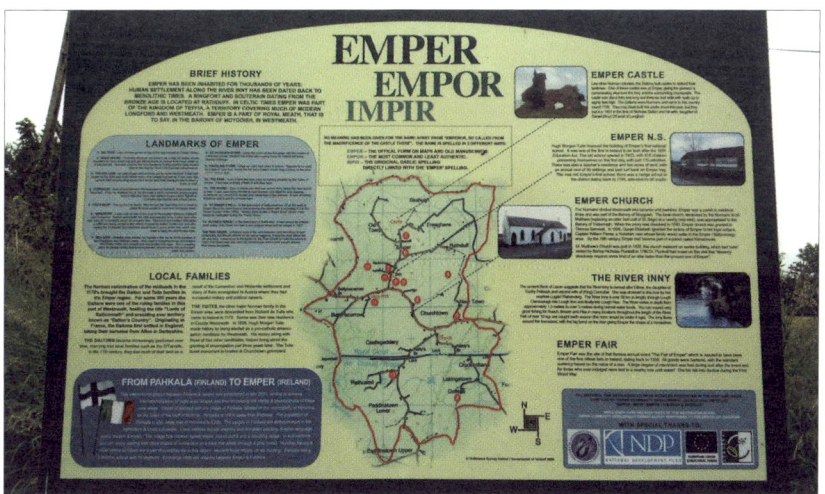
Information about Emper

Lost in the uplifting solitude, I suddenly find myself encountering the fourth lock over the last three kilometres. This is the 38th Lock. The name is missing from the bridge beside it, but my guide identifies it as Kelly's Bridge. The lockhouse could do with some tender loving care. However, there is a JCB close by, which might signal a restoration.

A nearby sign has information about this area, known as Emper. It shows a map and details of, among other things, a church, a castle and a fair. Emper has apparently been inhabited for thousands of years and human settlement along the River Inny dates back to Mesolithic times. In Celtic Times, Emper was part of the kingdom of Teffia, a territory covering much of modern Longford and Westmeath.

Emper Castle, with only two walls remaining, was built by the Normans in the twelfth century. The Fair of Emper is reputed to have been one of the first official fairs in Ireland, dating back to 1338. All goods were bartered, with the standard currency based on the value of a cow. A large degree of merriment was had during and after the event. Those who over-indulged were tied to a nearby tree until sober. This fair continued until the First World War, after which it fell into decline.

Beyond Kelly's Bridge, I proceed through a corridor of trees. After 500 metres I am approaching Ledwith's accommodation bridge,

Ledwith's accommodation bridge

through a wild meadow. A rough ledge, half a metre from its base, will suffice as a bench for me as I partake of a well-earned, solitary coffee break.

As I sip, I consider the name Ledwith. I know that Ledwithstown House, originally the seat of the Ledwith family, is approximately 20 kilometres west of here. As their estate was large, I think it likely that this bridge is named after that family.

From on top, I see wild, overhanging shrubs along the reed fringe in both directions, creating shadowy reflections in the water. The rounded green leaves of golden-saxifrage adorn a patch of the limestone bridge, making a home for itself there.

Feeling fully refreshed, I continue along the south towpath through this deserted countryside. I am suddenly brought to a stop by the sight of a dead pygmy shrew. I bend down to observe, captivated by this tiny mammal. Its body length is about four centimetres, while its tail length is slightly less. This little fellow is lying on its side and is covered in a brownish, thick fur, which is a shade lighter on its underside. It is an attractive, quirky little creature with its long snout, whiskers and very small eyes.

The pygmy shrew (*Sorex minutus*) is Ireland's smallest mammal, weighing typically three to six grams. It feeds on beetles, spiders, bugs and woodlice. It needs to eat up to 1.25 times its body weight each day in order to survive due to its small size and high metabolic rate. Thus, there is no rest for this species because if it goes without food for more than two hours it could starve to death. Although this shrew is common all over Ireland, it is seldom seen because of its size and its secretive nature. Thus, I am one of the lucky ones today, while unfortunately this tiny creature is not.

Dead pygmy shrew

The path ahead leads to yet another river called the Blackwater, in this case a tributary of the River Inny. It is ducted under the canal via a 3.7 metre wide tunnel.

From here, the canal passes through Ballymaglavy Bog, with signs of black soil by the grassy path's edge. It soon turns to a widespread, peaty surface. Every stretch of canal holds its own wonders. Out on the bog, there are occasional tracts of scrub, mostly gorse, ferns and heather, interspersed among the wild grasses that are alight with bog cotton. Then beyond that, signs of the brown sod, footed to dry, and behind that again a forest.

Ballymaglavy Bog is an example of a raised bog, a type generally formed in lowland areas. Blanket bog, the other type found in Ireland, is more expansive and is generally formed in wet or upland areas.

Slowly the grass returns to the towpath and I notice a small, dark heap on the trodden trail. Bending to take a closer peek, I realise it is otter spraints or poo, which signals the proximity of that mammal.

Now the grass has become about a foot high on either side of me, showing little sign of the tread of human feet in the recent past. However, there is a narrow corridor that allows me to continue on, with care, to the next accommodation bridge.

Surface explains the name Bog Bridge

When I reach Bog Bridge, as it is appropriately called, I discover that the road across it is completely overgrown with grass and large sections of the walls have been colonised by nature. Given its name and remoteness, I can only conclude that it was used by those working on the bog.

I ramble on through this peaceful, peaty landscape, as a light breeze fans my brow. After about 400 metres, I cross over the Westmeath/Longford county boundary. I spot a large barn and am soon surrounded by green fields once more, marking the end of my peatland haven.

A long streak moving across the water catches my eye. I stop and watch as this creature turns and begins to swim back to the far side. I realise from its size and head that it is an otter. Unfortunately, it disappears all too soon into the reed fringe. But it was a precious experience to have caught a glimpse of this elusive mammal at first hand. The otter is a mainly nocturnal creature and of the same family as the stoat, badger and pine marten. It has a long slender body, a flat head, a tapering tail and webbed feet. Otters are carnivores and eat a variety of foods, such as eels, fish, crab and aquatic insects. Its nesting place is called a holt, a large burrow in the bank of a river or stream.

A road coming from the south, takes a sharp turn west, so that it is now running parallel to the canal, replacing the towpath. A signpost indicates that walkers should continue along this road leading to Abbeyshrule. I walk along the strip of green on the far side of the road, beneath the welcome shade of hawthorn, ash and elder.

It takes me to Quinn's Accommodation Bridge, over which runs a well-worn tarmac road. Abbeyshrule Aerodrome and Airfield are now close enough for me to see the aircraft and the hangers. Within a short space of time, two planes take off and one lands. In fact, it is the only Midland airport in Ireland that provides opportunities for both pleasure flights and flight lessons, making it a popular destination. Occasionally it hosts air shows.

Minutes later, I arrive at the Whitworth Aqueduct, whose five splendid arches hold it solidly in place, as it carries the canal over the River Inny for a distance of 50 metres. It was built circa 1815, at a cost of £5,000, and was designed by John Killaly, the engineer responsible for the Royal Canal between Coolnahay and Cloondara. The sun is a shimmering ball of light on the water's surface below, while the river appears as a blade of light cutting through a rich corridor of green.

Abbeyshrule Aerodrome and Airfield

Whitworth Aqueduct over the River Inny

An interesting information sign references the Clonbrin leather shield, which was found in the nearby townland during peat cutting in 1908, the only one of its kind surviving from the Bronze Age. Possibly dating from the thirteenth century BC, it is now on display in the National Museum in Dublin. Except for bearing some marks of combat, its preservation is near perfect.

A young couple stroll by holding hands. As I pass a house beyond the aqueduct, a sheep dog comes running out, whose bark is answered by another dog further west.

There is an overflow from the canal here, with a sign that reads:

This cut stone structure is an overflow safety feature, ensuring that the canal water level does not rise too high, causing damage to its banks. There are two overflows on this approx. 8 kilometre level.

This brings to mind the overflow after Ledwith's Bridge.

Having crossed the Inny, the canal takes a sharp turn to the southwest and generally follows the river valley, which will lead me to Abbeyshrule. Soon I am passing Scally's Bridge onto a freshly mown towpath. This area is a haven for birds, such as mute swan, grey heron, teal, mallard, kingfisher, wigeon, whooper swan and moorhen, with both the river and canal providing a habitat in which to nest, feed and swim.

Indeed, on a subsequent visit here, I saw a bevy of wintering Whooper Swans preening themselves, their white plumage contrasting so vividly with the green surroundings. They have a long bill which is mainly yellow with some black.

As for the kingfisher, well they have been sighted but unfortunately not by me. They nest in tunnels dug into steep river banks or streams. Though having brightly coloured plumage of mainly orange-red and blue, they can be hard to spot as they sit on their favourite perch by the water ready to plunge-dive for a fish or large insect.

The road into the village is running parallel to the canal. A floral display and a blue sign welcome me to Abbeyshrule, and boasts of its Tidy Towns awards. The village won four consecutive gold medals in the national Tidy Towns Competition, in 2009, 2010, 2011 and 2012. It is still an outstanding contender in this competition to this day. However, the year 2012 was its real crowning glory, as it also won the gold medal in the prestigious European Entente Florale, surely testament to the hard work and commitment of the village's residents. This unique village entices me to explore further before completing today's journey.

Sign for Abbeyshrule

Planters, bursting with colourful flowers, adorn the walk towards the village, which is itself full of colour and innovation and where tidiness is pervasive. I pass a recessed area containing a bright-red, traditional water pump. At the entrance stand two brightly decorated milk pails with the words Bailte Slachtmhara 1958-2008, or Tidy Towns 1958-2008.

Water hand pump in Abbeyshrule

I am soon to discover that Abbeyshrule is a tight-knit community, with both Catholic and Church of Ireland congregations, and almost everyone is somehow involved with the Tidy Towns. Their work delivers to the community socially, economically and environmentally.

The walls of many buildings, and the windows and doors of vacant ones, are decorated with multicoloured murals and photographs, such as a fisherman reeling in his heavy catch and a woman leaning on a half-door, surrounded by hens, the contents of the traditional kitchen on view in the background. On the literary side, there is a quote on a plaque from a poem by Patsy Farrell:

> *I'm sad today cause I'm far away*
> *From that dear little village school*
> *But I can't forget fond days that I spent*
> *On the road to Abbeyshrule.*

The impression I get is that this village is set on welcoming the visitor. The airport, as a gateway to the Midlands, attracts anglers to the area. Besides the canal, the Inny is a top class river for fishing. A number of signs indicate the fish that can be found in the River Inny and Royal Canal.

Murals on building

Perch, pike, roach, tench, carp and bream, are among the species found in the canal, and all fish must be returned to the water. The River Inny contains brown trout, rainbow trout, pike, perch, roach and eel.

Abbeyshrule is most famous for its Cistercian Monastery, after which it was aptly named, so I take a stroll out to see it. The Irish place name, Mainistir Shruthla, means Monastery of the River, as it was sited on a major ford or crossing over the Inny River. The monastery or abbey was founded circa AD 1150, under the patronage of O'Farrell, Prince of Annally, and dedicated to the Blessed Virgin Mary.

Suppressed in the sixteenth century, under the reign of Queen Elizabeth I, the abbey was eventually granted to Sir Robert Dillon. The ruins consist of the abbey church and the outline of the cloister garth or courtyard. Sections of the church walls remain extant, and beneath the double bellcote there is a crossing arch. The ruins of the tower house are from a later century.

From the information at this site I learn that the monks who lived here rose at 3:15 am for silent meditation, followed by prayer. Then after a breakfast of porridge and bread, they gathered once again to prayer, before beginning their day's tasks, such as work in the kitchen,

Ruins of Cistercian Monastery

farm, mill, library and scriptorium, which allowed the monastery to operate self-sufficiently.

Some monks were involved in producing wine, honey or ale, while some took care of the sick and aged, while others taught the student monks. There were even those who were assigned to provide hospitality to passing pilgrim guests. With the day's work complete, they sat to a dinner of meat or fish with vegetables.

I mount my search for the special high cross I had read was located here. Unfortunately, I am unable to find it. I do, however, find a replica of it at the entrance to the abbey, which allows me see exactly what the real cross looks like. High crosses are free standing and can be located at churches, monasteries and occasionally at cross roads. The Abbeyshrule cross differs from the popular image of a ringed Celtic cross in that it is smaller, does not have arms and has a thistle-shaped head. Such high crosses are rare. Settling for this replica, I return to the village by crossing the double-arched Abbeyshrule Bridge, which traverses the Inny.

There was a large flour mill in Abbeyshrule, on Mill Lane, which used the canal for transportation. As railway transportation developed, the use of canals and mills declined. The area around Abbeyshrule then became somewhat forgotten and neglected. However, the development of the airstrip and airport from the 1950s on, improved its status. Furthermore, the official reopening of the Royal Canal in 2010, saw the villagers pull together to attract tourists, with festivals and events on the canal banks and walking trails for hikers.

Bio-diversity is a recurring theme throughout the village, with one of the information signs stating:

Replica of High Cross

To Bee or not to Bee.

Oh Yes it is a buzz!! A pollinating Eco-Friendly Village, Abbeyshrule has welcomed colonies of native black bees to help pollinate crops, fruits, flowers and vegetables in our local environment and beyond. Respect and be kind to them as if the bees die, we will die.

It is a grave reminder that without this pollination, many of our native plant species would quickly become extinct. It reinforces the role humans must play as caretakers of our environment.

Wildflowers provide nectar and pollen, which is food for bees and many other pollinating insects. Thus wildflower meadows, and gardens of diverse flower species, are essential for healthy bees.

An interview with the poet Michael Longley questioned the political nature of some of his poems, He replied:

In a way all poems are political. Poetry itself is a kind of conservation. Poetry gives things a second chance. Perhaps most political poems are concerned with how we treat the plants and the other animals. They are at our mercy. I believe that a poet's imagination should be like a Noah's Ark, with room for all the animals. I believe that we shall die if we let the wildflowers die.

Further on, the wondrous sight of a locally carved log hive, in the shape of a large head, complete with black hat and beard, is nestled among some apple trees. The piece is called 'Seanleaid na mbeacha', or 'The Aul Lad of the Bees'.

Some wonderful bog oak carvings by the Longford artist Brendan Collum are displayed about the village. One depicts the Cistercian Abbey's bellcote and arches. Another impressive piece is sited at the entrance to Corncrake Meadow housing estate, along with two bog oak benches. The original field here was known locally as Corncrake Meadow. It was wet and marshy and an ideal habitat for corncrakes.

The sculpture depicts three nests on three separate sturdy trunks of bog oak, while a number of corncrakes perched on top are delicately carved. This exquisite piece was commissioned by the Tidy Villages to raise awareness of the need for the revival of the corncrake.

Strolling back towards the village, my head is filled with marvellous bog oak sculptures, floral displays, local heritage and enhanced recycled materials.

I pop into the Rustic Inn, the heart of the village, for a sandwich, greeted warmly by the owner, Betty McGoey. I learn that the inn was established in the 1960s by the McGoey family, third generation residents of the village, as a grocery, hardware and petrol station. When a historical society came to visit the Cistercian Abbey, Betty McGoey catered for them. This paved the way for future enterprises.

Betty then relates some of the history of the Rustic Inn. She describes the tragedy of a fire back in 1979, which totally destroyed the inn. One of the newspaper clippings framed on the wall recounts how many local organisations had to find another venue for their dinner dances and functions during that time. Betty's husband Teddy was determined to rebuild the Rustic and it has been back in full swing for many years.

After lunch, I tell Betty of my disappointment at not finding the high cross with the thistle-shaped head.

'Come with me,' she says, in her friendly manner.

Corncrake Cluster Sculpture in Bog Oak

She leads me across the road to the presbytery. The front door is open and there is a great commotion inside, with cups of tea and chatter. Betty calls for the local priest, Father Charley, and he discovers my mission. He tells me that for fear of theft or damage, the cross had been taken from the abbey into safe-keeping by Betty's husband, now sadly deceased. He generously offers to show me this sacred artefact.

Driving me to its safe shelter, he lifts the heavy cross out into the open, with great difficulty. Standing around one metre high, it is indeed small, though very heavy. Though ancient and weather-worn, the front engravings, with latticing and spirals, are clearly visible on it. The cup and the flower of the thistle are also quite distinct. The sides have intricate patterns on them, while the back of the cross has a linear pattern. I feel privileged to see this rare cross at last.

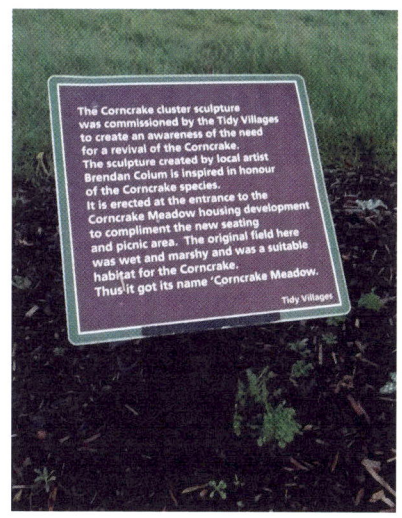

Corncrake Sculpture explained

Abbeyshrule Harbour

I chat with the light-hearted, humorous priest as we return to the presbytery, about how beautiful the village is, and of how deserving it is of all the awards it had won.

'A bit too clean for me!' he says, with a hearty laugh. 'Sure if you left something belonging to you down on the ground for a minute or two, you'd find it had been swept up before you got a chance to pick it up again!'

Having been dropped back to the village, I walk up onto the road that crosses Webb Bridge. Eastward, the canal widens into a tranquil harbour, demarcated by a stone wall, with a slipway for boats. Mooring posts line the way and two boats avail of their service.

Westward, the scene is predominantly rural, though there is a second stone harbour here, with a splendid, miniature replica of a traditional white-washed cottage adorning the north bank.

A large old building, at the edge of the canal, was most likely a store for materials that were transported along this waterway. The smaller

Wildlife to be found on the River Inny and Royal Canal

buildings close by may have been used as stables for canal horses. One is being used at present as a home for some delightful pygmy goats.

The waterway sweeps on through the lush countryside. Leaving Webb Bridge, I reflect on the beautiful Abbeyshrule and the friendliness and hospitality of the local people. To crown the day, light aircraft start to fly overhead, as if to bid me farewell.

17.

Abbeyshrule to Ballymahon

The Inny, Evictions, Bianconi and a Pleasure Park

With Ballymahon my destination, I find I am on a slightly overgrown, luscious green towpath, initially walking through a corridor of trees and shrubs with an avian chorus filling my ears. The scene then opens out briefly to expose the Inny to the south. The fields that stretch as far as the river are full of rushes, a sure sign of waterlogging. I can see from my map that for the next few kilometres the canal and river meander gently, close to each other. So for now, I have both waterways to keep me company.

The River Inny is known in Irish as An Eithne. In Irish mythology, Ethniu or Eithne was the daughter of the Fomorian leader, Balor of the Evil Eye. After hearing a prophecy foretelling his death at the hands of her son, Balor locked Ethniu in a tower. Cian, a member of the Tuatha Dé Danann, found a way into the tower and made love to Ethniu. She later gave birth to Cian's son, who was named Lugh. The prophecy came to pass and Lugh killed Balor in battle.

The Inny rises near Oldcastle in County Meath. After entering a number of lakes, including Lough Sheelin and Lough Derravaragh, it passes beneath the Whitworth Aqueduct. It then flows close to Tennalick, where Eithne is said to have drowned in the rapids, thus giving her name to the river. From there, its course is towards Ballymahon.

Soon I arrive at the 39th Lock and Draper's Bridge. Invasive shrubs have almost concealed what is left of the old lockhouse. There are no locks over the next 11 kilometres, so there will be no change in the water level over this distance. It is the longest level without locks on the western end of the canal.

I am in the townland of Tennalick, not too far from the ruin of the early eighteenth century Tennalick House, which lies between the canal and the Inny. The remains of the long avenue leading to the ruin is bisected by the Royal Canal, which it predates. The house and land was owned by the prestigious Gore family, who appear to have used it as an occasional country residence. This family also had a fine townhouse at No. 50, St. Stephen's Green, Dublin, which is now home to part of the Office of Public Works. Probably the most successful family member in politics was John Gore, who served as Attorney General of Ireland and Speaker of the Irish House of Commons.

Draper's Bridge

The canal continues to twist and turn, mimicking the Inny. Before long I arrive at Allard's Accommodation Bridge. Beyond it a marvellous wood of ash trees appears along the hedgerow. Conifers replace the ash for a short distance before the wood displays ash once again. The difference is quite noticeable, with the ash letting through quite an amount of light while the conifers block it completely. Blackbirds, crows and mallards are unanimous in their disapproval of my presence, as they take to the air shrieking. In contrast, two swans glide by, without so much as a glance my way. Their placid mood is a wonderful presence to be blessed with.

Molly Ward's accommodation bridge

The next two accommodation bridges, with their intriguing names, come in quick succession. They are Guy's and Molly Ward's respectively. I smile at their intimate names as I ponder their origin.

The Inny follows the canal closely for a short distance and then turns south, its course taking it through Newcastle Woods, once part of Newcastle Demesne. Here, its waters can be appreciated to the full along the River Inny Walk. It then meanders through Ballymahon, flows south, then west, before entering Lough Ree, the second largest lake on the River Shannon, via a channel known locally as the Owenacharra River. The Inny now becomes part of Ireland's longest river.

In the early nineteenth century, Lady Jane King-Harman owned the largest estate in County Longford, the principle part being Newcastle Estate, situated at Newcastle House near Ballymahon. She was the Dowager Countess of Rosse, known in Longford lore as Lady Rosse. For the last thirty years of her life, she was an absentee landlord, living in England. During the 1820s and 1830s, her agents evicted large numbers of Catholic tenants in favour of Protestant ones, with the aim of securing a loyal electorate.

When she died in 1838, her twenty-two year old grandson, Lawrence Harman King-Harman, became the new owner. He proved to be a different kind of landlord than his grandmother. To begin with, he made Newcastle House his home and so witnessed the ongoing struggles of his tenants at first hand. History records him as a fair man, at least in comparison to other landlords. Lawrence set about enhancing the housing of his tenants and employed an agricultural advisor to improve the quality of the land and grow different varieties of crops.

Unfortunately, these visionary ideas were just taking off when famine struck, and an entire way of life died, with County Longford suffering one of the sharpest declines in population anywhere in Ireland. However, King-Harmon's advances in local agriculture are thought to have helped prevent a repeat of the Great Hunger.

Newcastle Demesne is now home to Center Parcs holiday village and the lime trees planted by Lawrence Harman King-Harman still line the avenue leading to it. This 400 acre resort caters for up to 2,500 guests, in 466 lodges and 30 apartments. There are 10 eating options, a supermarket and an Irish pub.

The resort boasts over 100 activities, both indoor and outdoor, including aerial tree walks, zip lines, an indoor swimming pool, water slides, a spa and even a beach, situated right in the heart of Ireland.

As I part with the Inny, my ears rejoice at the melodic song of the chaffinch, which now modulates the airwaves. The sights also astound me, as a swarm of dragonflies enliven the reed fringe.

I pass some beech and alder, which triggers a memory of a Michael Viney article in *The Irish Times*. In it, he explains that of our native trees, the buds of the alder are the first to open up in early spring. The leaves of the alder, which are four to seven centimetes across, are broadly oval and on short stalks. Separate male and female catkins are produced in early spring.

Long ago, alder was used for making shields. There is an alder shield in the National Museum in Dublin, which is an amazing whole metre across – a diameter unlikely to be offered by any alder trunk in

Ireland today. The alder is a poor conductor of heat. It thrives in boggy soil and in moist woodlands, its wood being useful and long lasting where moisture is present. It is ideal for making clogs and sluice gates for canals. In addition, much of the city of Venice rests on alder piles.

The buds of the beech on the other hand are the last to open up. Like the sycamore, it is not native to Ireland. However, its smooth grey bark is a relatively common sight here. Its leaves are alternate, short stalked and oval and can be up to ten centimetres long by six centimetres broad. The crunch of fallen beech nuts beneath one's feet is a delightful experience, with its own special timbre. These nuts provide food for squirrels and other woodland animals.

Just beyond a large farmhouse a conspicuous telephone pole hides among the trees, as if apologising for its intrusion on rural life. Yet it is surely a necessary modern lifeline in this secluded setting.

For about 10 minutes, I find myself on a straight stretch of canal as it takes a short break from its meandering. Slowly, my ears tune into the increasing sound of traffic, passing over the N55 on Fowlard's (or Cloonard) Bridge, linking Athlone to Cavan. From on top I can see two dark brown and well-groomed horses grazing in a meadow close by. Looking ahead, I am rewarded with a fabulous view along the undulating landscape, a patchwork of hedgerows and fields with a mixture of tightly grouped small trees.

Returning to the south towpath, I continue on a barely discernible, though manageable, trail through grass averaging half a metre in height, with splashes of yellow wildflowers. I feel as if I am eavesdropping on the meadow. The road has moved away from the canal and it is so quiet now that I can hear my thoughts as never before. A small tortoiseshell flutters among the tall grasses, looking quite at home in its chosen biosphere.

On I plod through this dense, wild meadow, becoming slowly aware of traffic up ahead. Finally, I am greeted by the queen of the reed fringe, the yellow flag of summer, appearing in clumps on my approach to Toome Bridge. This was formerly one of the principle places on the canal, where Bianconi coaches operated in conjunction with the passenger boats.

Coaching connections were an important aspect of the passenger trade on the Royal Canal. There were a number of these services at particular points along the waterway. With over 40,000 passengers travelling per year on the canal in the 1830s, these services were indispensable contributors to the transport network.

Charles Bianconi was Ireland's principal operator of horse-drawn coaches, which were frequently referred to as cars. He was born in Italy in 1786 and when he came to Ireland he sold prints and mirrors for a living from a shop in Clonmel, before becoming involved in the transport business. When the Napoleonic wars ended in 1815, there were many ex-war horses for sale and Charles saw an opportunity to set up his passenger horse-drawn car business, which became very successful. Bianconi was a devout Catholic and a friend of Daniel O'Connell. He later sold his business to his employees on good terms and spent the last years of his life still rich and active in politics.

Toome Bridge

From on top of Toome Bridge, a scattering of houses are visible, signalling proximity to some nearby community. Descending a dozen or so moss-covered steps down an embankment past a welcoming bench, I find myself on a path of gravel and grass. Care has been lavished on this area, as the slope is neatly mown and planted with a variety of colourful shrubs.

Passing a wall of greenery, the bellowing of a bull from behind it echoes through the hinterland with menacing intensity.

The canal now recommences its seemingly ceaseless meandering. I am greeted by a cow sunbathing on the green-carpeted towpath. As I slip by her, she seems totally undaunted by my invasion of her privacy.

Cow sunbathing by the Canal

A Waterways Ireland sign informs me that I have finally reached Ballymahon, and beyond it stands the exotically named Chaigneau Bridge. From it, I gaze down on the magnificent cut stone Ballybrannigan Harbour. The water below acts as a three dimensional canvas, reflecting the blue, grey and white shapes of the fluffy clouds up above.

From here I could walk one kilometre to my lodgings in Ballymahon. Alternatively, I could walk another 2.3 kilometres as far as Archie's Bridge, accessing the town from the western side, thus saving me a little time tomorrow morning. I decide to continue along the towpath, taking a gulp of water from my diminishing supply.

There is an eye-catching garden arch close to the harbour, which is enhanced by yellow and red climbing roses. Beyond it, I am greeted by a row of fourteen mallards sitting by the water's edge, like spectators awaiting some imminent event. Two women, relaxing on a bench, are soaking up the harbour's beauty, as am I. The old, ivy-covered canal

Ivy-covered canal store

store, with two windows and a door still exposed, is holding its own against nature's encroachment.

Just a short stroll ahead, the blue and white passage-boat ticket office, which has been recently restored by the Ballymahon branch of the RCAG, is a wonderful sight. Such buildings tell the story of the canal when it was in its heyday, and I begin to realise that Ballybrannigan Harbour was once an industrious and busy place. Curiously, although the harbour and passenger boat station were here at Ballybrannigan Harbour, the passengers actually alighted at Toome Bridge to connect with Bianconi's cars journeying to Athlone.

Leaving this splendid harbour behind, I catch my first glimpse of Ballymahon's buildings across a field to the south, with the church spire rising high in the distance. As I walk along, I spy through a gap in the reeds a heron on the far bank, his reflection in the calm water below almost as real as the bird itself.

As I pass through sheep country, their whiteness striking on the low-lying hills, I arrive at the relatively new Longford Bridge, which carries traffic between Ballymahon and Lanesborough. A fine old rowing boat has been transformed into a garden display, striking in the evening sun, embellishing the mown embankment.

Old passenger boat ticket office

Ballybrannigan Harbour

The towpath leads me under the bridge and my tired legs take me down a long, straight corridor of elder and ash as I delight in the shimmering light dancing up and down the canal water.

The welcome sight of Archie's Bridge and Quay signals that I am almost at the end of my walk for today. The third-class road coming from over the bridge will lead me into Ballymahon. On my way, I pass a mixture of cottages, bungalows and some large houses, all with neatly manicured lawns and planted with a mixture of flowers and trees.

After about half an hour, I reach the town. Walking through its wide, main street, I admire some impressive buildings that line the footpaths, encouraging me to explore them before tomorrow's departure.

Feeling the tiredness of my 20 kilometre trek, my goal is to reach Cooney's Hotel where I am booked in for the night. The pleasant hotel staff welcome me warmly. A cheerful girl checks me in and shows me my room. She is interested in my canal adventure, evident by her enthusiastic questions.

After a refreshing shower, I relax, before writing up my notes. Later, I have pizza in the bar with a pint of refreshing Carlsberg. The lively music and dancing feet of the teenage disco continues until midnight, and exudes a youthful energy which I now lack. Its cessation allows my older bones to retire to a well-earned sleep that will sustain me on tomorrow's long adventure.

Line of ducks near Ballybrannigan Harbour

18.

BALLYMAHON TO MOSSTOWN

Authors, a Medic, an Ancient Trackway and a Notorious Banker

As soon as my eyes open, the enthusiasm for today's walk grips me on this the ninth day of my journey. My stay at Cooney's Hotel, though short, has helped to revitalize me, along with a breakfast from the extensive menu. It sets me up for today's trek.

Ballymahon is a sizeable regional town with an interesting history. Baile Uí Mhatháin, in Irish, means Mahon's town. Some say it is named after a chieftain called Mahon (Mathgamain mac Cennétig), the eldest brother of Brian Boru.

The earliest documented evidence of Ballymahon was in the year 1578, when houses and lands were granted to Robert Dillon and his heirs. Later on, the Confiscation and Settlement Act of 1650 changed the ownership of properties, with the old landed farmers forfeiting their property to the Crown. With the coming of the new property owners, the notable Irish surnames, such as Dillon, Murtagh and Sleator, were replaced with English names, which included the Molyneuxs, Gores and Sandys. Following on from this, there began the construction of great houses.

Commerce and industry in Ballymahon began to take on a business footing in the eighteenth century. Flax, corn, wheat and potatoes were plentiful due to the fertile soil in the surrounding area. The arrival of the Royal Canal in 1817 marked the beginning of a booming period in the town and hinterland. Mills were constructed, mainly for corn and flax, and the town was developed.

It was hoped that the railway would come through Ballymahon in the mid-nineteenth century to continue boosting exports. However, it took a different route and with the railway becoming the preferred mode of transport over the Royal Canal, Ballymahon began to decline.

Matters were not helped by the advent of the Great Irish Famine of 1845-1851. When the potato crop failed, many people died and others were admitted to the workhouse, called the Ballymahon Union.

In the early years of the twentieth century, the mills closed down one by one. It would not be until after the Second World War, and a national economic recovery, that Ballymahon would see economic growth again.

I decide to briefly explore Ballymahon before I depart. Main Street's spacious thoroughfare is lined with buildings of mostly late Georgian architecture, with two and three storey gabled houses, colour-washed and in rows of three and four.

Anglicanism, and other reformed faiths, arrived in Ireland in the late sixteenth century, and St. Catherine's Anglican Church, dating to 1736, stands near the southern end of the town. An impressive addition since is the bell tower, with four small outer spired pinnacles, and a magnificent cut stone spire soaring from its centre. Unfortunately, it is closed when I arrive, depriving me from investigating the box-style pews, each with their own door, for which it is renowned.

Dr. Kathleen Lynn was one of the first female medical graduates in Ireland. Her father was a Church of Ireland clergyman associated with this church. In 1882, when Kathleen was nine, he took over the Ballymahon parish. Kathleen studied medicine at Cecilia Street, Dublin. Legislation introduced during her lifetime allowed women to qualify in the medical profession 'without distinction of sex'.

Following her graduation, she worked in a number of Dublin hospitals. She also set up her own private practice in her home at 9

Belgrave Road, Rathmines. She was an advocate for the rights of women and became a member of the Irish Women's Suffrage.

Kathleen helped with the relief efforts for workers and their families during the 1913 Lockout and became a friend and supporter of James Connolly. She joined the Irish Citizens Army and was appointed Chief Medical Officer with the rank of captain. During Easter Week, her presence had a comforting effect on her comrades, through her calmness on the roof of City Hall, 'with bullets smacking all around her'.

Following the Rising, instead of being imprisoned Kathleen was sent to assist a doctor in Bath. In 1917 she was elected to the Sinn Féin Executive. She was also active in the War of Independence. Although arrested, she was released to assist with the Great Influenza epidemic, which had first appeared in 1918. Kathleen was elected to the Dáil, but having opposed the Treaty of 1921 did not take her seat.

Kathleen Lynn and her partner Madeleine Ffrench Mullen founded St. Ultan's Hospital for infants in 1919 in Dublin. In 1934, Dr. Maria Montessori, the first female medical doctor to qualify in Italy, visited St. Ultan's Hospital. Both women readily exchanged ideas, which soon led to the opening of a Montessori ward at St. Ultan's. Kathleen died in 1955 and left her cottage in Glenmalure, County Wicklow to An Óige.

Leaving St. Catherine's, I continue on down the street to where the substantial waters of the River Inny flow beneath a triple-arch stone bridge. This stretch of the Inny from Newcastle Bridge to Ballymahon town is a renowned route for beginner to intermediate kayaking, canoeing and time trials. The Inny is also a top class river for coarse fishing. Visiting anglers can also enjoy coarse fishing on the Royal Canal.

Gazing down along the river, I try to imagine the spirit of Eithne being carried along by the water, yet always being present there. It is a nice little conundrum to figure out, as I retrace my steps, heading to the other side of town. I soon arrive at the former courthouse and market house.

This building now serves as Ballymahon Library. Outside stands a very impressive bronze sculpture of the famous poet, playwright and novelist Oliver Goldsmith, complete with satchel and flute, affirming his prominence as a writer to the local people. An even better known sculpture of Goldsmith stands in Dublin, at the main entrance to Trinity College.

Inside Ballymahon Library, I find that the librarians are especially enthusiastic about their many local writers, and there are related artefacts, books and information on display throughout the library. Three of these writers, in particular, are of interest to me: John Keegan Casey, Mary Flynn and Oliver Goldsmith.

John Keegan Leo Casey, poet, songwriter, teacher and Fenian, was born in 1846. His father was a teacher in nearby Gurteen. When John was fourteen he became his father's assistant. Such informal training was common among Catholics at the time and it led to a teaching post for John, first in the school at Cleraune and later at Keenagh.

Statue of Oliver Goldsmith

Casey wrote many songs and poems. His most famous, 'The Rising of the Moon', a tribute to the insurgents who had assembled at Skeagh Hill, near Rathconrath, County Longford, during the 1798 Rebellion, was published in *The Nation*.

> *'Oh! then tell me, Shawn O'Ferrall,*
> *Tell me why do you hurry so?'*
> *'Hush, ma bouchal, hush and listen,'*
> *And his cheeks were all a-glow.*
> *'I bear orders from the captain,*
> *Get you ready quick and soon,*
> *For the pikes must be together*
> *At the risin' of the moon.'*

However, Casey's writings brought him to the attention of the authorities. In March 1867, he was interned in Mountjoy Prison on suspicion of inciting others to rebellion and high treason, but was released later that year. Sadly, in March 1870, Casey was thrown from a cab that collided with a dray and died a few days later at the young age of twenty-four. His coffin was draped in green, white and orange banners, the first recorded use of a tricolour for this purpose. Thousands of people marched from his home in a procession to Glasnevin Cemetery, Dublin. His wife Josephine never remarried and survived him by fifty years.

Mary Flynn, a teacher and author of children's books, was born in Ballymahon in 1911. By that time Beatrix Potter (1866-1943) had become famous for her children's books, such as *The Tale of Peter Rabbit*. It seems probable that Mary was familiar with the tales of Beatrix and it inspired her to carry on the tradition.

Mary told her pupils stories about the adventures of Cornelius Rabbit and his friends. She wrote her stories during her summer holidays in Tang, which is a little south of Ballymahon. One of her books is entitled *Cornelius Rabbit of Tang*. She died in 1984 and is buried in Shrule cemetery, which lies between Ballymahon and Tang.

Having told a very helpful member of the library staff that I was always a great admirer of Oliver Goldsmith's work, she gives me access to the Goldsmith Room for a short period. What a wonderful surprise to behold this large collection of beautifully bound books, some first editions, either written by Goldsmith or about him, housed for protection in large glass bookcases!

Oliver Goldsmith was born in 1728 in Pallas, between Abbeyshrule and Ballymahon. His father, the Rev. George Goldsmith, was curate of Forgney church, just 2.5 kilometres south of the family home. Oliver was still a young child when they moved southwest to Lissoy, a village between Tang and Glasson. He was awkward and often undignified in social circles, particularly among the upper class, and he suffered from a lack of confidence.

Oliver entered Trinity College Dublin in 1745 shortly before his sixteenth birthday. He did not always apply himself to his studies having 'no taste for the tortuosities of academic learning'. Despite this, he managed to leave Trinity with a B.A. Degree in 1749.

For the next few years he travelled aimlessly throughout Europe, moving from job to job, sometimes earning his board and keep by playing the flute and singing. On his travels he mingled mainly with the peasants and workers, and through this he acquired a sense of real values, which is the main strength of his serious work.

In 1756, Goldsmith arrived in London, where he was to spend the rest of his life. In England at this time, patronage by which men of letters had hitherto lived was finally dead. The public was the new patron and the editor-publisher their deputy, and Goldsmith's fortune began to change. He started to write and translate prose on diverse subjects, leading to his essays being published and to the establishment of his reputation as an original voice. He should have been financially secure because of the success of his poems, plays and novel. Instead, he was perpetually in debt, partly due to his drinking and gambling, but also due to him lending money to needier men of letters. He was only forty-three when he died on 4 April 1774. He is buried in Poet's Corner in Westminster Abbey.

Some of Goldsmith's works have stood the test of time. Testaments to this are his long poem 'The Deserted Village', loosely based on memories of Lissoy, his comic play *She Stoops to Conquer* and his novel *The Vicar of Wakefield*, one of the most influential works of the eighteenth century and still in print to this day.

Goldsmith remained an enigma to his contemporaries. Sometimes seen as an absurd clown, most still acknowledged his literary genius. His epitaph at Westminster Abbey was written in Latin by his friend Dr. Samuel Johnson. Perhaps the translation of an extract from it best sums up his legacy.

Oliver Goldsmith: A Poet, Naturalist, and Historian, who left scarcely any style of writing untouched, and touched nothing that he did not adorn.

Satisfied with my exploration of Ballymahon, I rejoin the canal at Archie's Bridge. Stepping onto the potholed, gravel towpath on the north bank, I start off westward on this warm, overcast day.

Two old buildings, covered with invasive shrubs, are the remains of two large stores, a legacy from the busy trading days of this waterway around Ballymahon. They must have been associated with the former mill at Archie's Bridge.

Although the canal is only three kilometres from Lough Ree on the River Shannon at this point, it takes a very definite turn in a northerly direction, keeping more or less to that course all the way to Cloondara. The Grand Canal Company objected to the Royal Canal terminating in Lough Ree. The government agreed, saying that the purpose of the Royal Canal was to serve north Shannon, and in particular to provide a route for Lough Allen coal. There was also a problem associated with

Remains of two large stores near Archie's Bridge

terminating the canal in a large lake, where poor weather conditions could hold up traffic for long periods, causing timetable rescheduling. As a result, the canal continued for another 19 kilometres to the junction with the Shannon at Cloondara.

Following the waterway's new northerly course, I stop to observe an emerald damselfly, which stays on the ground below me, just long enough to take in its magnificent green colour, from its head down along its folded feather-like wings. When I look up I notice a man approaching.

'Grand day!' he says.

'It is to be sure!' I answer.

'You're out for a stroll so?' he comments.

'Well, I'm walking the canal in stages and I'm on my way to Killashee today,' I state with satisfaction.

'Good for you,' he nods in approval.

'I noticed some loose stone and low sections of crumbling wall just back the way a little,' I say. 'Do you know what the former buildings were?'

Damselfly

'Most likely the ruins of some old farmhouses,' he answers. 'In fact they would have looked very much like that old farmhouse on the far bank,' he continues, as he points to a building very much intact.

'Ah yes, I see!' I reply. 'Are you from around here?'

'I am indeed,' he answers. 'I live in an old house on Main Street in Ballymahon, which had been associated with the canal. Back then, it was advertised as a hotel but had actually just been a lodging house.'

'A little misleading!' I exclaim.

'Yes it was. In fact, you might often have had to share a bed with another lad,' he comments humorously.

As we both smile, there is a lull in the conversation before he continues. 'I remember, too, that agents were sent down periodically from Dublin, to take orders for supplies required in surrounding towns and villages. Orders were often known to include that most formidable of items: a coffin!'

I am delighted to learn this information from such a good-humoured and witty local. I thank him and we part company.

As I approach the 40th Lock, the first in 11 kilometres, I discover that I am now in a prominent position to view the local landscape. The fields to the west fall away from the towpath. Beyond them is a forest of silver birch. The land to the east rises into the occasional hillock.

Reaching the lock, I find that the old lockhouse has had a small porch added for shelter. The canal's cascade into the lock chamber mingles with birdsong in the otherwise stillness and quietness. This rhythmic sound of flowing water is only heard where rivers or streams flow under the waterway or at locks when a sluice is open.

Mullawornia Accommodation Bridge is just after the lock, with a modern house the far side of it. A warm greeting is mounted on the bridge:

> *Welcome to*
> *McLoughlin's*
> *40th Lock*
> *Mullaworna*

40th Lock and Accommodation Bridge, Mullawornia

The website Logainm.ie gives the Irish for this place as Mullach Bhoirne. *Mullach* means hilltop or summit and explains my panoramic view of the surrounding countryside.

I tread along a path of compacted clay, with a ribbon of grass forming a disjointed backbone. A short distance ahead, as I approach a bend, I see a rock face rising from the far towpath. The marshy land is still falling away from the bank, sweeping down to the shores of Lough Ree.

The writer and engineer Tom Rolt passed through here aboard the chartered *Le Coq*, a twenty-six foot by eight foot converted ship's lifeboat in 1946, on his journey around the waterways of Ireland. In his excellent book, *Green & Silver*, he relates how a Mr. Cafferty had described very vividly this section of the canal to him as the hundred feet of rock and hundred feet of bog, a very apt description indeed. Cafferty's boat was one of only two operating on the Royal Canal at that time. He carried general cargo, mostly between Dublin and Mullingar. The other boat, owned by Leach of Killucan, carried bog ore into Dublin.

Across the water, a brown horse, with a black horse blanket draped over his back, is eating from a prickly furze bush and thoroughly enjoying it. As a food source, it is highly nutritious, being full of protein. Despite that, there are many farmers who look upon it as a

Horse eating gorse

pest and actually remove it. Some articles talk of the necessity to crush the spines before feeding it to horses. However, one particular article claimed that horses can eat the furze straight from the bush because they cleverly turn the tips of the prickly branches around in their mouths, so that it is swallowed with the spikes backwards. The horse I am watching appears to have mastered this technique to perfection.

Ballymahon and the surrounding areas have a lot to offer those interested in equestrian activities as one comes across horse trainers, stables and interschool equestrian events.

Beyond some low-lying bramble, I see little Drum Lough to the west. With the land falling down to it, then rising tree-studded beyond, it presents a placid, picturesque scene.

As I approach the Pake Bridges, a flock of chaffinch whizz in and out of the trees, flying in a mesmerizing wave. The general name for a finch in Irish is glasán, literally meaning grey or green bird. There is more than one collective name for them, but my favourite has to be a charm of finches.

The splendid old Pake Bridge is in danger of being camouflaged out of existence by nature's heavy growth. From on top, I see that the new Pake Bridge traverses the canal diagonally, carrying traffic on the busy road that links Lanesboro with Ballymahon and Mullingar.

The towpath leads under both bridges to a grassier path beyond, made more colourful by the buttercups and clover that are peeping up above the blades of grass. A hill covered in a woolly whiteness is recorded on my map as being merely 88 metres high. Notwithstanding, it is another substantial elevation along this flat plain. I am dwarfed as I am led through a corridor of mature trees, spreading out over the towpath and towering high above me.

View beneath Pake Bridges

As I arrive at Foigha Bridge and Harbour, I notice a beautiful mistle thrush perched on the bridge. Bigger than a blackbird, it stands erect with spotted pot-belly. When it takes flight, I watch the wings go into action, exposing a white flash on its underbelly, as its long tail trails behind.

Chaffinch

Looking southeast from Foigha Bridge

My pace soon slows, as the grass rises to half a metre high. I emerge from it to find myself walking through another corridor of trees, towering from both banks. An increasing awareness of isolation creates a special space in my head that is relaxing and uplifting.

Suddenly, a bright blue butterfly floats by, but that vivid colour soon flits away across a red rowing boat. The song of a blackbird fills the air, shrill and piping. In the background, smaller birds tweet and chirp in harmony, adding to the melodious soundtrack enveloping me.

A cruiser appears up ahead and I wave to the boaters as we fleetingly pass each other, and they wave back excitedly, until I am alone once again. A pretty line of bright reeds, with their darker subdued reflection, greets me on the way to Cloonbreany Accommodation Bridge. Beyond it, trees continue to act as a guard of honour for me, as I stroll along this majestic waterway.

I disturb two moorhens that flutter in panic, unused as they must be to a human presence. I love this timid, black-coloured bird, with its red and yellow beak and white patches on its tail and flanks.

Ballymahon to Mosstown

A beautiful display of bright reeds

Within minutes, I round a bend leading to a beautiful long stretch of canal. The waterway has widened now as it passes through Cloonbreany Bog, with views stretching over this ancient terrain of expansive peatland for long distances.

Silver birch are now predominant all about. This hardy tree loves peat, though it grows in a variety of habitats. Coleridge referred to it as the Lady of the Woods. It is indeed most graceful, with its silvery white bark, peeling artistically in places, exposing darker shades beneath the silver skin, and its loosely hung delicate leaves swaying in the breeze. Birch is of little value for timber. However, its twiggy branches made it ideal in the past for use as a broom, and dye made from birch bark was used for tanning leather.

I pass a pedestrian walkway on my left, leading to the Visitor Centre at Corlea Bog. The road over Island Bridge passes close to its main entrance. Back in the 1960s, Bord na Móna started to extract peat from Corlea Bog, and over time a large network of wooden trackways was uncovered, some dating as far back as 3,500 BC in a vast tract of bog that lies between the canal and the Shannon.

Path from canal to Corlea Bog Visitor Centre

Later, in 1984, a major pre-historic one kilometre long trackway of large oak planks was discovered. The Visitor Centre is built on the exact axis of the trackway in the bog, with 18 metres of the excavated and conserved timber trackway on display, along with other artefacts of interest.

Bogs are oxygen-free environments, thus the bacteria which bring about the normal processes of organic decay are absent. Bogs will often yield information about past cultures, which has long since disappeared from dry land sites.

The construction of the trackway at Corlea, as narrated in the Visitor Centre, was a huge undertaking. We can only speculate as to where it led. It could have been part of a dry land route, leading to a Shannon crossing at Lanesborough. Or more dramatically, it may have been part of a highway that had the royal site of Crúachain as its destination. Crúachain or Rathcroghan, as it is known today, was the home of Queen Medb, from where she ruled all of Connacht. It is sad that after all the marvellous workmanship involved in crafting this wooden structure, its weight caused it to eventually sink into the bog.

The Granard poet, Noel Monahan, captured the trackway succinctly in his poem 'The Corlea Road'. It begins:

After a long silence
The bog heaved, delivered a road

and finishes:

Dream road, wooden road,
A road raised up to the light
That will talk,
If you give it time to speak.

As I continue along the towpath, I notice on its fringe, three wonderful orchids, one white, one a pinkish purple and the third purple, each perfectly displayed on their own upright stem. Orchids often hybridise, making identification difficult. Because of my location it is likely that these ones are heath spotted-orchids.

Off to the northeast, the dense woods of Mosstown Estate rise and spread over a distance. Then I meet the oxeye daisies, setting the grass aflame with their bright-yellow, sun-like centre disc, from which white petals spread out like rays of light.

Orchids

By the time I snap from beneath their spell, I find I am passing a line of mooring posts, with one boat moored. They lead me to Island Bridge, Mosstown Harbour. The bridge is a new structure mostly of metal. To the south, on the far bank, is a semi-derelict house. To the east, a large gaggle of white geese are scattered about a field. Mosstown Harbour opens out like an Olympic swimming pool, with some kids taking the plunge. When I descend, I ask the swimmers if the water is cold, and I am given a very definite 'No.'

The harbour is a spacious, well-kept amenity area with picnic tables. A council worker is busy on the far bank, wheeling a barrow with a spade protruding from it, testament to the ongoing maintenance. This was not the case when Ruth Delany and friends travelled the length of the Royal Canal in 1955 on *The Hark*. It was the last boat to pass through this waterway on an official pass, before the canal was closed to navigation in 1961. She talks of reaching Island Bridge where 'an overgrown harbour indicated its former role as a trading place'.

Approaching Island Bridge, Mosstown

A short distance east of here is the estate village of Keenagh. The name Keenagh comes from the Irish *caonach*, which means moss. There is little doubt that Mosstown Demesne derived its name from the same source. Parts of Mosstown Estate stretch from the village down to the banks of the Royal Canal.

In 1789, Mosstown Demesne passed to Charlotte Newcomen who had married William Gleadowe, a Dublin banker, in 1772. He adopted the name Gleadowe-Newcomen, and he also took ownership of Charlotte's extensive family properties in Longford. With his wife's influence, he gained a seat in the Irish Parliament and earned himself a Baronetcy.

When the Royal Canal Company was formed in 1789, William Newcomen became a director and its first treasurer. Shortly after the work commenced, the company met with severe financial difficulties, until Sir William and his bank came to the rescue with a loan to help carry on the work. However, the price this villain charged was very high indeed, at 30 per cent interest, being described by fellow directors

Mosstown Harbour

Mosstown Estate gates

as a most exorbitant and illegal profit. Sir William died in 1807, never witnessing the canal's completion. Nevertheless, Newcomen Bridge, at Ballybough, on the Royal Canal in Dublin, is named in his honour.

In 1800, Sir William had voted in favour of the Act of Union, despite his constituents being solidly against it. Somehow it was discovered that his support came at a price. He had owed up to £10,000 to the public treasury, all except £2,000 of which had been cancelled by Attorney-General John Toler, that infamous Hanging Judge with links to Cabra. William's near-neighbour, Richard Lovell Edgeworth, father of the famous writer Maria Edgeworth, scornfully penned the following lines regarding him:

With a name that is borrowed, a title that's bought,
Sir William would fain be a gentleman thought;
His wit is but cunning, his courage but vapour,
His pride is but money, his money but paper!

The impressive entrance gates to Mosstown Estate, with a large stone eagle perched on each of the prominent stone pillars, are still standing in Keenagh village. This estate became a part of the large Newcastle Estate during the ownership of Lady Rosse. Mosstown House was demolished in 1962.

The remains of an old Wesleyan Church beside the entrance are an added attraction. It is still possible to walk through the old grounds and soak up the sensation of past life on such an estate. The beautiful Dovecote or Pigeon House, now privately owned, supplied eggs and pigeon meat to the Big House.

An elegant 60 foot tall clock tower, dated 1878, in memory of the Hon. Lawrence Harman, King-Harman of Newcastle House, dominates the village of Keenagh. The plaque attributes its erection to his tenants and friends. Lawrence died in 1875. The clock tower has been restored to perfect working order, and is one of few in Ireland of such design.

This small village has many links to the Royal Canal's chain of stories. It is said that Ireland is a small country. I have found that recurring titles and characters, such as Sir William Newcomen and Judge John Toler, have journeyed with me from the east coast into Ireland's heartland.

19.

Mosstown to Killashee

Swimmers, the Famine Way, Dams and Merchants

Leaving Mosstown Harbour, I find myself on a quiet and peaceful towpath, bordered by the crumbling walls of Mosstown Estate. Behind them, I have a wonderful view of both the native and introduced species within the widespread and dense woodlands.

I notice holly growing along the edge. The common holly, a familiar native tree, is slow growing and is pollinated mainly by bees. The holly is dioecious, meaning the male and female flowers are produced on separate trees, with only the female tree producing berries.

The contrast between the glossy green leaves and the scarlet berries makes the holly particularly attractive. When blackbirds, wood pigeons, thrushes and robins are finished feasting on the holly tree in my garden, I am lucky if there are enough berried branches left for my Christmas decorating.

Rhododendron is also very prevalent in Mosstown Estate. During the early nineteenth century, it was introduced to Ireland and planted in large estates for its ornamental elegance and also as cover for game, in particular pheasants. Although it displays the most beautiful pinkish-purple blossoms during summer, it is a highly invasive species and is posing a threat to our oak woodlands. In Killarney National Park, millions of euros have been spent to date in the battle to eradicate it.

In contrast, the splendid row of native ash along the woodland edge has been of huge benefit to man. In early Irish law the ash was classified as one of the seven Nobles of the Wood. Its high quality timber has had many uses, such as the manufacture of furniture and hurleys. Ash bark could be used for tanning and the dried leaves were sometimes used as fodder for livestock.

A blackbird sings from a nearby hedge and I start to hum that Beatles song in which the protagonist, on hearing the blackbird at night, urges it to take flight on broken wings. Ah, but it is day, that moment has passed, and he has risen!

Snapping out of my reverie, I arrive at the end of the Mosstown Estate wall. Beyond it in a field of rushes are two delightful black donkeys, each with a white snout. Falling apart behind them, are two roofless ruins.

The towpath converges here, with the road coming through Mosstown from Keenagh village. I walk along this road for 20 metres as far as Coolnahinch Bridge and the 41st Lock. The original lockhouse has been extended and the wheelbarrow in the tidy garden is testament to some avid gardening.

Old ruins and two donkeys

Cruiser in lock chamber

As I stand on the bridge, I hear the engine of a cruiser in the distance and shortly after see it approaching from a northerly direction. This is a pleasant place to stop for lunch and a good vantage point to observe the progress of the boat. A Waterways Ireland employee, sitting in his van on the far bank, is also enjoying a sandwich. Unlike the early lockkeepers, these modern keepers cover a lot of ground and can be in charge of a dozen or more locks.

I take a seat on a mooring post and wait for the cruiser's arrival. Soon it enters the lock chamber and the crew secure the bow and stern, using ropes wrapped around mooring posts on the far bank. Although I had witnessed the whole operation from Jenny Wren's boat at the 13th Lock back near Leixlip, viewing it from the towpath offers a different perspective.

The lad from Waterways Ireland springs into action. I see how he bends his back with arms outstretched, and with hands on the tail gate, pushes hard down through his legs into his anchored feet to begin closing it. He does this first on the east bank then on the west. Next he produces the windlass or lock key, which operates the sluices via a rack and pinion system. First he closes the lower sluices, then he slowly opens the upper sluices and the chamber begins to fill with water. At the same time, the crew are tensioning the ropes appropriately, shortening them as the boat rises. It is very much a cooperative effort, and so far it appears to be proceeding like clockwork.

Eventually, the water in the chamber equalises with the water in the canal's high level. The breast gates are then opened by one of the boaters with help from the Waterways Ireland chap, each on opposite sides of the canal. Soon the cruiser is on its way again, heading southwards. The whole process took approximately 15 to 20 minutes.

Canal turns northwest just after Coolnahinch Bridge

The man from the lockhouse appears and I ask him if he knows what speed the cruiser might do on average. He estimates about 8 miles per hour, approximately twice my walking speed. If there were no locks that boat could do this journey twice as fast. Luckily, I don't have forty-six locks to delay me.

As I move along, I see a rider exercising a horse in a nearby paddock. Two other horses are wearing waterproof blankets, usually done to protect the horse from rain, snow or high winds, helping to keep it dry and warm. Loud bellowing from the fields across the canal informs me of a different type of husbandry in the distance.

The heron up ahead knows its hunting ground, as the canal is alive with fish, which are breaching the surface in order to catch flies.

As I arrive at Ards Bridge, a car pulls up alongside me.

'Hello there, lovely day,' the elderly gentleman remarks.

'Marvellous,' I answer, 'I'm so lucky that it's staying dry for my walk. I left Ballymahon earlier and hope to get to Killashee later today.'

'Well it's only three o'clock now and you've just about five kilometres more to walk,' he says. 'I think it will be no bother to you.'

'Yes, I'm about two-thirds of the way there already,' I reply.

'I'm eighty-five years old now,' he tells me, 'but when I was young I used swim with my pals to the lock above the bridge and back again.'

Interestingly, the 42nd Lock is 400 metres beyond Ards Bridge and not beside it, as is usually the case. Those youths would have done a round trip of 800 metres, equivalent to completing sixteen lengths of an Olympic swimming pool. Taking into account the canal's vegetation, it would have been a more difficult swim. It was an era before swimming pools, but this waterway served the same function.

'That's quite a swim,' I say. 'It must have kept you all fit.'

'Sure, we were kept fit alright,' he replies. 'You know, during the war we used walk as far as Longford and back, as there was little or no transport.'

I thank him for sharing some of his memories with me as he switches on the ignition to continue his business. I must say, he doesn't look his age and his eyes reflect the joyous music of his speech.

I ramble along the tarmac road as far as the 42nd Lock or Ards Lock, passing an occupied, whitewashed lockhouse.

On my approach to the Lyneen or Ballinamore Bridges, I encounter the old, arched cut stone beauty first. It is followed by one of modern construction, with some tasteful stone work below, facilitating traffic on the regional road between Newtown Cashel and Longford.

As I leave these two contrasting structures behind, I notice some smashed duck eggs in the grass near the bank and wonder what predator might be responsible.

Cascade of water at 42nd Lock

Approaching Crossover or Lower Lyneen Bridge

Walking past dense hedgerows, I am totally isolated from humanity. The bank is like a narrow linear meadow, with grasses 0.5 metres high and well established saplings rising from the reed fringe.

The grassy path becomes rougher approaching Crossover or Lower Lyneen Bridge. It was built to allow horses pulling barges to cross over to the far side of the canal at this point, providing access to the Longford Branch towpath, which diverges from the main branch 0.75 kilometres from here. Since my original walk, the Royal Canal Greenway project has resulted in this once overgrown and impassable towpath being cleared and tarmacked, completely transforming it.

Further on, the towpaths from Crossover Bridge and Killashee curve away from the canal towards the Longford Branch, creating a wide expanse of water. However, shortly after this turning, the canal is dammed, thus terminating the flow of water towards Longford Town. This 8.3 kilometre branch is dry, except for the final 1.5 kilometres, which has been re-watered and is fed by springs.

Following the closure of the Royal Canal in 1961 by Córas Iompair Éireann (CIÉ), a dam was built across the canal west of Mullingar, which prevented water flowing westward from the summit level.

Junction with Longford Branch

This dam here on the Longford Branch was also built at that time. The section of canal west of Mullingar was allowed to dry out and the lock gates, chambers and harbours sadly fell into complete disrepair. This has since been restored, with the necessary finances and a huge amount of voluntary dedication.

The Royal Canal Amenity Group is still involved in an effort to have the Longford Branch restored. Their target is to have it reinstated by 2030, which would be 200 years after the branch first opened in 1830.

Ruth Delany tells us that emigrants used to join the passenger boats here at this junction, having travelled by coach from the west of Ireland. However, most emigrants did not share this luxury and had to make the journey by foot.

During the famine, Major Denis Mahon, the landlord of Strokestown Park House, Roscommon, evicted large numbers of his tenants. Forced into assisted emigration, 1,490 of these mistreated people were marched from Strokestown to Cloondara and along the Royal Canal towpaths to Dublin. They were then loaded onto the *Virginius* and the *Naomi*, two of the so called coffin ships, bound for

Canada. Typhus was rampant on board during the voyage. Both ships eventually arrived in Quebec, but with many of the passengers having died en route. In one vessel alone, 268 persons were alleged to have died at sea.

This disaster would appear to have sealed the fate of Major Mahon. He was assassinated in November of 1847, the first landlord to meet this fate during the famine. Within days, the murder came to define the misgovernment of Ireland and the event was being publicised and discussed worldwide.

Consequently, the route from Strokestown along the towpaths of the Royal Canal to Dublin has been designated the National Famine Way. This trail is waymarked with over thirty small bronze sculptures of nineteenth century style shoes, an apt marker for this poignant pathway.

Strokestown House, now home to the National Famine Museum, is at one end of the National Famine Way, while EPIC, the Irish Emigration Museum, is at the other end in Dublin. As I move on, I look forward to exploring the Longford Branch a couple of days from now.

Sculpture of Famine shoes

The next kilometre or so is a pleasant tree-lined walk that opens up in places, so that a distant forest is visible. Pink-tinged wild angelica is growing among the grasses along the bank and its sweet fragrance fills my nostrils. The lacewing moth feeds on it. The plant is said to yield a yellow dye, while the stems have traditionally been used to decorate sweetmeats and to flavour liqueurs.

A lovely display of tufted vetch

Blips of yellow flag rise up from the bankside vegetation here and there, and the hedgerows renew their love of the yellow gorse, which now appears in constant clumps.

A robin is singing close by. I spot the feathered beauty and, staying motionless, watch spellbound. Its tiny beak moves rapidly to its musical notes. Of course, that same robin could be reprimanding me for daring to come too close to the nest. The male and female of this species both sing and look alike, even to each other. There are many beliefs as to how this bird obtained a red breast. In one story, a robin is said to have helped Christ on the cross by trying to pick thorns from his head to staunch the flow of blood, some of which fell on the robin.

Mooring posts lead me to the 43rd Lock, Aghnaskea Bridge, and yet another classic lockhouse. Some kayaks for hire are stacked, resting beside a large van. A road sign points the way to the small village of Killashee where I will spend the night in Magan's Airbnb and pub.

I pass a grassy quadrangle, forming a square in this quaint village, arriving at Magan's three storey house on a sharp bend on the main

View South from Aghnaskea Bridge of 43rd Lock

Lanesboro to Longford Road. Close to the farm entrance beside the house, there is an old red weighbridge inscribed H. POOLEY & SON, LIVERPOOL AND GLASGOW, dated 1850.

Staying at Magan's proves to be a real trip into a different time. The pub's window display contains a variety of earthenware jugs, lanterns, mineral dispensers, medicine bottles, an antique iron (non-electric of course), books, a sewing machine, an old scales, beer bottles, a blowtorch, a bread bin, a dated Jacob's Cream Crackers box, and many more items from days long gone. This establishment is here since 1826. Dan Magan, who runs the pub and B&B, shows me to my room and invites me down for a cuppa when I am ready.

My room has wooden shutters on the window and a high ceiling. The old, solid collectable furniture creates the perfect ambience for the large bedroom. The large bookcase contains a huge variety of books, including one beautiful illustrated volume of Goldsmith's works.

Various crafts from far flung places adorn the room. A hand-crafted wooden duck that opens to expose a collection of coloured marbles would have delighted any young boy. An engraved vintage jewellery

Magan's Pub

Part of Magan's window display

box, sitting on an antique chest of drawers, would have stored the delicate treasures of the lady of the house. There are also various paintings on the wall, some of eastern influence, and one beautiful landscape painted by Marjorie Magan. A collage of photographs shows her at various stages of her life, from childhood to adulthood, including one of her in a swimming costume.

Downstairs, Dan welcomes me with tea and biscuits. I learn that his brother runs the large farm located behind this Georgian house and that it was originally a one and a half storey thatched building. His paternal great-grandmother had the height of the house extended to serve her large family.

Dan then brings me into the sitting room to meet his mother Marjorie, an elegant lady who is ninety-one years of age, but whose appearance does not betray her years. She is a most cordial woman who shows great interest in me and my canal walk. I am equally intrigued by her life. I had learned from Dan that when Marjorie was a young girl she was a great swimmer and was a member of Pembroke swimming club in south Dublin. Encouraged by her father, she went on to be a ten times All Ireland swimming champion. Marjorie relates her story enthusiastically. She tells me that she was married at nineteen and that she had reared eleven children. I also learn that her husband, who died a few years previous, enjoyed breaking horses and entering them in point to point races.

Marjorie's maiden name is Beckett. The famous author Samuel Beckett was her cousin and his portrait hangs on the landing wall. It is interesting to come across a second connection to this famous writer on my trip. Marjorie married one of two Magan brothers. Her nephew Manchán Magan, the writer, traveller and documentary-maker,

Portrait of Samuel Beckett

visits them regularly. Marjorie is an engaging host, intriguing me with family stories and facts. When we part company I retire to my room. Needing a good rest, my head takes to the pillow early.

At breakfast, Dan informs me that he too had walked the 146 kilometres along the Royal Canal from the Liffey to the Shannon, so we spend some time swapping anecdotes of our long treks.

Dan tells me that in the past the premises served not only as a pub, but also as an inn, bakery and hardware shop, supplying the local farming community. Pearse in Waterford was the supplier of the hardware, while Shackleton Mill in Lucan used to deliver flour to Magan's bakery, shipping it along the Royal Canal. Sharing stories over breakfast with a kindred spirit is a great way to begin my day.

I bid goodbye to the Magan household, appreciating my pleasurable and informative stay with this family.

Retracing my steps of the previous day, I arrive at St. Patrick's Roman Catholic Church, set slightly back from the Royal Canal. It dates from 1829, has a bellcote, stained glass windows and was built on a site donated by the Royal Canal Company. Inside, one of the plaques on the wall reads:

> *For the love of Jesus and Mary, pray for the soul of Michael Magan, Killashee who departed this life, January 3rd 1883 aged 56 years. A token of affection from his sorrowing widow, Margaret.*

The Magan family's historical links to Killashee go back generations. This little village is snugly tucked away, just off the route of the canal. It has enriched my understanding of those folk who live in small communities close to the Royal Canal, and how their lives are entangled in the history of the waterway.

20.

Killashee to Cloondara

Raised Bogs, the Táin, a Glorious Harbour and the Shannon

Back on a light gravel towpath, I leave Aghnaskea Bridge to begin the tenth day of my walk, heading towards Cloondara, six kilometres from here. However, I plan to use the extra time today to explore both Cloondara and Termonbarry.

After a pleasant stroll, I arrive at Killashee Harbour and the 44th Lock, with Savage Bridge visible on the cut stone. Killashee village can also be accessed from the road that crosses this bridge. The lockhouse here has an interesting story associated with it. A plaque naming it Frances' Cottage tells me that it was built in 1840 at a cost of £45. It was restored in 1990 by Frances K. Kelly of New York, who loved old historic buildings. The bright whitewashed walls contrast with the dark blue door and surrounds. A lighter blue picket fence perfects the scene.

As I proceed beyond Savage Bridge, light rain starts to fall. It soon becomes heavy, so I rummage for my raingear as I gaze amused at some horses prancing playfully in a field across the rain-spattered water, oblivious to the weather.

I soon arrive at the sturdy Ballydrum Accommodation Bridge. The main Killashee-Cloondara road runs parallel to the towpath, and this bridge can be accessed from it through a gate. Chaffinches fly from the bridge to the tall hedgerow trees in a wavelike motion.

Lockhouse and 44th Lock

Sign on Savage Bridge

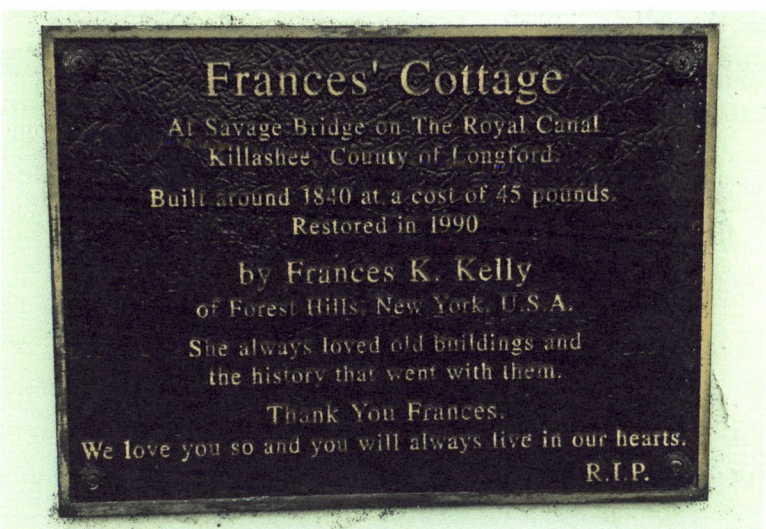
Plaque on lockhouse

With difficulty, I try to follow their playful antics as they swoop about with ease. Out on the water, a mother duck with her ducklings slowly glides away on my approach.

The canal widens for a long stretch, lined with trees all the way to the Begnagh Bridges. I am enjoying the cool rain on my face and how it punctures the normally mirror-like water surface. A murder of crows descends, with raucous voice, on the alder trees up ahead. Their stay there is short lived as they flock to a line of silver birch.

Off the far bank, through the hedgerow, a raised, dark embankment at least two metres high appears. This is my first sighting of the expansive Begnagh Bog.

The towpath comes to an end at the Begnagh Lifting Bridge, which replaced the old humpback structure in 2007, carrying the Killashee-Cloondara road across it. The design incorporated a lifting mechanism and a level crossing so that the bridge could be raised to allow boat traffic to pass, while also accommodating road traffic. It all works automatically so boats are warned to approach it slowly, allowing time for the road barriers to be lowered to stop traffic, and for the bridge to lift, before they get the green light. The canal takes a sharp turn beneath the lifting bridge, changing direction to northwest.

Crossing the road, I arrive at the old limestone Begnagh Bridge. The view from it looks out over the expansive Begnagh Bog, a perfect example of a raised bog. The vast, neat platform of deep-brown peat seems to stretch in both directions, like a dark desert spreading out for miles. Yet this brown landscape is far from a desert, being a rich habitat for a variety of species.

The story of how raised bogs are formed is interesting. At the end of the last ice age, around 10,000 years ago, many hollows left by glacial moraines were filled with water, forming shallow lakes. Reeds and other plants grew around the edges of these lakes, and also extended into the water. When these plants died, they were unable to decompose completely because of the wet environment and ended up on the bed of the lakes. Over time, a thick layer of peat was formed that slowly rose to the lake surface and was eventually invaded by sedges to form a fen. As time passed, the fen continued to grow as the lake reduced in size. Hence a raised bog was formed.

View north from Ballydrum Bridge

A fen wetland system is fed by groundwater, which is rich in nutrients such as calcium, and the habitat is predominantly alkaline. In contrast, rainwater becomes the only source of water for plants in a raised bog, being poor in minerals and thus acidic.

This unique habitat supports sphagnum moss, which thrives in such conditions, appearing in a variety of colours such as red, yellow or green, depending on how wet or dry the soil is. The bog also supports some

Two elder trees in flower

carnivorous plants, such as sundews, butterworts and bladderworts that eat insects for extra nutrition. Probably the best known plant is bog cotton, whose brilliant white, fluffy flowers, on narrow bare stems, wave at you as you pass.

Peatlands are also home to the Irish hare and the common frog, as well as red grouse, lapwing and curlew. Many insects thrive here, including dragonflies and damselflies.

Walking northwards, I notice to the west the big Cats at work in Begnagh Bog extracting peat. On one side, there is a tract of bog covered in grass, looking untouched. In contrast, on the other side, there is a vast carpet of deep brown, patterned by the bucket's work, and the tracks of these enormous machines. However, the low, distant hum from them does not interfere with the soothing, peaceful experience walking through this peaty paradise. Further on, an ESB power line from Lough Ree Power Station at Lanesborough crosses the canal.

After 1.5 kilometres, I arrive at the Bord Na Móna Bridges. The first one is a light, non-automatic railway lifting bridge and is normally kept in the open position. The rail line runs to the power station at Lanesborough, carrying supplies of turf. A branch of it also crosses the Shannon, about two kilometres north of the station, joining a network

Canal widens after Savage Bridge

of light railway lines traversing this huge bog east and west of the river. A sign at the edge of the bog warns the pedestrian:

> *BEWARE*
> *RAILWAY CROSSING*
> *STOP*
> *LOOK*
> *LISTEN*
> *BEFORE CROSSING*

The second bridge is a very solid structure and is a high-level machinery crossing. After a gulp of refreshing water, I carry on.

The protection of our bogs has become a controversial issue. Ireland has a high proportion of Europe's few remaining peatlands, placing an international responsibility on us to conserve them. A bog must be drained before it can be harvested. As peat dries out, some of the carbon stored in it is released into the atmosphere. The remainder is released when the peat is burned as fuel. According to An Taisce, of all the fuel sources used to generate electricity and heat in Ireland, peat is the most damaging to the climate.

View south of Begnagh Lifting Bridge

Bord na Móna had produced fuel for the domestic market since the early decades of the new state, as well as supplying fuel to ESB's peat-fired power stations. Both of these companies have, for a long time, given huge employment, especially in the Midlands, helping to stem emigration from these vulnerable areas.

Since my walk through this beautiful habitat, all has changed. Bord na Móna had been winding down since 2018. Their 'brown to green' strategy sees the company now fully focussed on renewable energy generation, recycling and the development of other low carbon enterprises. Word is that employees have been retrained for new roles and that these changes have not impacted on staff numbers.

Following on from this, the ESB peat-fired generating stations at Lanesboro and Shannonbridge have been decommissioned.

On a smaller scale, Irish families have been cutting turf for heating their homes for centuries, after Ireland lost its source of timber for fuel through deforestation. Many families still own turf banks, and turf is now generally cut by machine, rather than the traditional method of using a sleán. These remote rural households depend on the turf as their primary source of fuel.

Big Cats at work on Begnagh Bog

After a short distance, I arrive at the 45th Lock, Rinnmount. This is the penultimate one on the canal, and so I am on the home stretch now to Richmond Harbour. Joy surges through me with the expectation of what might lie at my journey's end.

Beyond the 45th Lock, there are mooring posts along the canal bank, with a number of boats tied up displaying such names such as *Lé Cheile* and *Royal Blue*. As I carry on, I become aware of traffic, and then voices from a nearby house. Further on, a man is preparing his fishing tackle.

'You look like you're just starting out,' I say.

'Just about to make my first cast,' he responds.

'Well, I wish you luck. I hope you catch something for supper,' I continue.

'Maybe you'll bring me luck,' he says. 'But there's actually a catch and release policy along here, so I won't be seeing any on my plate.'

'I'm sure you'll enjoy the fishing anyway,' I reply.

'Oh, that's for sure,' he says.

'What type of fish are you hoping to catch?' I ask him.

'It will most likely be perch or roach,' he replies. 'Although if I hooked a tench I'd be delighted, as they put up such a good fight.'

Bidding him goodbye, I continue on.

The towpath now leads onto a road for the last few hundred metres to Richmond Harbour. Back when the canal was in its heyday, it was one of the two biggest harbours on the Royal Canal, the other being Broadstone.

Having walked 146 kilometres, Richmond Harbour now awaits me. The view from Richmond Bridge is a perfect panorama out over this wonderful cut stone construction, which opens out to the east and west, sheltering at least twenty boats, a mixture of barges, cruisers and small craft.

Cloondara village, which takes its name from the Irish, Cluain Da Rath, meaning the Meadow of Two Ringforts, was a purpose-built terminal to cater for the canal traffic, with the harbour at its centre. On the east side it is lined with old, stately Georgian buildings of one, two and three storeys, one dated 1817, the year the canal was completed to Richmond Harbour. They were built to house the harbour master, the lockkeeper and the inn, as well as storage and office facilities.

Thrush

View north from Richmond Bridge to Richmond Harbour

I stroll to the far end of the harbour and finally reach the 46th Lock, where the Royal Canal ends as it meets up with the Camlin River. A Waterways Ireland sign welcomes me to the Shannon Navigation. I gaze elated, lost in time, taking in this man-made confluence, filled with a deep sense of accomplishment.

The Camlin River is a tributary of the River Shannon, rising near Granard. After it splits in two, one branch enters the Shannon near Lough Forbes. The other branch flows south to Cloondara, connecting with the River Shannon, via the Cloondara Canal, just below the weir at Termonbarry. The three waterways form a 10 kilometre loop, one of the paddling trails of the Shannon Blueway.

I stroll curiously along the river bank and discover a weir straddling the Camlin and a five arch bridge crossing it. Returning to the lock, I admire the fine lockhouse, with its original grey stone exposed. A dry dock with lock gates at its entrance, standing off this east bank, serves for boat repairs.

Back at Richmond Bridge, I cross over to a prominent three and four-storey industrial type limestone building. It was originally built

46th Lock

Sign for Shannon Navigation at confluence of Camlin River and Royal Canal

as a corn mill in 1771 during a boom period for the corn milling industry. In 1827 it was converted for use as a whiskey distillery, when it produced over 10,000 gallons of whiskey annually. However, during the Father Matthew Temperance crusade it was reinstated as a corn mill in 1843.

The building eventually fell into a state of disrepair, before being refurbished in 2005 and converted into apartments. The round-headed arch that carried the former millrace through the building is preserved and the remains of the timber and iron water wheel can be seen beneath it. Still functioning, this building remains a special part of the village's heritage.

It starts to rain again. Although still early, I enter the Richmond Inn, with its inviting cream walls and contrasting red door, to see if it is possible to check in. The friendly young girl shows me to my clean and cosy room. I chat with her while enjoying a sandwich and a cup of coffee in the bar. She outlines the route to the Shannon along the Cloondara Canal.

Dry dock

After lunch, I set off full of enthusiasm to see that huge river, the largest in Ireland, which swallows up numerous channels of water along its course. I cross over Richmond Bridge, passing the old mill apartments.

I stop at the relatively modern church in Cloondara. In the graveyard beside it stand the roofless remains of an old church, with a beautiful arched stone entrance.

Further on, a small gate to my left, next to an old school building, leads me along a passageway onto the banks of the Cloondara Canal, which is less than one kilometre long. The

Termonbarry Lock on the Shannon

sun is now glistening through the trees, casting diverse shadows on the water. I soon arrive at Cloondara Lock, known locally as Bourke's Lock after the lockkeeper John Bourke who was once in charge of both it and the lock at Termonbarry.

Alas, the rest of the pathway from here is closed for renovation. The River Shannon is visible in the distance, but not close enough to satisfy. A little dispirited, but undaunted, I decide to seek out this elusive river by the longer route, via the N5 to Termonbarry. Soon I am standing on an enormous bridge spanning the broad expanse of the Shannon, which carries heavy traffic between Longford Town and Strokestown. A control hut operates a lifting section of the bridge to allow larger boats pass beneath it.

The river is relatively shallow at this point and boats need to follow the navigable channel rising or falling through the large lock here at Termonbarry. As an alternative, some boats use the route that loops around via the Cloondara Canal and the Camlin River.

When I cross the bridge at Termonbarry, I have also crossed the County Longford boundary, entering County Roscommon. I feel as if I am standing in the centre of Ireland as it is here Leinster meets Connaught, east meets west.

Termonbarry Lifting Bridge

Turning left at Keenan's Boutique Hotel, I follow the path leading down to the weir and lock on the Shannon. The limestone weir, which dates from circa 1845, is a very impressive piece of engineering, given that the Shannon is approximately 150 metres wide at this point. In the mid-twentieth century sluice gates were added, designed to regulate the water levels in the Shannon Navigation, and can be accessed by a railed walkway. The lock, with its walls of cut stone, is close to the weir. It is a huge structure compared to locks on the canal, and the chamber seems enormous.

Standing on the bank of this great river I begin to feel the pulse of Ireland's heartland. As I look across at the entrance to the Cloondara Canal, I picture it connecting with the Camlin River, which in turn connects into the Royal Canal. I begin to fully realize that this confluence of waterways allows a vessel to travel from the mouth of the Liffey to the Shannon Estuary.

Beyond Termonbarry Lock, the Shannon bulges into what resembles a small lake, before continuing on south towards Limerick. I stand for a while listening to the water lapping against the bank, and the sound of the reeds above it moving in rhythm to the gentle breeze.

I ponder on these villages of Cloondara and Termonbarry, once hubs of trade and economic activity, with barges loading and unload-

The weir at Termonbarry

ing. They now attract tourists interested in the navigation of pleasure craft, following waterway trails, or seeking to get close to nature.

This heartland beats with ancient stories of the Táin and of Cúchulainn, who took on Queen Medb's huge army single-handed. It vibrates with the footsteps of evicted tenants from Strokestown Estate in County Roscommon, as they travelled to the waiting coffin ships in Dublin Port. It throbs with the enthusiasm of the newly independent Irish Free State, as it sought to harness the power of the River Shannon to generate electricity at Ardnacrusha, approximately 150 kilometres downstream from here. It succeeded in keeping the Shannon navigable by building a 30 metre deep lock, the deepest lock in these isles. I picture these waterways as the heart of the past, present and future of this place. They are an intrinsic part of the connectivity of our country.

As I stroll back to the village, I see a sign explaining that the Irish name, Tearmann Bearaigh, means Barry's Sanctuary, or more commonly, the Church of St. Bearaigh, who lived at the end of the sixth century. From a notable Leitrim clan, he was under the tutelage of St. Dagaeus, who sent him to Glendalough for further instruction under St. Kevin.

Dagaeus presented the boy with the Bachall Gearr Bearaigh or the Short Crozier of St. Berach. Made of yew wood and yellow bronze, this sacred relic was known for solving disputes. The two parties involved would clasp their hands together over it and swear their agreement to the proposed solution. It now rests in the National Museum in Dublin. After his schooling at Glendalough, Berach founded his church at what came to be known as Kilbarry or Termon Barry.

A beautiful grotto is at the core of its main street. Our Lady stands in a cut stone wall from which water trickles, reminiscent of a lock chamber. A solitary devotee is kneeling in prayer. On top of the grotto is a sculpture of a heron, a bird which has been my loyal companion for so many stretches of towpath along this canal. I smile as I see it and almost expect it to flap away down the street.

An information sign and map of the Táin Cycle Route shows the route Queen Medb of Connaught set out on with her army in the legendary Táin Bó Cuailnge or Cattle Raid of Cooley. Her intention was to look for a loan of the Brown Bull of Cooley for one year, from the Ulsterman Dáire mac Fiachna, as it was the only one in the country that could match her husband's prize white bull. When Dáire refused, she decided to steal it, while the Men of Ulster were suffering under a curse called the Pangs of Ulster, so were unable to fight. The defence of Ulster rested with the seventeen year old Cúchulainn. Over a number

Grotto at Termonbarry

Shannon Waterway

of days he slaughtered thousands of Medb's warriors, until finally, the Men of Ulster began to recover their strength.

However, Medb managed to capture the brown bull and fled back to Connacht. A fight ensued between the white bull and the brown that lasted all day and all night. By morning, the brown bull had defeated the white bull. But its victory was short lived and it died two days later. Medb and her husband Ailill made peace with Cúchulainn and with Ulster, a peace that lasted seven years.

The Táin Cycle Route follows along parts of what used to be another of the five great Slí or roads through ancient Ireland, linking Rathcroghan to the Hill of Tara.

I saunter back to Cloondara with a warm sense of fulfilment. Back in my room I write up my observations of the day. A generous feed of fish, chips and salad satisfies my hunger. As the sun sits low in the west I take a final stroll about this enchanting harbour.

Back at the inn, the jukebox in the bar is entertaining people brimming with energy. I enjoy the music over a couple of pints before bedtime. However, it won't be a late night, as I need to replenish my resources before I embark on the final stretch of my walk tomorrow, the yet unexplored Longford Branch. When I return contented to the bedroom, my body and mind are so weary that sleep comes fast.

21.

CLOONDARA TO LONGFORD TOWN

Butterflies, a Buried Harbour, a Cathedral and a Workhouse

Early next morning I am ready to embrace the final stage of my journey which will take me to Longford Town. When I've had my fill from the tasty Richmond Inn breakfast I find I have enough left over to make a substantial sandwich for my lunch, with the helpful owner offering tinfoil.

Today's forecast is for a mixture of overcast skies, sunshine and a cool refreshing breeze. I have been blessed on this trip with very little rain and temperatures requiring me to wear the minimum of clothing.

Judging by my observations yesterday, it should be possible to walk the opposite towpath all the way back to the Longford Branch Junction. So I decide to give it a go but soon discover that the path is rough and uneven. Although the grass has been cut somewhat, it is still concealing the dips and hollows underneath. However, by proceeding with care, it does not pose too much of a problem.

Making good progress I soon arrive at the Bord na Móna Bridges. I discover that it is not easy to skirt around them on this east towpath, with no obvious track through this boggy ground. While weighing up my options, I have the good fortune to disturb a frog, which surprises me as he leaps. I bide my time examining this amphibian, with its slimy skin mottled with varying shades of brown, with white stripes on either side of its body. Amphibian comes from a Greek word

Cruiser near Richmond Harbour

meaning both lives, referring to the fact that frogs start their lives in water, before making themselves at home on land. Frogs need water, or a moist environment, to survive. So this expansive bog provides the perfect habitat for them.

The grass here is coloured by bird's-foot-trefoil. Some of the flower clusters are yellow and some orange, presenting a bright, warm image to savour. With care and patience, I manage to arrive back on the rough grassy towpath once more.

The white flowers of wild angelica flush pink, as if in shyness, as I pass sights I had seen yesterday. The bankside vegetation is in full bloom on this stretch, in particular the most wonderful display of spotted orchids I have ever seen, a row of mauve delight. The occasional yellow buttercup presents itself amid this floral flourish. My next few steps take me by the tiny, white flower clusters of some marsh-bedstraw, a little closer to the water. They dance delightfully in the breeze on their delicate stems.

Spotted Orchids

Passing by a wood of silver birch, I arrive at the junction with the Longford Branch. Having put 8 kilometres behind me to reach this confluence, I already have half my journey for today complete. I follow the gravel towpath as it curves away from the main line of the canal, making its way towards the northeast and Longford Town.

The Longford Branch presented some difficult engineering problems because part of the canal was through boggy terrain. This was compounded by opposition to its construction by local people from Killashee and Richmond Harbour. They had concerns regarding the effect it would have on their trade, and the canal works were breached maliciously on several occasions. When the branch was officially opened in January 1830, local fears were soon realised as Longford Town became the centre for the trade boats and a passenger boat terminus.

The Longford Branch of the Royal Canal is mostly dry. I see now that the water flows about 25 metres into the branch and is then stopped by an earthen bank, which effectively acts as a dam and serves as a path over the canal. From here on, the walk is totally different. The absence of water is strange at first, but I soon become accustomed to shrubs and trees replacing it in the canal bed below me.

Typical bridge growth on Longford Branch

Cloonsheeerin Accommodation Bridge

A few scattered oxeye daisies rise gloriously from the grass near the junction, enhanced by the magenta of willowherb. The protruding stamens of devil's-bit scabious give it a fluffy appearance. My ears are drawn to the buzzing in those violet-blue flower heads, nodding on their long, narrow stems. Industrious bees hum as they extract nectar from these rich storehouses, and in the process transfer pollen to other plants, thus maintaining the cycle of growth. The abundant variety of wildflowers along the Longford Branch make this a haven for insects and butterflies, and on this increasingly sunny day I encounter them in great numbers.

Reeds rise to a good height along the water's edge leading up to the dam. Beyond it, the canal bed itself is full of reeds and sallies all the way to Cloonsheerin Accommodation Bridge, where I stop for coffee and a biscuit. As I eat, I have the company of a herd of cattle in a nearby field.

I can see through the tangle of shrubbery that this towpath goes under the bridge, which would have given ease of passage to horses pulling the barges.

Feeling refreshed, I set out again along a corridor of trees and shrubs. The taller growth in the hedgerow is recessed, so that the closer ferns have space to stretch out their fronds. The scorching sun glares down from the south. However, I can find shade by these tall trees, as well as the lower trees stretching up from the canal bed, two metres below me.

Bird's-foot-trefoil

View of trees and canal bed from Newtown Bridge

I notice the growth in the hedgerow being replicated again and again along the canal bed, evidence of nature's ability to reproduce and multiply.

As I pass a small hazel wood, the towpath is suddenly transformed into a yellow carpet of bird's-foot-trefoil, which is under investigation by a peacock butterfly. Its red wings are stunningly coloured with large eyespots. The small tortoiseshell flitting past is quite different. Although it is our most common butterfly, it is still exceedingly beautiful. Its colour is predominantly reddish-orange, with black markings and blue spots around the wing border. A few more steps and there is no mistaking the pale-pink petals of herb Robert. Everything I pass is eye-catching as I walk through nature's wonderland.

As I approach Aghantrah Bridge, I see that its walls and capstones are overgrown and wild strawberries have rooted there. The view is like eavesdropping on a forest canopy as I look out across the treetops that have risen from the canal bed below. The towpath on the east side again runs under the bridge.

I continue along the west towpath within my green enclosure. The Fallon River runs below a wooden fence. It is a tributary of the Shannon, but also links into the Camlin River.

The canal bed becomes more open as the vegetation is slightly lower than the towpath. The delicious fragrance of woodbine fills the air, and I see its slender, creamy-yellow, trumpet-shaped flowers outshining the other delights of the hedgerow. This highly perfumed climbing plant is also called honeysuckle due to the practice of children sucking the flower for its sweet tasting nectar. However, its wood becomes hard as it matures, and can choke off the growth of any tree it wraps around. This has

Canal towpath

made it a symbol in Irish legend of strength and slow, inexorable power. I wonder how long these entangled shrubs will survive under her tight hold!

The vegetation rising from the dry bed keeps changing. Sometimes there are trees such as sycamore, beech, hawthorn or elder, and sometimes bulrush or ferns. In one case, dog roses had spread their colour up the full height of one tree, presenting an astounding display. A row of silver birch leads me to Newtown Accommodation Bridge. Ivy is beginning to engulf it and there are a number of ash tree saplings growing from the capstones. I never cease to wonder where seeds might find a niche in which to germinate.

I pick my steps over cowpats on the towpath, evidence that cattle have been herded along here. Looking skyward, I am rewarded with the sight of a marvellous buzzard soaring high overhead. It hovers in the air above, seeking out its prey in the dense vegetation below. This dry, overgrown canal bed must be a rich source of food for such predators.

I have now arrived at a beautiful, traditional whitewashed cottage, set just back off the canal bank, with its door, windows and gables painted red, and a well-tended lawn surrounded by a cut stone wall.

Lovely cottage on the canal

The weather vane, which incorporates a depiction of a swan, is a distinctive feature.

I soon arrive at Cloonturk Accommodation Bridge. Clumps of grass are growing between the capstones, and ferns are emerging from its side. The canal bed here is a wild growth of mostly hazels and sallies.

A passing cyclist dismounts, stopping for a chat.

'Grand day,' he says.

'Perfect for a stroll or cycle,' says I.

'Ah sure it's the life, so it is,' he proclaims. 'I'm retired and I keep myself fit by cycling the paths of the canal.'

'Oh, a bit like myself,' I reply, 'except my pleasure is walking, which helps to keep me fit too.'

'Wonderful,' says he. 'I've had an extra-long ride today, as I cycled from Longford Town all the way to Cloondara. I'm on the way home now, so I best be away.'

'That was some cycle. Nice talking to you and safe home,' I answer, as he mounts and cycles off.

It's as if the passers-by on the canal, whether walker or cyclist, have found a kindred spirit through their love of this lovely waterway.

The towpath switches to the east bank. As I leave the bridge, I have an open view of a number of houses across green fields and can also see Stonepark National School, helping to identify where I am. It has the beautiful sounding Irish name of Gort na Cloiche, or Field of Stone.

Traffic on a nearby road is now audible and the towpath runs alongside it. Local people can access the canal on foot from this road. However, I continue along the towpath, passing through a gate across it on the way. There is a large bath tub in the next field, which acts as a convenient container to hold drinking water for animals.

Resuming my walk I soon arrive at the old Knockanboy Bridge. After stopping at a yield sign, I cross the minor road that traverses it. A man leaning on the bridge salutes me and I wave back. After a short stroll along the towpath, another yield sign, beside a wooden gate, halts me again. I have arrived at the N63 culverted road crossing, under which the waterway is ducted. I cross this busy thoroughfare with care, where a second wooden gate leads me safely back onto the towpath.

Knockanboy Bridge

The menacing presence of giant hogweed looms before me on the canal bank. An unwelcome invasive species, this specimen is about one metre tall, but they can grow as high as three metres. It is phototoxic and can cause severe blistering of the skin if touched.

Bees are busy visiting the reddish-purple flowers of the nearby knapweed. Horsetails now become quite prevalent among the plants growing in the canal bed.

There is another culverted road crossing over the N63, just before Churchland Bridge. To the northeast I spot a sign for Longford. Crossing the road, I am presented with a manicured bed of flowers, shrubs and heathers, in bloom right now. What a display of colour: red, cream, orange, white, pink and a very vivid blue, richly impacting on my senses.

The original cut stone bridge at Churchland was built circa 1829 and is sadly gone. It was replaced completely in 1935 by this functional bridge of reinforced concrete. This in turn has been made redundant by the culverted road crossing, which was part of a road straightening and widening scheme. The history of the changing bridges highlights the modernisation of Ireland, and in particular the increased use of cars as a means of transport.

Flower beds at Churchlands Bridge

Community walkway at Churchlands

Beyond the bridge, I discover a picnic table and some interesting information signs. There is a five kilometre looped walking route, using both towpaths, from Market Square in Longford Town to Churchlands Bridge and back. Public lighting adds to the safety of an evening stroll.

A sign here reads Bird and Bat Boxes, and yet another proclaims this to be an Alcohol Free Area. An information chart, close to the picnic table, outlines the bird species that might be seen along the canal, such as mallard, mute swan, moorhen and song thrush.

After Churchlands Bridge, I find myself walking through a beautiful tree-lined avenue along the east towpath. A couple pass, then a lone girl, followed by a mother pushing her baby in a buggy, all enjoying this accessible towpath. I sense the closeness of civilization.

Some factories on the outskirts of Longford Town signal the approach of the urban. However, nature persists with its rural variety as a maple tree in the hedgerow dwarfs a snowberry bush. A curious mossy growth patterns the trunks of the nearby ash, while chaffinches sing cheerfully from among their branches.

Tree-lined avenue

In the hedgerow, the small, violet bells of Russian comfrey are in full flower. This tall plant is rich in potash, a gardener's delight. The hairy leaves can be put in a compost bin with other compostable materials. Alternatively, they can be steeped in a bucket of water until they become smelly, just like any good fertiliser. The resultant fluid can then be used to feed tomatoes and potatoes.

There is a dam across the water on the approach to Farranyoogan Bridge. From here to Longford Town the canal has been re-watered, fed from local springs and developed as a local amenity. Leaks occurred here at some masonry culverts carrying streams under the canal, and the building of this dam was one of the measures taken to combat this.

Except for patches of ivy and moss, Farranyoogan Bridge is reasonably clear of growth, and the lovely patterned stonework is visible. There is a good view of Longford Town to the west, with the spires of St. Mel's Cathedral and of the Church of St. John getting gradually closer.

Beyond the bridge, the canal bed is full of reeds, bordered along the bank's edge by the brightness of yellow flag, but as the reeds slowly recede to their proper place in the fringes, water becomes more and more

Farranyoogan Bridge

evident, with lily pads floating on top. It is all starting to look more like the familiar canal again, as the beauty of the waterway is restored.

The water is alive with ducks and moorhens, living in close proximity to each other. Perhaps a continuous supply of food from local people encourages this, as well as the abundance of reeds providing camouflage for what must be dozens of hidden nests.

On the bank, I come across a mature moorhen accompanied by its young. To my surprise, they do not flutter off at speed, as they are prone to do elsewhere on the canal. These birds are fearless, having become accustomed to the walker and passers-by.

Across the fields lies the local GAA Club, with the wonderful name of the Longford Slashers. Soon after, I pass Longford Greyhound Stadium, which is quite close to the canal.

The rural and the urban now suddenly meet. Behind a farm gate, cattle graze in an overgrown field, and beyond them a tractor is busy cutting grass. All this is taking place next to a housing estate, a hedgerow the only separation between them.

Moorhens

A charm of finches flies overhead, before dancing through the foliage of the trees. They are answered by the laughter of children having fun in the gardens of the nearby houses.

Suddenly, I am at the end of the Longford Branch. A murder of crows screeches overhead, as if to reflect my creaking bones. However, my head and spirit rejoice as the air is filled with the ringing of bells from St. Mel's Cathedral, as though the town is celebrating my arrival. A sign reads:

> *Royal Canal Longford – Transforming Ireland – this project has been funded by the Irish Government under the National Development Plan 2007-2013.*

The ground rises towards the railway line and some old railway buildings 100 metres away. Originally, the canal continued on from here and having passed under the railway, opened out into an expansive harbour at Market Square. Unfortunately, like Broadstone Harbour, all of this has been infilled. Apparently the original stonework of the harbour is in situ under it; a buried heritage. Perhaps the effort of the Royal Canal Amenity Group to have the Longford Branch re-watered in its entirety will uncover this lost harbour. It would certainly be an attractive proposition to boaters, as there are only four locks between Longford Town and the River Shannon.

Set on limestone slabs, a series of bronze sculptures by Mel French are interspersed on this grassy embankment. They explore and celebrate the theme of emigration. An introductory piece states:

> *Longford Town Council dedicates this public sculpture as recognition and celebration of the achievements of Longford emigrants worldwide.*

French sculpted each piece as a bronze suitcase, with a section cut out, within which are figures representing the skill sets of each occupation that left for distant shores: science, business, politics, anthropology, sport, performance arts and academia. Accompanying each is a

One of many sculptures at end of Longford Branch

definition of some aspect of the particular profession. I stop to ponder these visual delights and the circumstances of each person's departure,

Soon after, I continue on under the railway bridge and out onto Market Square. It is easy to visualise how this large square was once the terminus of the Longford Branch of the Royal Canal. The former Harbour Master's house lies to the west side and is testament to this. The distinctive building is a detached two-storey structure, built of cut limestone, with a pitched roof of grey slate and a gable at each end. There is a timber canopy, with decorative bargeboard over the front door, adding to its attraction. It is currently in use as offices. The beige-coloured four and five-storey apartments on either side are completely out of character with most of the older buildings that encompass the square.

My stroll along the Longford Branch of the Royal Canal has given me time to reflect on the demise of its original function and on its slow resurrection as an amenity. The infilled harbour and the de-watered branch tell the story of a time of change in Irish transport.

Beginning in the mid-nineteenth century, the gradual transition to moving goods by rail instead of by water eventually saw the Royal Canal becoming redundant to a large extent.

Former Harbour Master's house

When this canal closed in 1961 it seemed that its fate had been sealed. However, a number of interested groups had a vision that entailed a different purpose for it. In 1974, Dr. Ian Bath founded the Royal Canal Amenity Group with the aim of highlighting the amenity potential of a restored canal. Work began on clearing the channel and towpath. The group spread to towns and villages along the canal. In 1986, the ownership was transferred from CIÉ to the OPW, who together with the RCAG worked on the canal's restoration. Waterways Ireland was set up in 1999 as part of the Belfast Agreement. By 2011, the Royal Canal had been completely restored from the Liffey to the Shannon.

If this gem of waterway heritage had been appreciated earlier, perhaps the Longford Branch might never have been de-watered. However, it remains an access route to the restored Royal Canal, facilitating the use of the towpaths by local people and visitors. It is also a route that is abundant with plant, animal, bird and insect life; an area of unique biodiversity.

Leaving Market Square, I set off to explore Longford Town. I make my way to St. Mel's Cathedral, the principle landmark, which first opened in 1856. St. Mel is the patron saint of the combined diocese of Ardagh and Clonmacnoise.

On entering the cathedral courtyard, I am faced with an enormous stepped base, from which rise the majestic Ionic columns of the portico, framing the cathedral entrance. The pediment above it depicts St. Patrick consecrating St. Mel, as the first bishop of the diocese. Rising high above it all is an Italianate campanile tower, which is a dominant feature on the town's skyline. The interior is elaborately decorated, containing a mosaic tiled floor and pine confessionals and pews. The windows are stained glass, the ones in the chapels of the two transepts being originally designed in the famous Harry Clarke studios.

I say originally, because on Christmas Day, 2009, fire spread through the building. The daunting task of rebuilding the cathedral was eventually completed, with the cherished stained glass reinstated.

St Mel's Cathedral

The dedication of all involved resulted in St. Mel's being officially re-opened at Christmas 2014.

Exiting the cathedral, I walk to Ballymahon Street, where I pass many brightly painted, terraced business premises before continuing onto Main Street. Here, at the junction of Dublin Street and Geraldine's Terrace, believed to be close to the original site of the Cunard Shipping Line booking office, is an emigration memorial in brass and limestone by the County Mayo sculptor Rory Breslin. It is very much in tune with Mel French's series of suitcases on the canal bank. It depicts a man and a woman, each clutching their passage ticket. Curiously, although the setting is nineteenth century, the figures are dressed in modern clothes, perhaps to highlight the ongoing nature of emigration. The circular limestone plinth bears an inscription by Catherine Lynch:

> *Some leave by choice, some by necessity. All are missed. Always welcome home.*

Rory Breslin's emigration memorial

The well-groomed figures in this sculpture are in stark contrast to the emaciated figures in Rowan Gillespie's famine memorial on Custom House Quay in Dublin.

Longford Courthouse, which stands three storeys high, is one of the oldest buildings in the town, dating back to 1793. Interestingly, it had an underground tunnel to the jail on Battery Road through which prisoners were taken on their way to be hanged.

A building further along Main Street, with a coach arch and pedimented door and windows, was formerly a gentlemen's club which was founded in the 1890s and operated until the

1920s. Its members were mainly local shop owners and men from the legal profession. It was essentially a men's social club, away from female interference, where men could relax and converse. The building is now a business premises.

I arrive at a bridge where steps lead down to a peaceful walk by the Camlin River in the Albert Reynolds Peace Park, which has a children's playground, a swimming pool, and a number of sporting facilities, including an outdoor gym and astro-turf.

I continue along the short length of Bridge Street. At a sharp bend in the road, I see the gates leading to Seán Connolly Barracks, built in 1815 and known as Longford Town Cavalry Barracks. It was renamed after Brigadier Seán Connolly of the Longford Brigade who, during the War of Independence, was fatally wounded in action in 1921 by British forces.

As I have discovered, while visiting Ballymahon, County Longford is very proud of its prolific literary genre. Longford County Council has acknowledged this in a unique way by naming roundabouts on the Longford N4 bypass after three of them. One is named after John Keegan Leo Casey, whose acclaim I discovered at Ballymahon Library.

Another roundabout is named after Charlotte Brooke who died in 1793. Charlotte was the daughter of the playwright and novelist Henry Brooke. She was educated by her father, who rejected strong discipline, letting the child's curiosity be part of her learning. Her most famous book, *Reliques of Irish Poetry*, contains her translations of poems, alongside their original Irish versions. Brooke herself acknowledged the difficulty of the task, assuring her readers that it is a reflection of the inadequacy of English to convey the beauty peculiar to the Gaelic language. Thus Charlottes takes her place in the history of Irish literature, as a forerunner of the literary movement for the revival of Irish in the nineteenth century.

The third roundabout has been dedicated to Padraic Colum, one of Longford's most famous writers. Colum was born in Longford Town, in 1881, in what was then the workhouse, where his father Patrick was master. The workhouse environment, where he made acquaintance with the homeless men who stayed there, helped inspire his work. He had a long and productive career as a poet, playwright, essayist, editor, folklorist, biographer and a writer of children's stories. Colum had also played a major part in the founding of the Abbey theatre.

In 1912, Colum married the teacher and activist Mary (Mollie) Maguire. In 1914, they decided to visit America, staying there eight years. After this they lived in Europe and later Hawaii. It was here that Colum was employed by the legislature to collect folklore. The couple finally settled in New York, where both lectured at Columbia University.

After his wife's death in 1957, Colum continued lecturing, writing and editing volumes of poetry until the late 1960s. In 1963, he became a member of the American Academy of Arts and Letters. He died at the age of ninety in 1972 and is buried in Sutton, County Dublin.

Sculpture in Longford

Padraic Colum, of necessity, worked into old age as he had no pension. Some writers, such as Anthony Cronin, considered this disgraceful and began a campaign directed towards Charles Haughey and his government. It eventually led to the establishment of Aosdána (translated as people of the arts) in 1981, which was set up to support Irish artists, some of whom would receive a State-funded stipend from the Arts Council.

The beautiful haunting ballad, 'She Moved Through the Fair', which Colum adapted from traditional material, was published in his book *Wild Earth and Other Poems*.

Encountering the tragedy of homelessness in his youth, Colum was moved to write 'An Old Woman of the Road'. We first hear of her wish for her own little house. However, in a later verse we are suddenly confronted with the reality of her life.

> *Och! but I'm weary of mist and dark,*
> *And roads where there's never a house nor bush,*
> *And tired I am of bog and road,*
> *And the crying wind and the lonesome hush!*

Finally she prays to God on high for a little house that is,

> *Out of the wind's and the rain's way.*

I retire to the comfort of the Longford Arms, where I sit to appease my hunger before walking to the station. Boarding the train, I sit back to savour the sights of the Central Plain as we chug our way eastwards. At Edgeworthstown, the train stops for about 20 minutes.

My thoughts turn to Maria Edgeworth, who together with her father Richard wrote *Practical Education* in 1798. One of its main principles argued that a desire to learn is best achieved through play. This system was way ahead of its time and in some ways emulated the beliefs of Charlotte Brooke's father. Maria went on to write *Castle Rackrent*, in which she was critical of the exploitative practices of many Protestant land owners.

Finally, as the train pulls out of Edgeworthstown I sit back and enjoy the scenes that flash past my window. This wonderful rhythmical ride brings me towards a more northerly stretch of the River Inny, crossing it close to the haunting Lough Derravaragh, before swishing me south by the great canal feeder of Lough Owel. Finally, at Mullingar, the railway meets up with the Royal Canal, and I am back on familiar territory. I am swept past lines of native trees, forests of conifers, bogs, vast crops of cereal, church spires, fields dotted with cows and sheep, landscaped studs and bales of hay, as I nurture a deep sense of satisfaction and accomplishment on completing this amazing journey.

A final look at the Royal Canal

BIBLIOGRAPHY

Canal History and Guides

Clarke, Peter, *The Royal Canal: The Complete Story*, Elo Publications, 1992

Clarke, Peter, *Walking the Royal Canal: History and Local History*, Published by Canalwalks in association with the Royal Canal Amenity Group Ltd., 2016

Cox, Ronald and Donald, Philip, *Ireland's Civil Engineering Heritage*, Collins Press, 2013

Delaney, Ruth and Bath, Ian, *Ireland's Royal Canal, 1789–2009*, Lilliput Press, 2010

Delaney, Ruth, *Ireland's Waterways: Map and Directory*, Waterways Ireland & Euromapping, 2006

Delaney, Ruth, *Ireland's Inland Waterways: Celebrating 300 years*, Appletree Press, 2004

Guide to the Royal Canal, Waterways Ireland & Inland Waterways Association of Ireland, 1994

Rolt, L.T.C., *Green & Silver*, Canal Book Shop, Fifth Edition, 2015

Nature

Anderson, Glynn, *Birds of Ireland: Facts, Folklore & History*, Collins Press, 2017

Conroy, Don & Wilson, Jim, *Bird Life in Ireland*, O'Brien Press, 1994

Dempsey, Eric and O'Clery, Michael, *Pocket Guide to the Common Birds of Ireland*, Gill & Macmillan Ltd, 1995

Devlin, Zoe, *The Wildflowers of Ireland: A Field Guide*, Collins Press, 2014

Mac Coitir, Niall, *Ireland's Trees: Myths, Legends and Folklore*, Collins Press, 2015

Mac Coitir, Niall, *Ireland's Wild Plants: Myths, Legends and Folklore*, Collins Press, 2015

V. Vetvicka and D. Tousova, *Wildflowers of Field and Woodland*, Magna Books, 1995

Wilde, Jane (Lady) *Ancient legends, Mystic Charms & Superstitions of Ireland*

Woodward, Marcus, *How to Enjoy Wild Flowers*, Hodder & Stoughton, 1927

Wyse-Jackson, Peter, *Irish Trees and Shrubs*, Appletree Press, 1994

Local History and Landscape

Curran, Linda; Twomey, Valerie; Donohoe, Patricia; and Pegley, Suzanne, *Aspects of Leixlip: Four Historical Essays*, LPSV Publishers, 2001

Horner, Arnold, *Irish Historic Towns Atlas: Maynooth*, Royal Irish Academy, 1995

Jebb, Matthew and Crowley, Colm, *Secrets of the Irish Landscape*, Atrium, 2013

Kelly, Martin J., *Cloncurry Through the Years*,

Kelly, Seamus, *A Walking Tour of Leixlip*,

Leixlip 2000, *Celebrating 100 Years: People, Place, Memory*, Leixlip Town Commissioners, 2000

Leixlip I.C.A., *Leixlip: A Local History*, Leixlip I.C.A., 1990

Manning, C., *Irish Field Monuments*, National Parks and Monuments Service, 1985

Literature

Behan, Kathleen & Behan, Brian, *Mother of all the Behans*, Poolbeg Press, 1994

Bolger, Dermot, *County Lives: The Clondalkin Suite*, Commissioned by South Dublin County Council through In Context 3 and funded under the Department of Environment, Heritage and Local Government's Per Cent for Art Scheme, 2008

Bolger, Dermot, *Reading Ireland, Interview with Adrienne Leavy*, 2020

Brayton, Teresa, *In an Irish Twilight*, The Teresa Brayton Heritage Group, 2002

Dáibhís, Bríd, Cosán Na Gréine, *Dánta le Bríd Dáibhís*, Coiscéim, 1989

Goldsmith, Oliver, *The Poetical and Prose Works of Oliver Goldsmith*, National Press, Dublin

Harvey, Francis, *Collected Poems*, Dedalus Press, 2007

Joyce, James, *Ulysses*, Penguin Edition, 1968

McMahon, Sean and O'Donoghue, Jo, *Brewer's Dictionary of Irish Phrase and Fable*, Weidenfeld & Nicolson, 2004

Monahan, Noel, *Curse of the Birds*, Salmon Poetry, 2000

The Táin: From the Irish Epic Táin Bó Cuailnge, translated by Thomas Kinsella

Bibliography

General

Bourke, Edward J., *The Guinness Story*, O'Brien Press, 2009

Byrne, Art amd McMahon, Seán, *Lives of 113 Great Men and Women*

Mac Thomáis, Shane, *Glasnevin: Ireland's Necropolis*,

Websites

buildingsofireland.ie

duchas.ie

https://irelandswildlife.com/squirrel-pine-marten/

https://www.academia.edu/38347463/Charlotte_Brooke

imdb.com

Irish Men of Learning. Studies by Father Paul Walsh, Edited by Colm O' Lochlainn. Dublin: Three Candles 1947

irishwildflowers.ie

kathleenlynn.net

kildare.ie/leixliphistory

kildarelocalhistory.ie

logainm.ie

longford.ie

moxhamireland.wordpress.com/newcomens-of-mosstown

nationalfamineway.ie

samueljohnson.com/goldsmith

sci.esa.int

waterwaysireland.org

wildflowersofireland.ie

www.antaisce.org

www.ipcc.ie

www.nli.ie/darcy_of_hydepark

Index

1st Lock, 13
2nd Lock, 19
3rd Lock, 20
4th Lock, 21
5th Lock, 28–9
6th Lock, 31, 33
7th Lock, 36
8th Lock, 44
9th Lock, 45
10th Lock, 46–7
11th Lock, 49–50
12th Lock, 52, 55, 65
13th Lock, 52, 65, 84–6
14th Lock, 102
15th Lock, 104
16th Lock, 105
17th Lock, 113
18th Lock, 54, 143
19th Lock, 144
20th Lock, 144
21st Lock, 144
22nd Lock, 146
23rd Lock, 151
24th Lock, 152
25th Lock, 152
26th Lock, 152, 181
27th Lock, 186
28th Lock, 186
29th Lock, 188–9
30th Lock, 188–9
31st Lock, 188–9
32nd Lock, 189
33rd Lock, 189
34th Lock, 190

35th Lock, 192
36th Lock, 200
37th Lock, 202
38th Lock, 203
39th Lock, 219
40th Lock, 240
41st Lock, 249
42nd Lock, 252
43rd Lock, 256
44th Lock, 261
45th Lock, 268
46th Lock, 270
Abbeyshrule, 207–17
Abbeyshrule Aerodrome and Airfield, 207
Aghnaskea Bridge, 256
Albert Reynolds Peace Park, 295
Allard's Accommodation Bridge, 219
Allen Bridge, 110
Amanda Levete Architects, 6
Archie's Bridge and Quay, 227, 234
Ards Bridge, 251
Ashton House, 47
Ashtown Mill, 47

Bailey's Accommodation Bridge, 102
Ballasport Bridge, 138
Ballinamore Bridges., 252
Ballinea Bridges, 36, 178
Ballybrannigan Harbour, 224–6
Ballydrum Accommodation Bridge, 261
Ballymahon, 219–29

Index

Ballynacargy, 192–9
Ballynacargy Harbour, 192–3
Ballymaglavy Bog, 205
Balroe Bridge, 190
Baltrasna Bridge, 163–4
Bardwell, Leland, 80
barges, 27, 53, 73, 92, 141
Battle of the Boyne, 132–3
Beckett, Samuel, 80, 259
Begnagh Bog, 263, 265
Begnagh Bridges, 263
Behan, Brendan, 15–17, 20
Behan, Kathleen, 16
Belvedere House and Gardens, 168–9
Bianconi, Charles, 223
Binns Bridge, 17–18
Binns, John, 18
Blackshade Bridge, 133
blackthorn, 34, 74, 90
Blackwater Aqueduct, 125–6
Blanchardstown Mill, 53
Blaquiere Bridge, 22
Boardstown Bridge, 165
Bog Bridge, 206
Bolger, Dermot, 42
Bond Bridge, 100
Bord Na Móna Bridges, 265
Brayton, Teresa, 117–8
Breslin, Rory, 294
Broadstone, 3, 21, 26, 73
Broadstone Harbour, 21, 27–8, 163, 177, 290
Brogan, Alan, 45
Brogan, Bernard, 45
Brooke, Charlotte, 295
Broome Bridge, *see* Hamilton Bridge
Broome, William, 39
Brú na Bóinne, 132
buttercups, 180

Cabra, 37–8
Cahill, Frank, 10
Callaghan Bridge, 62
Camlin River, 270, 273–4, 282, 295
canal boats, 53
Cappagh Bog, 115

Carton House, 78, 87, 91, 97–8
Carton Wharf, 90
Casement, Roger, 32
Casey, John Keegan Leo, 231–2, 295
Cassels, Richard, 89, 96
Castletown House, 79, 81, 99
Central Plain, 153, 163, 187, 189
Center Parcs holiday village, 221
Chaigneau Bridge, 224
Chamber's Bridge, 104
Churchland Bridge, 286
Cistercian Monastery, 211–12, 214
Clarke Bridge, 12, 14
Cloncurry Bridge, 112, 119–20
Clonliffe Bridge, 15
Cloonbreany Bog, 241
Cloonbreany Accommodation Bridge, 240
Cloondara, 269, 272, 274
Cloonsheerin Accommodation Bridge, 281
Coll, John, 19
Collins Bridge, 66–7
Collinstown Bridge, 82
Collinstown House, 83
Colum, Padraic, 295–7
Confey, 68–70
Conolly, Katherine, 81, 89
Conolly, Louisa, 78
Conolly, Thomas, 77, 99
Conolly's Folly, *see* The Obelisk
Coolnahay Harbour, 152, 181
Coolnahinch Bridge, 249
Cope, William, 72
Cope Bridge, 29, 69, 72
Corncrake Meadow, 214
Corlea Bog Visitor Centre, 241–2
cowslips, 124–5
Croke, Thomas, 14
Croke Park, 6, 14–15
Cross Guns Bridge, 21, 28
Crossover Bridge, 253
Cúchulainn, 276–7
cuckooflower, 164
Cunningham's Hideout Pub, 147–50
Curley, Barney, 195–6

da Vinci, Leonardo, 19
D'Arcy's Bridge, 141
daffodils, 105
Dáibhís, Bríd, 106–7
damselflies, 67, 202, 235, 265
dandelions, 109
Deep Sinking, 56–62, 75, 121
Deey Bridge, 84
Devlin, Anne, 32
Dolan, Joe, 171
Dolan Bridge, 183
Donleavy, J.P., 172
double-chambered locks, 19, 20, 29, 46, 47, 52, 105, 113
Downs Bridge, 161
Draper's Bridge, 219
Drew, Ronnie, 9
Dubliners, The, 50
Dukes Harbour, 94
Dunphy, Eamon, 18
Dunsink Observatory, 47–9

Edgeworth, Maria, 79, 246, 297
Emmet, Robert, 32–3, 38
Emper, 203
Enfield, 121–3
Ennis, Séamus, 41
Evans, Richard, 102, 104, 113

Fallon River, 282
Farranyoogan Bridge, 288
Fern's (Ferrans) Lock, see 17th Lock
Finglas, 41–2
Finglas River, 41
FitzGerald, Edward, 97
FitzGerald, James, 98
FitzGerald, Robert, 96
FitzGerald Castle, 96
Flynn, Mary, 232
Foigha Bridge and Harbour, 239
Footy's Bridge, 153
Foster, John, 26
French, Mel, 290, 294
Furey's Select Bar, 127–8

Gaelic Athletic Association (GAA), 14–15
Gandon, James, 26
George's Dock, 29

Glasnevin, 29–30
Glasnevin Cemetery, 31, 34–5
Goldsmith, Oliver, 231–4
gorse, 60, 92, 133
Granard Bridge, 56
Grange Bridge, 174
Great Famine, 6, 89
Green Bridge, 171
Griffith, Arthur, 84
Guinness, 5
Guinness, Arthur Ernest, 63

Hamilton Bridge, 39, 42
Hamilton, William, 39–40, 47
Harrington, Kellie, 11
Harvey, Francis, 130
hawthorn, 112–13, 133, 154, 180
hazel trees, 125–6
Heaney, Seamus, 34
herons, 129–31
High Bank Walk, 163–4
Hill of Down, see Killyon Bridge
Hone, Evie, 64, 80
Hone, Nathaniel, 80
Hone, Pat, 80
Hopkins, Gerard Manly, 33
horsetails, 139
How to Enjoy Wild Flowers, 124, 177
Hyde Park, 139–40

Irish Turf Company, 73
Inland Waterways Association of Ireland (IWAI), 154

Jackson Bridge, 102
Jonathan Swift Park 170
Joyce, James, 22, 48, 171–2

Kelly, Luke, 9
Kelly's Bridge, 203
Kennan Bridge, 61
Keoghan, Barry, 9
Kerrigan, Gene, 38
Kilcock, 105–9
Kilcock Canoe Polo Club, 105
Kilcock Fair, 108
Kildallan Bridge, 188
Killashee Harbour, 261
Killucan Barge, 141

Index

Killyon Bridge, 133–5
Kilmore Bridge, 125
Kilpatrick Bridge, 176
King-Harman, Lawrence Harman, 221
Knockanboy Bridge, 285

Ledwith's accommodation bridge, 203
Ledwithstown House, 204
Leixlip, 79–82
lesser celandine, 103
lichens, 93
Lonely Battle of Thomas Reid, The, 88
Long Level, 115, 121
Longford Branch, 199, 253–4, 280–1, 290–2
Longford Bridge, 46–7
Longford Town, 278, 280, 286–90, 292, 294–5
Longley, Michael, 213
Lough Allen, 234
Lough Derravaragh, 218, 298
Lough Ennell, 168, 170
Lough Forbes, 270
Lough Iron, 198
Lough Owel, 143, 168, 172, 298
Lough Ree, 220, 234
Lough Sheelin, 218
Louisa Bridge, 75, 78, 99
Luttrellstown Castle, 62–3
Lynn, Kathleen, 229–30
Lyreen River, 102

MacGreil, Father Michael, 95
Magan's Pub, 257–60
Mahon, Denis, 254–5
Mallett, John, 29
Mallett, Robert, 29
Mary Lynch's Bar, 155
Matt Goff Bridge, *see* Collinstown Bridge
Maynooth, 92, 94–6
Maynooth Harbour, 94
McLoughlin's Bridge, 113–16
McQuinn, Austin, 25
meadowsweet, 154
Middleton Park, 195–6

Midland Great Western Railway Company, 3, 6, 144
Molly Ward's accommodation bridge, 220
Monahan, Noel, 242
Mosstown Harbour, 243–5
Mosstown Estate, 245–7
Mountjoy Prison, 21
Moyvalley, 27, 127
Mullawornia Accommodation Bridge, 240
Mullen Bridges, 93
Mullingar, 165–73
Mullins, Bernard, 73

Nanny Quinn's Bar and Restaurant, 141–2
narrow boats, 53
National Famine Way, 255
Newcastle House, 220–1
Newcomen Bridge, 7, 12–13
Newcomen, William Gleadowe, 12, 245

O'Casey, Sean, 10
O'Connell, Daniel, 31, 223
O'Connell Tower, 31
O'Hehir, Michael, 30, 195
O'Rourke, Laurence, 145–6
Ó Sé, Maidhc Dainín, 109
Ogham stone, 90
Old City Basin, 24

Pake Bridges, 238–9
Pakenham Bridge, 64
Parnell, Charles Stuart, 32
Phoenix Park, 47
Pig's Nostril, 165
Pike Bridge, 90, 92
Piper's Boreen, 167–8
primroses, 74
Prospect Cemetery, 31

Queen Medb, 276–7
Quinn's Accommodation Bridge, 207

Raven Arts Press, 42
Reid, Thomas, 87–8
Reilly's Bridge, 44

Ribbonmen, 129
Ribbontail Footbridge, 129
Richmond Bridge, 269–70
Richmond Harbour, 269
River Blackwater, 125, 131, 205
River Brosna, 166, 168
River Boyne, 125, 131, 144
River Inny, 203, 205, 207, 211, 217–20
River Inny Walk, 220
River Liffey, 3, 5, 9, 68–9, 76, 79, 102, 274
River Shannon, 3, 168, 199, 220, 234, 270, 273, 275, 290
Riverstown Bridge, 146
Riverstown Feeder, 141
robins, 256
Rochfort, Robert, 168
Rock, Dickie, 37
Royal Canal Amenity Group (RCAG), 68–9, 105, 129, 141, 154, 225, 254, 292
Royal Canal Company, 3, 131
Royal Canal Greenway, 2, 156, 190, 253
Royal George Reservoir, *see* Old City Basin
Rye Water Aqueduct, 75
Rye water feeder, 113–4

Saint Laurence O'Toole church, 7–8
Saunders Bridge, 166
Savage Bridge, 261
Scanlan's Bridge, 168
Scherzer Bridges, 29
Shackleton, Ernest, 80
Shackleton Mill, 80, 260
Shalakabooky, 58, 91
Shandonagh Bridges, 181
Shannon Navigation, 270, 274
Shaw's Bridge, 105
Sheridan, Jim, 10
Sheridan, Peter, 10–11
Sheriff Street Bridge, 6
Spencer Dock, 3, 5–6, 13, 29
Spencer Dock Bridge, 5
Spin Bridge, *see* Allen Bridge

Spook of the Thirteenth Lock, 85
spotted orchids, 279
Springfield Tunnel aqueduct, 168
squirrels, 159–60
St. Catherine's Park, 67–8
St. Mel's Cathedral, 288, 292–3
St. Oliver Plunkett GAA Clubhouse and Sports Grounds, 45
St. Patrick's Chair, 190
St. Patrick's College and Seminary, 95–6, 100
Strokestown House, 255
swans, 14, 23, 35, 43, 131, 174–5, 200–1
Swift, Jonathan, 170

Táin Cycle Route, 276–7
Talbot Bridge, 52
Termonbarry, 273–4, 276
Termonbarry Lock, 273–4
The Obelisk, 89–90
'The Old Bog Road', 117–8
Thomastown Bridge, 143
Toler, John, 38, 246
Tolka River, 30, 43, 45, 47
Toome Bridge, 223–4
Tristernagh Abbey, 197

Walsh, Father Paul, 179
Walsh's Accommodation Bridge, 187
Waterways Ireland, 78, 92
Webb Bridge, 216–7
Westmoreland Bridge, *see* Cross Guns Bridge
Whitworth Aqueduct, 207, 218
Wicked Earl, *see* Robert Rochford
Wonderful Barn, 80–1
Woodword, Marcus, 124, 178
Wren, Jenny, 58–62, 66–7, 86, 91–2

yarrow, 157–8
Yeats, W.B., 125
yellow iris (yellow flag), 151–2, 160, 222, 256, 288